长城

THE GREAT WALL

LAST SURVIVOR

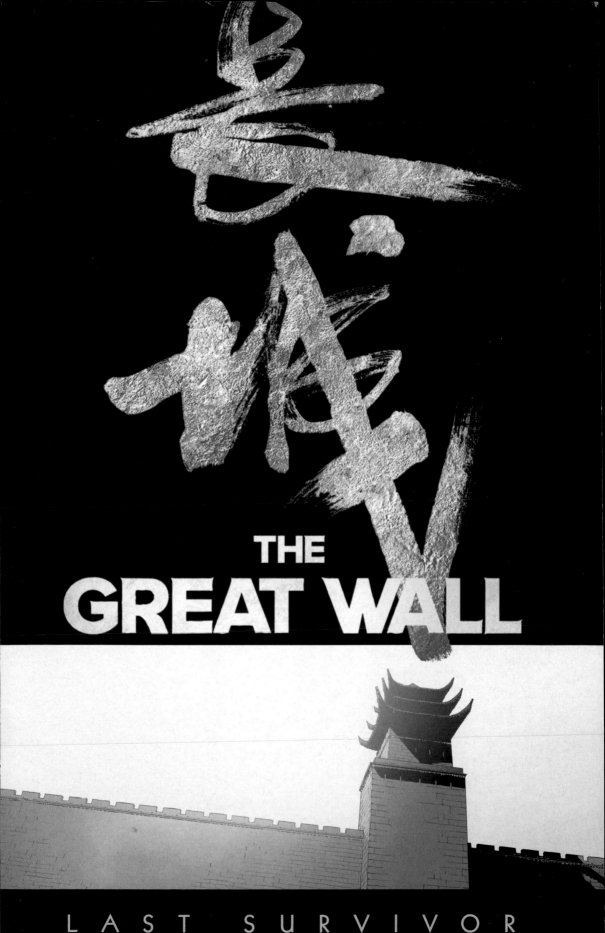

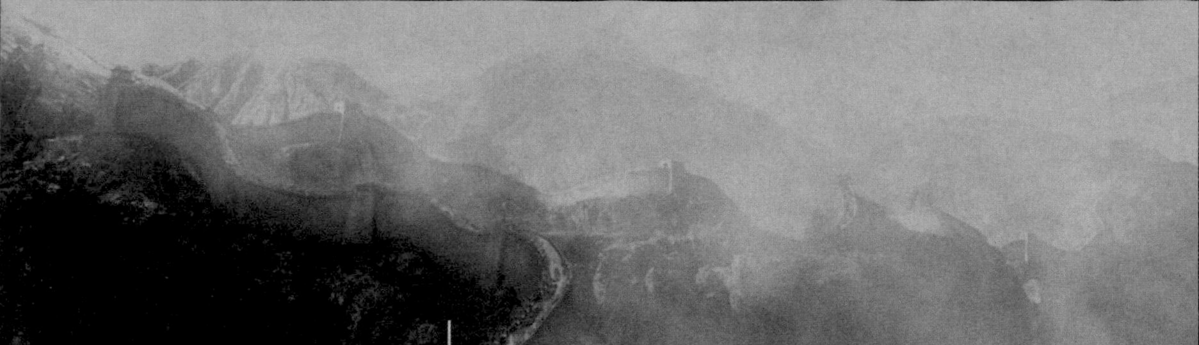

WRITER
ARVID NELSON

ARTIST
GIAN FERNANDO

COLORS
GUY MAJOR

COVER
WHILCE PORTACIO

BACKGROUNDS
(CHAPTER 3 AND 4)
JOEL GOMEZ

STORY DEVELOPMENT
BARNABY LEGG

LETTERS
PATRICK BROSSEAU

BOOK DESIGN
JOHN ROSHELL
OF COMICRAFT

EDITOR
ROBERT NAPTON

SPECIAL THANKS
PETER LOEHR
ALEX HEDLUND
ZHANG YIMOU
JON JASHNI
JILLIAN SHARE
TENG ZHANG
CYNTHIA HE
LEGENDARY MARKETING
JENNIFER STEWART
LAURA CURRAN
DIPESH PATEL
NIKITA KANNEKANTI

LEGENDARY

THOMAS TULL
CHIEF EXECUTIVE OFFICER

MARY PARENT
VICE CHAIRMAN OF WORLDWIDE PRODUCTION

MARTY WILLHITE
CHIEF OPERATING OFFICER AND GENERAL COUNSEL

PETER LOEHR
CHIEF EXECUTIVE OFFICER, LEGENDARY EAST

EMILY CASTEL
CHIEF MARKETING OFFICER

BARNABY LEGG
VP, THEATRICAL STRATEGY

MIKE ROSS
SVP, BUSINESS AND LEGAL AFFAIRS

DAN FEINBERG
VP, CORPORATE COUNSEL

BAYAN LAIRD
VP, BUSINESS AND LEGAL AFFAIRS

LEGENDARY COMICS

BOB SCHRECK
SVP, EDITOR-IN-CHIEF

ROBERT NAPTON
VP, EDITORIAL DIRECTOR

DAVID SADOVE
PUBLISHING OPERATIONS COORDINATOR

GREG TUMBARELLO
EDITOR

FIRST PRINTING: JANUARY 2017
10 9 8 7 6 5 4 3 2 1

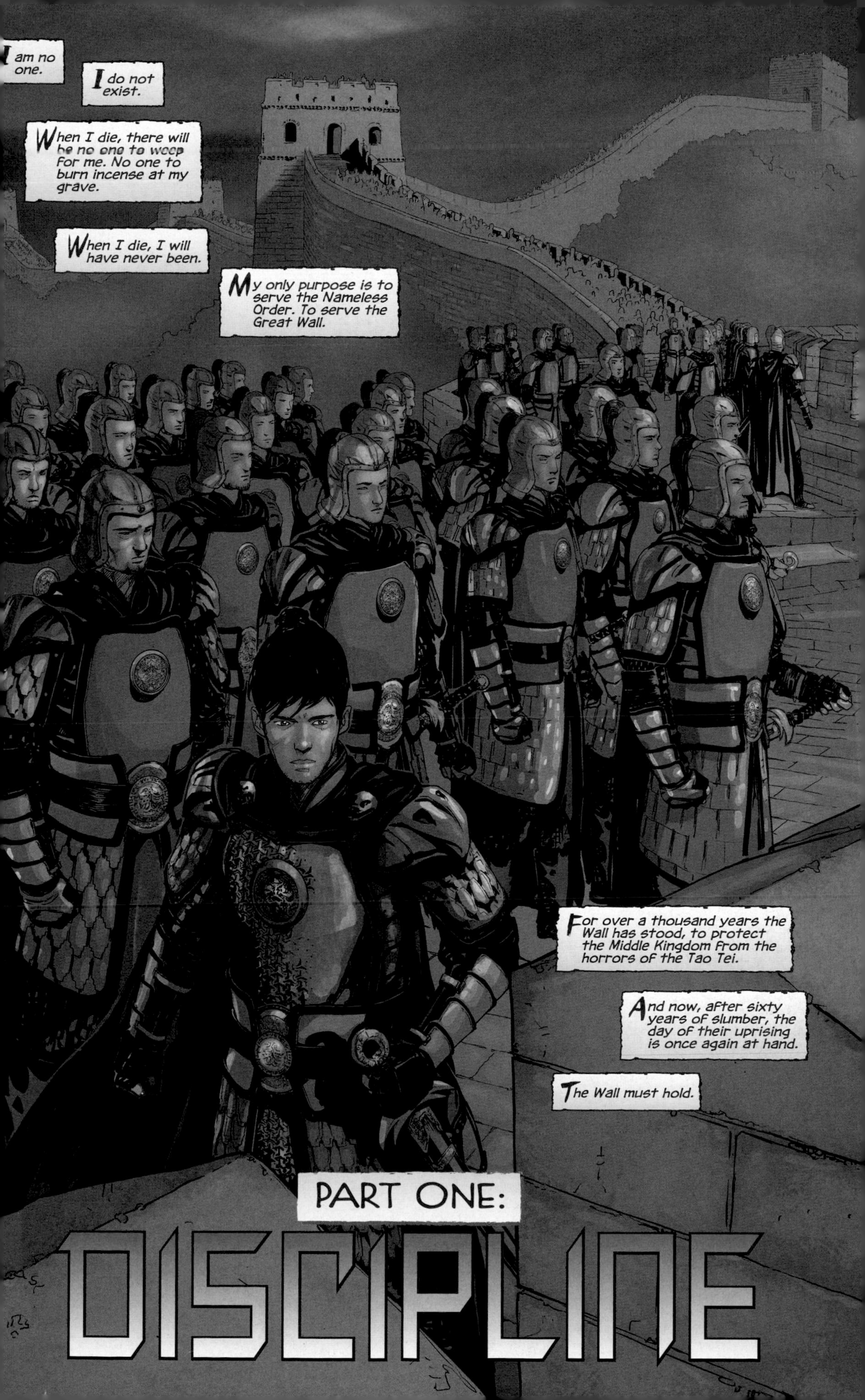

I am no one.
I do not exist.
When I die, there will be no one to weep for me. No one to burn incense at my grave.
When I die, I will have never been.
My only purpose is to serve the Nameless Order. To serve the Great Wall.
For over a thousand years the Wall has stood, to protect the Middle Kingdom from the horrors of the Tao Tei.
And now, after sixty years of slumber, the day of their uprising is once again at hand.
The Wall must hold.
PART ONE:
DISCIPLINE

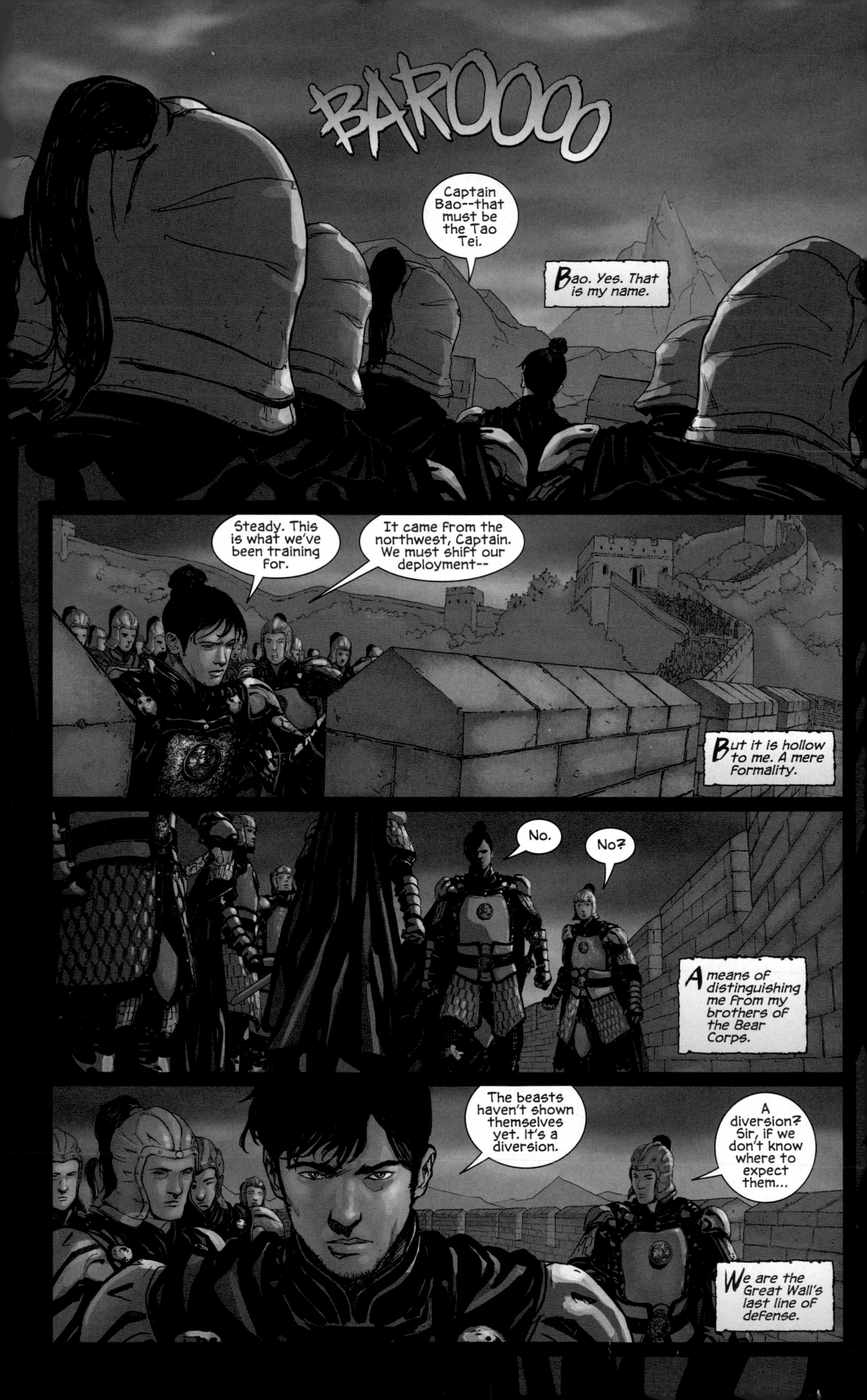
BAROOOO
Captain Bao--that must be the Tao Tei.
Bao. Yes. That is my name.
Steady. This is what we've been training for.
It came from the northwest, Captain. We must shift our deployment--
But it is hollow to me. A mere formality.
No.
No?
A means of distinguishing me from my brothers of the Bear Corps.
The beasts haven't shown themselves yet. It's a diversion.
A diversion? Sir, if we don't know where to expect them...
We are the Great Wall's last line of defense.

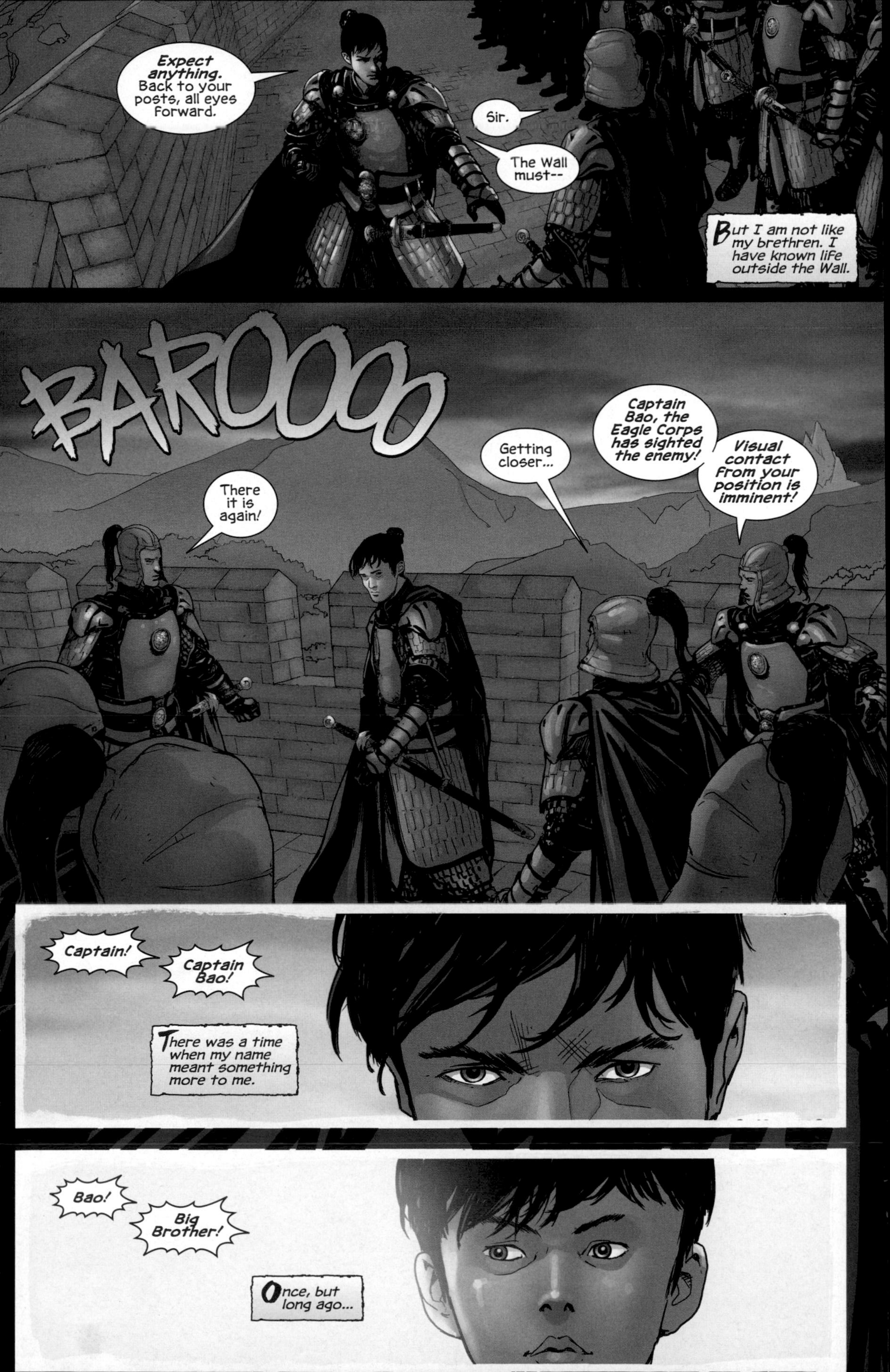

Expect anything. Back to your posts, all eyes forward.
Sir.
The Wall must--
But I am not like my brethren. I have known life outside the Wall.
BAROOOO
There it is again!
Getting closer...
Captain Bao, the Eagle Corps has sighted the enemy!
Visual contact from your position is imminent!
Captain!
Captain Bao!
There was a time when my name meant something more to me.
Bao!
Big Brother!
Once, but long ago...

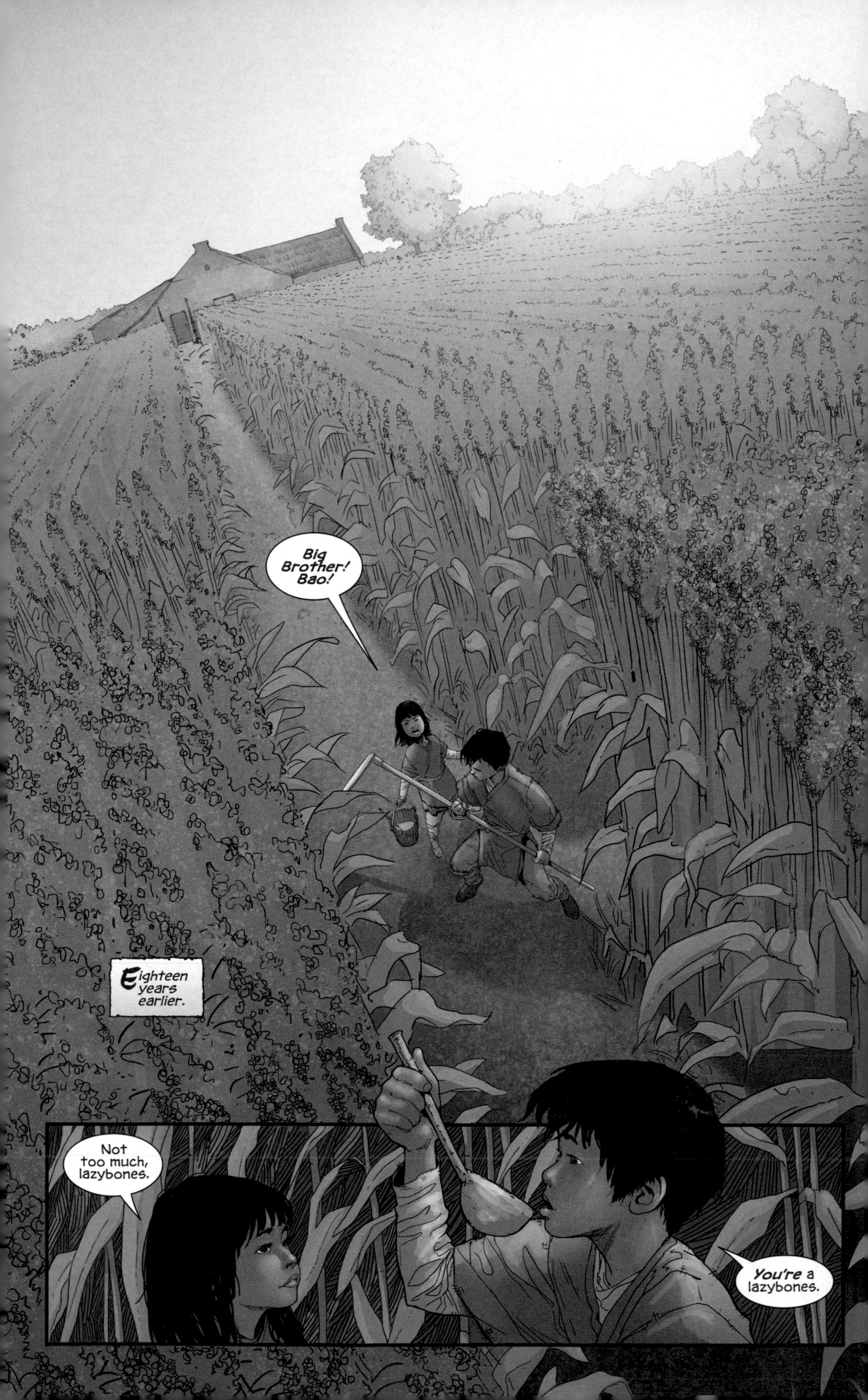
Big Brother! Bao!
Eighteen years earlier.
Not too much, lazybones.
You're a lazybones.

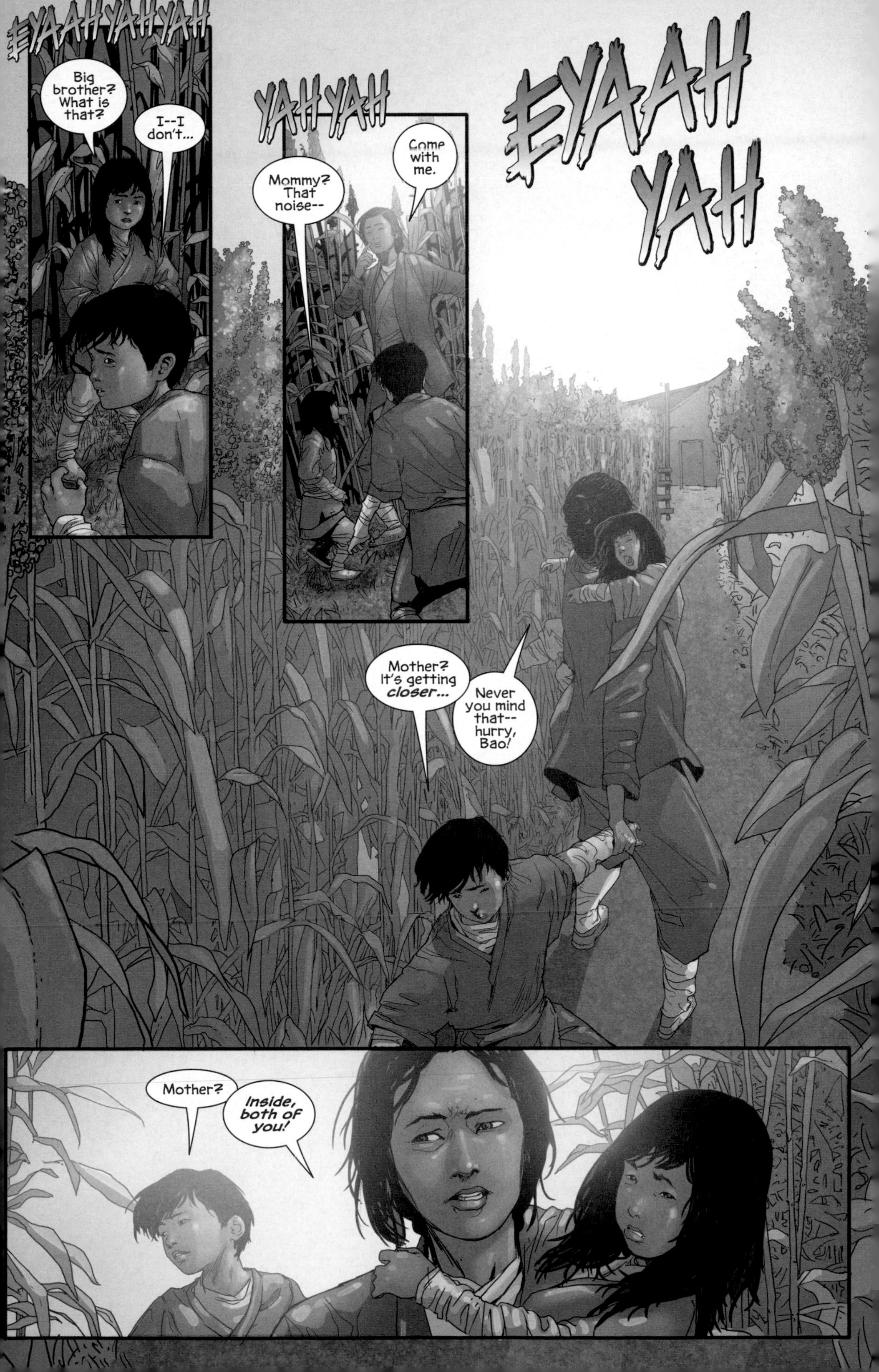
EYAAHYAHYAH
Big brother? What is that?
I--I don't...
YAHYAH
Mommy? That noise--
Come with me.
EYAAH YAH
Mother? It's getting *closer...*
Never you mind that-- hurry, Bao!
Mother?
Inside, both of you!

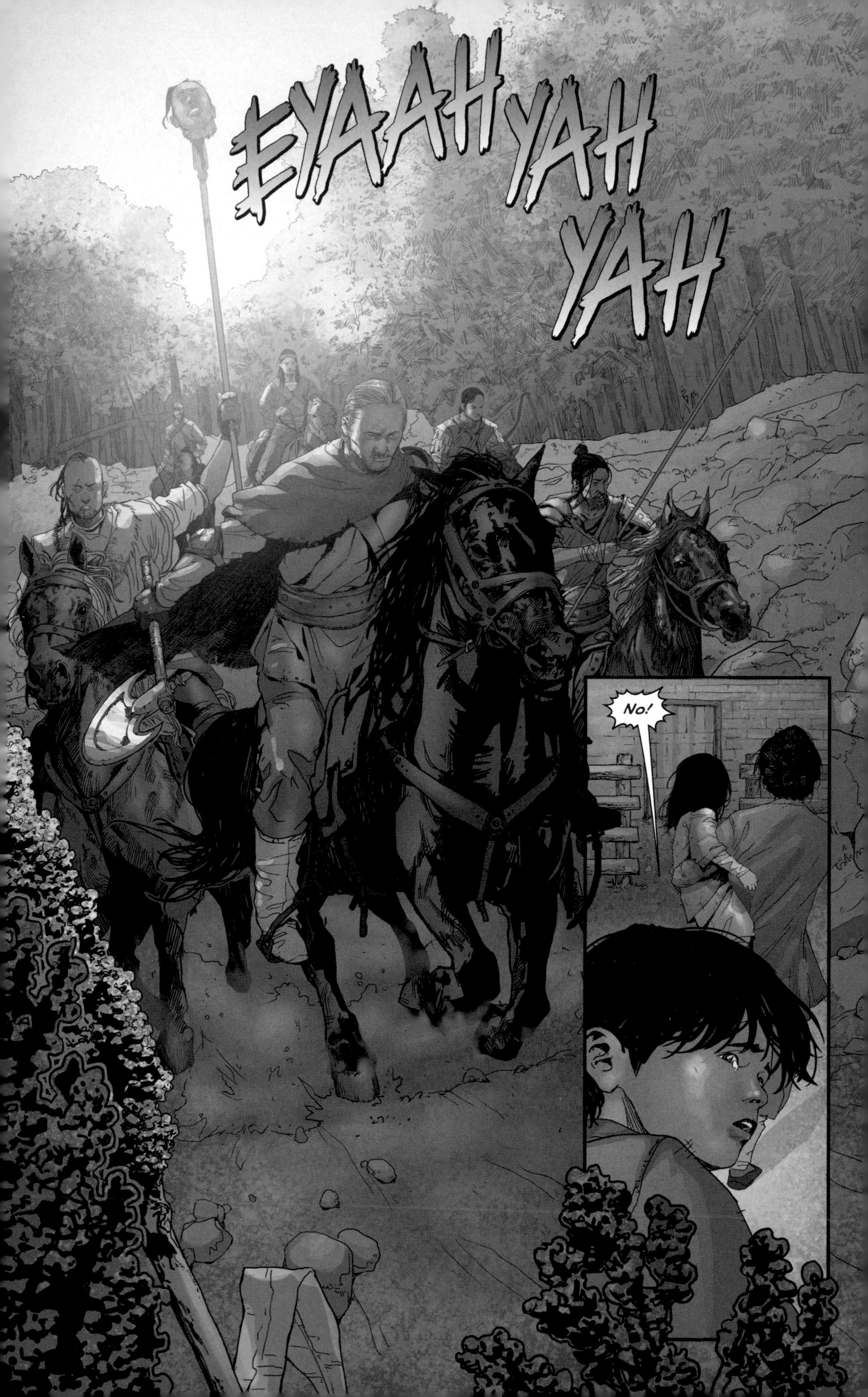
EYAAH YAH YAH
No!

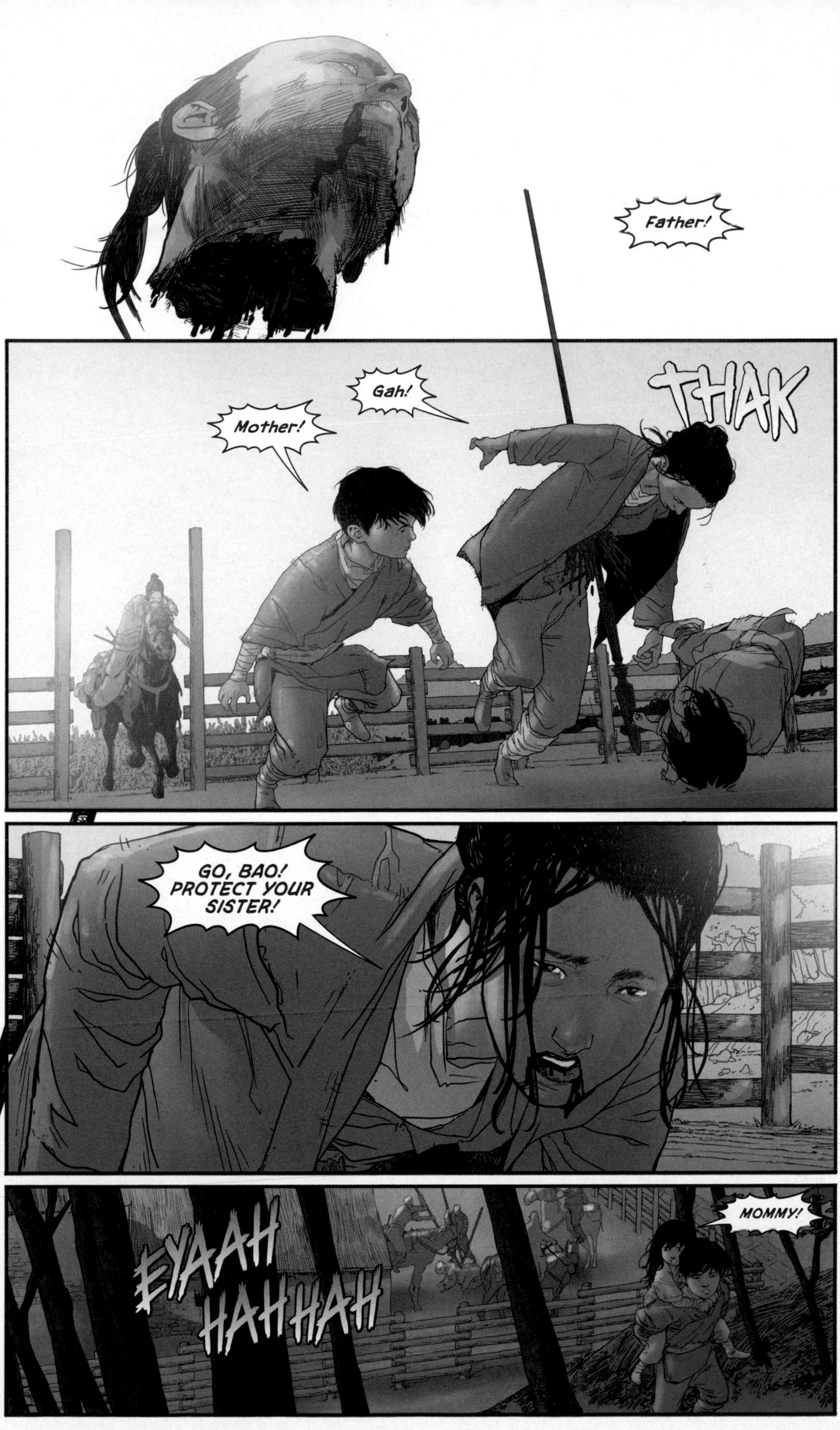
Father!
Mother!
Gah!
THAK
GO, BAO! PROTECT YOUR SISTER!
EYAAH HAHHAH
MOMMY!

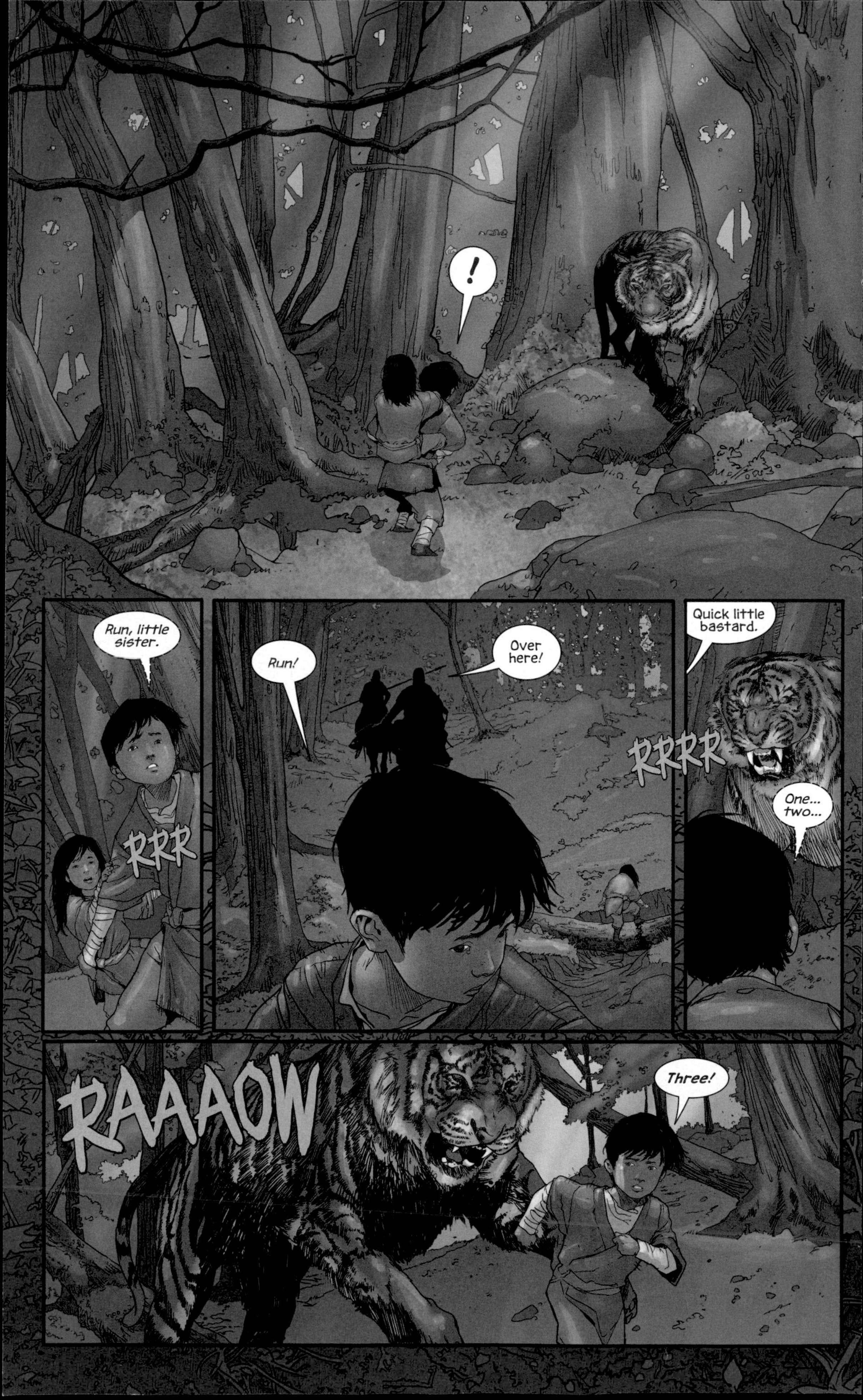
!
Run, little sister.
RRR
Run!
Over here!
Quick little bastard.
RRRR
One... two...
RAAAOW
Three!

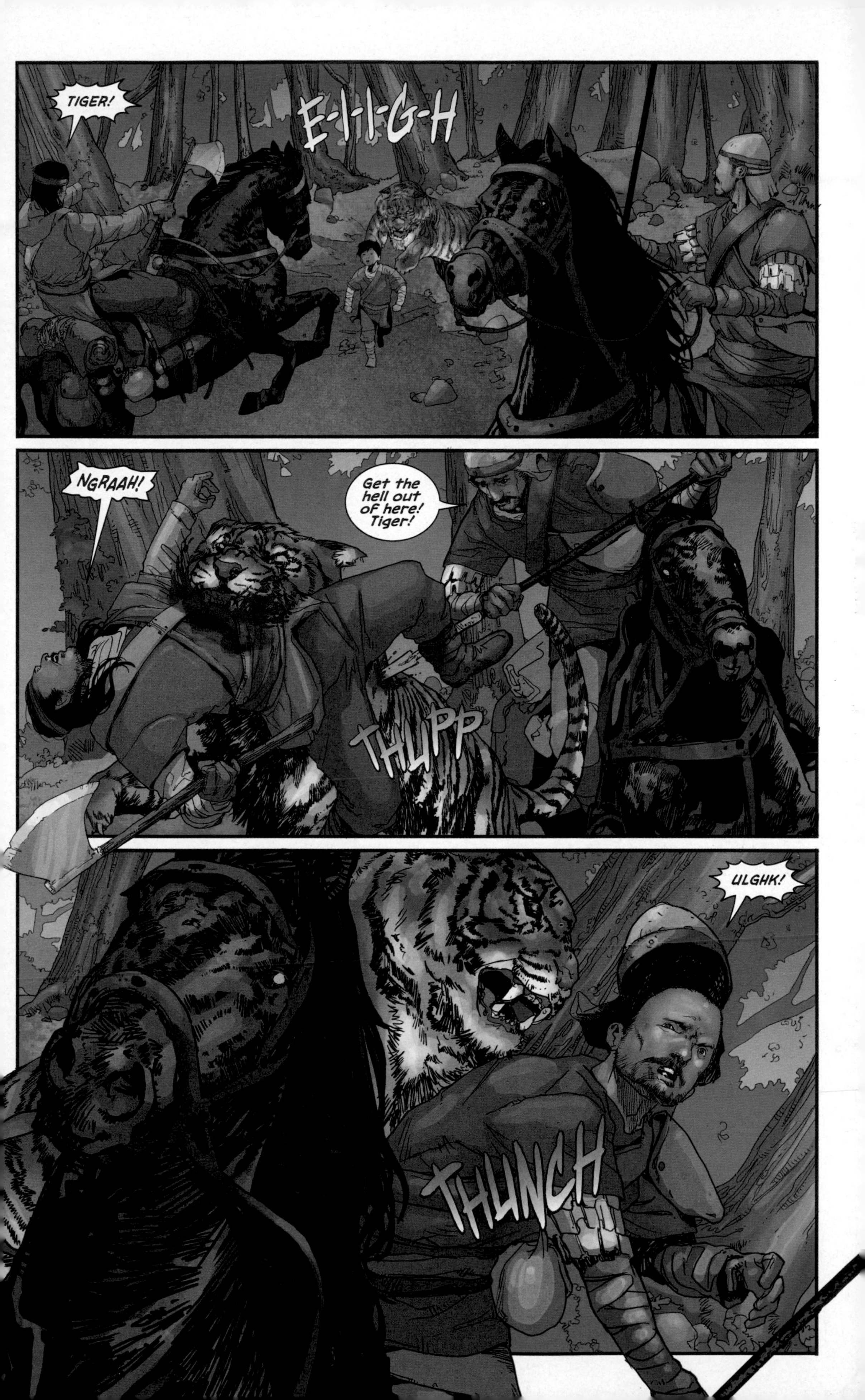
TIGER!
E-I-I-G-H
NGRAAH!
Get the hell out of here! Tiger!
THUPP
ULGHK!
THUNCH

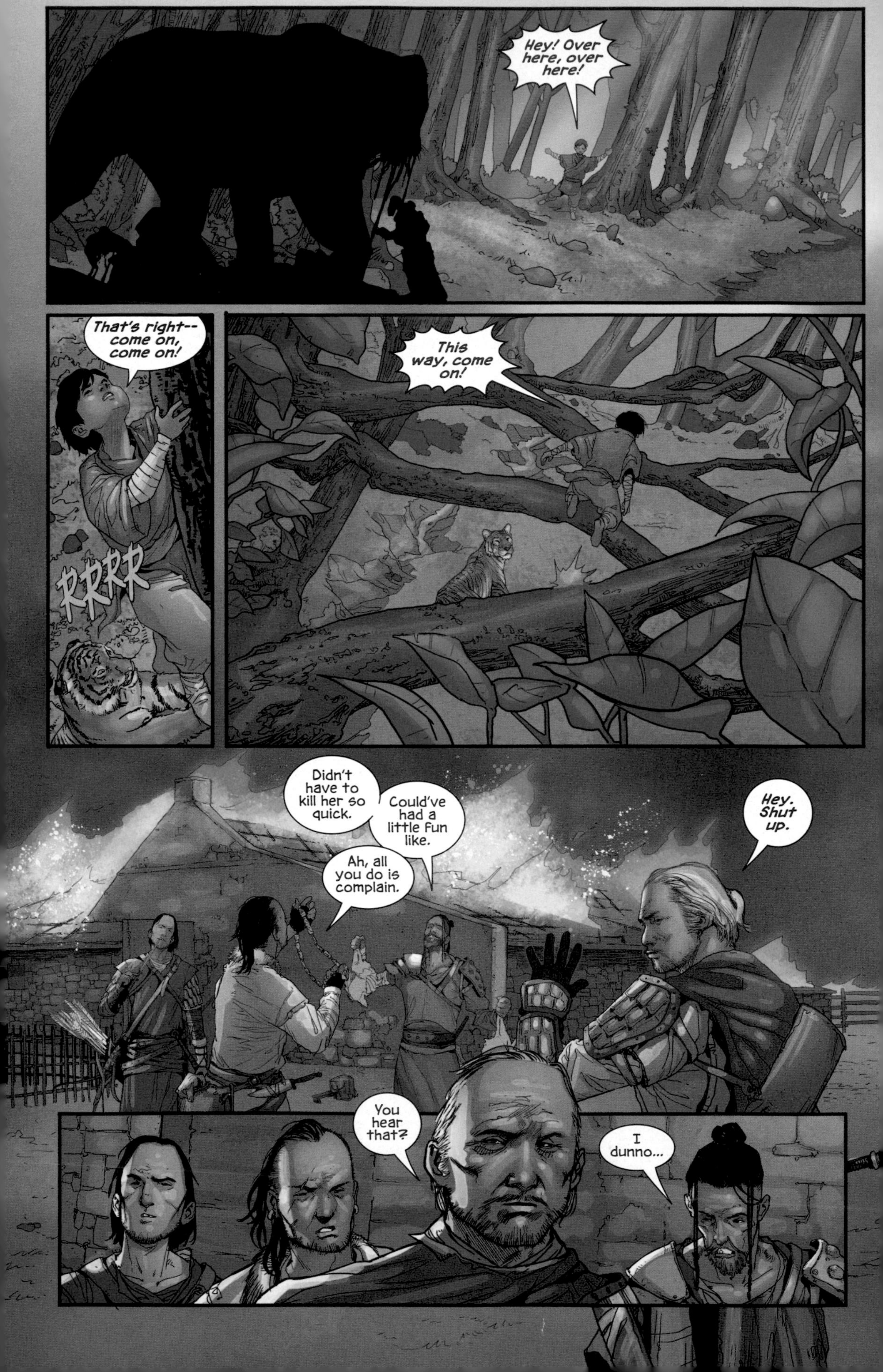
Hey! Over here, over here!
That's right-- come on, come on!
RRRR
This way, come on!
Didn't have to kill her so quick.
Could've had a little fun like.
Ah, all you do is complain.
Hey. Shut up.
You hear that?
I dunno...

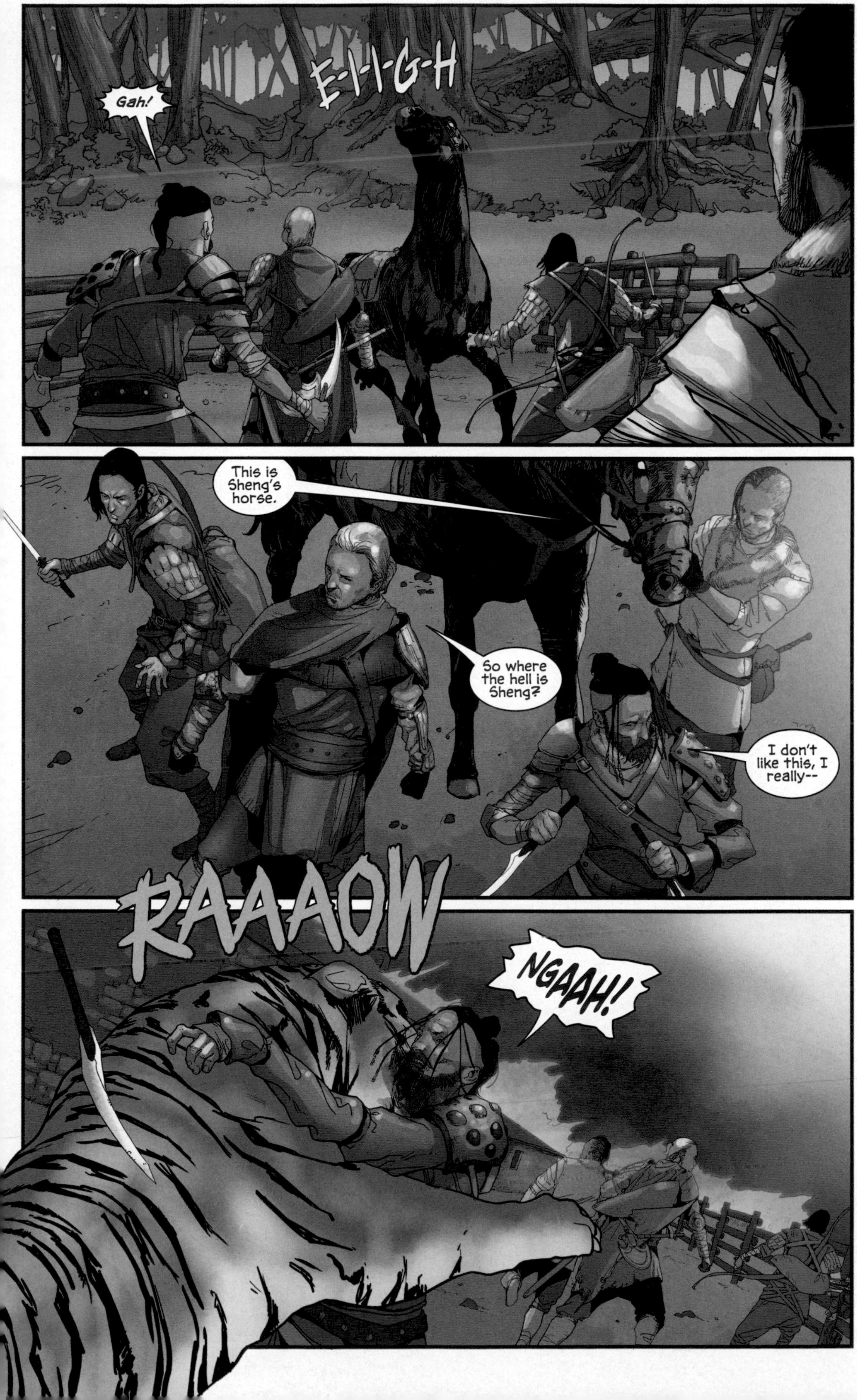
E-I-I-G-H
Gah!
This is Sheng's horse.
So where the hell is Sheng?
I don't like this, I really--
RAAAOW
NGAAH!

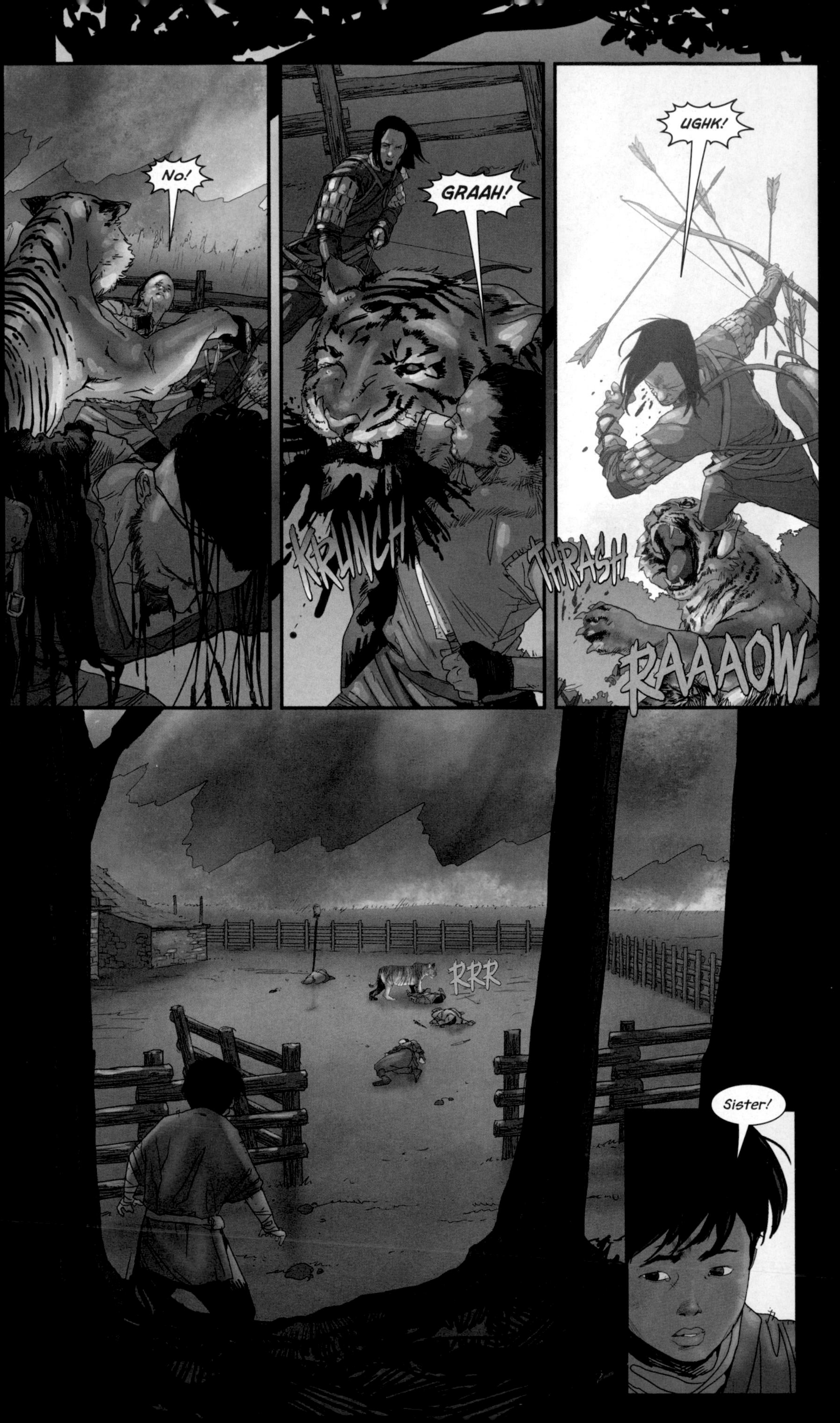
No!
GRAAH!
KRUNCH
UGHK!
THRASH
RAAAOW
RRR
Sister!

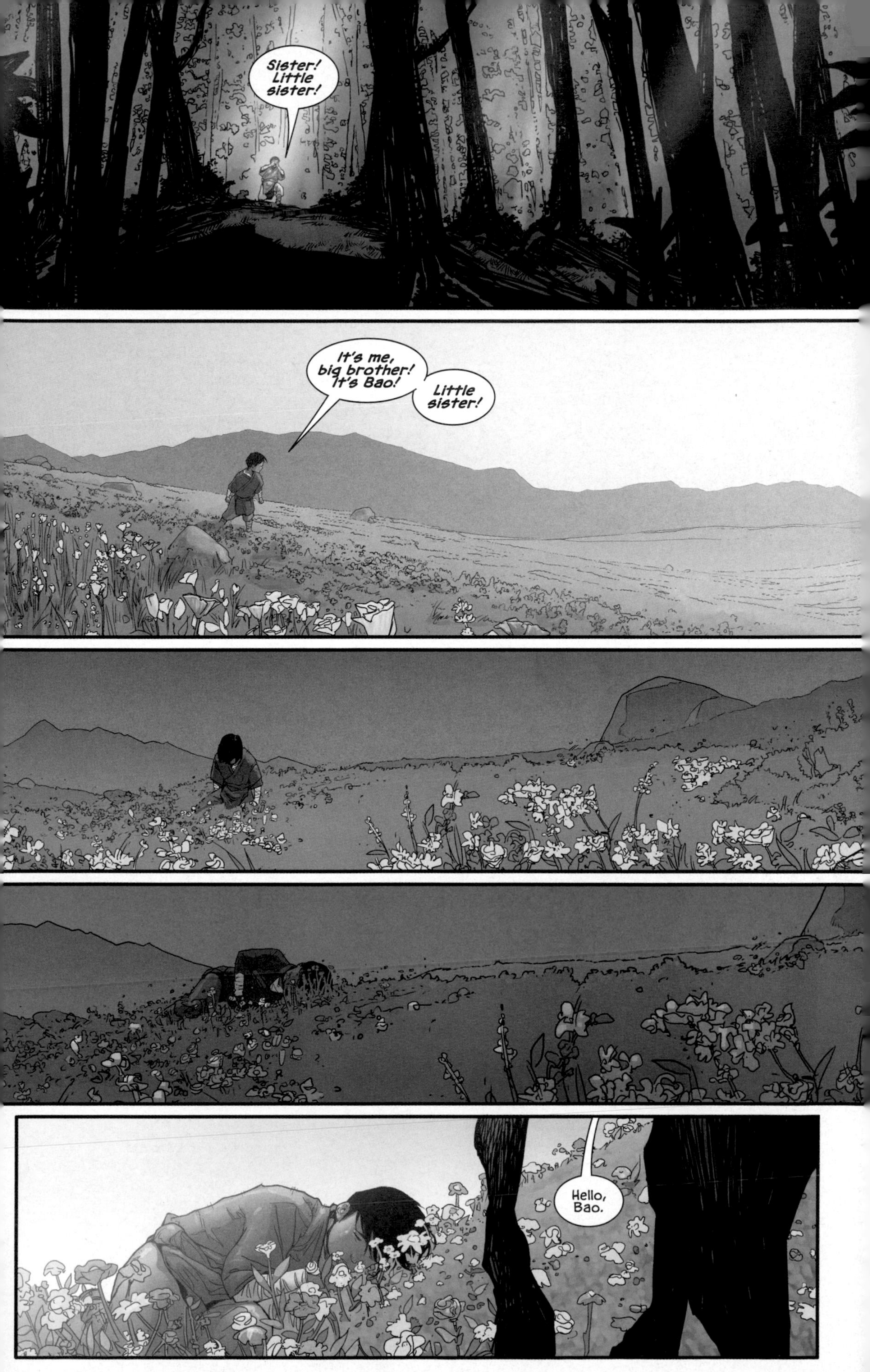
Sister! Little sister!
It's me, big brother! It's Bao!
Little sister!
Hello, Bao.

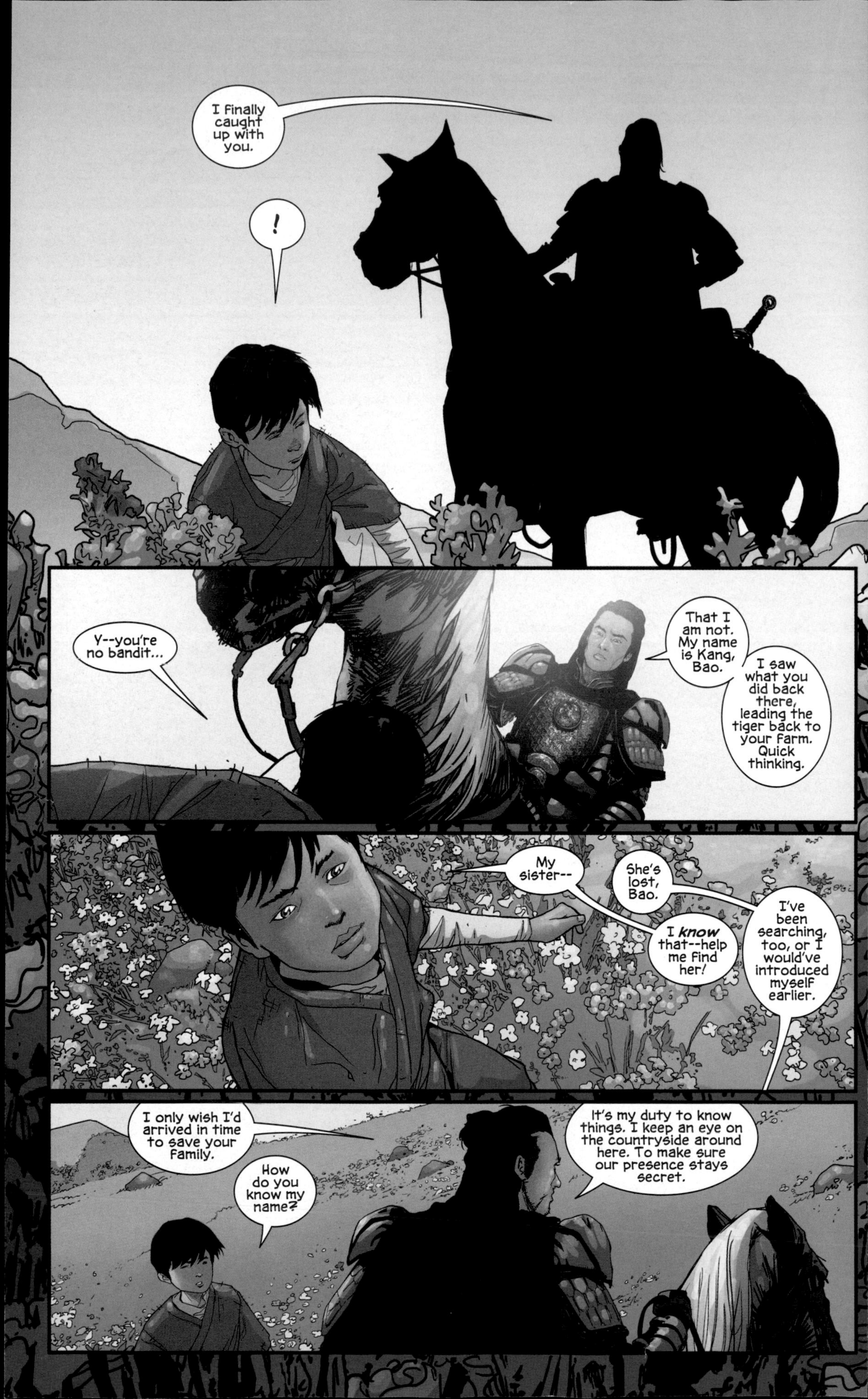
I finally caught up with you.
!
Y--you're no bandit...
That I am not. My name is Kang, Bao.
I saw what you did back there, leading the tiger back to your farm. Quick thinking.
My sister--
She's lost, Bao.
I *know* that--help me find her!
I've been searching, too, or I would've introduced myself earlier.
I only wish I'd arrived in time to save your family.
How do you know my name?
It's my duty to know things. I keep an eye on the countryside around here. To make sure our presence stays secret.

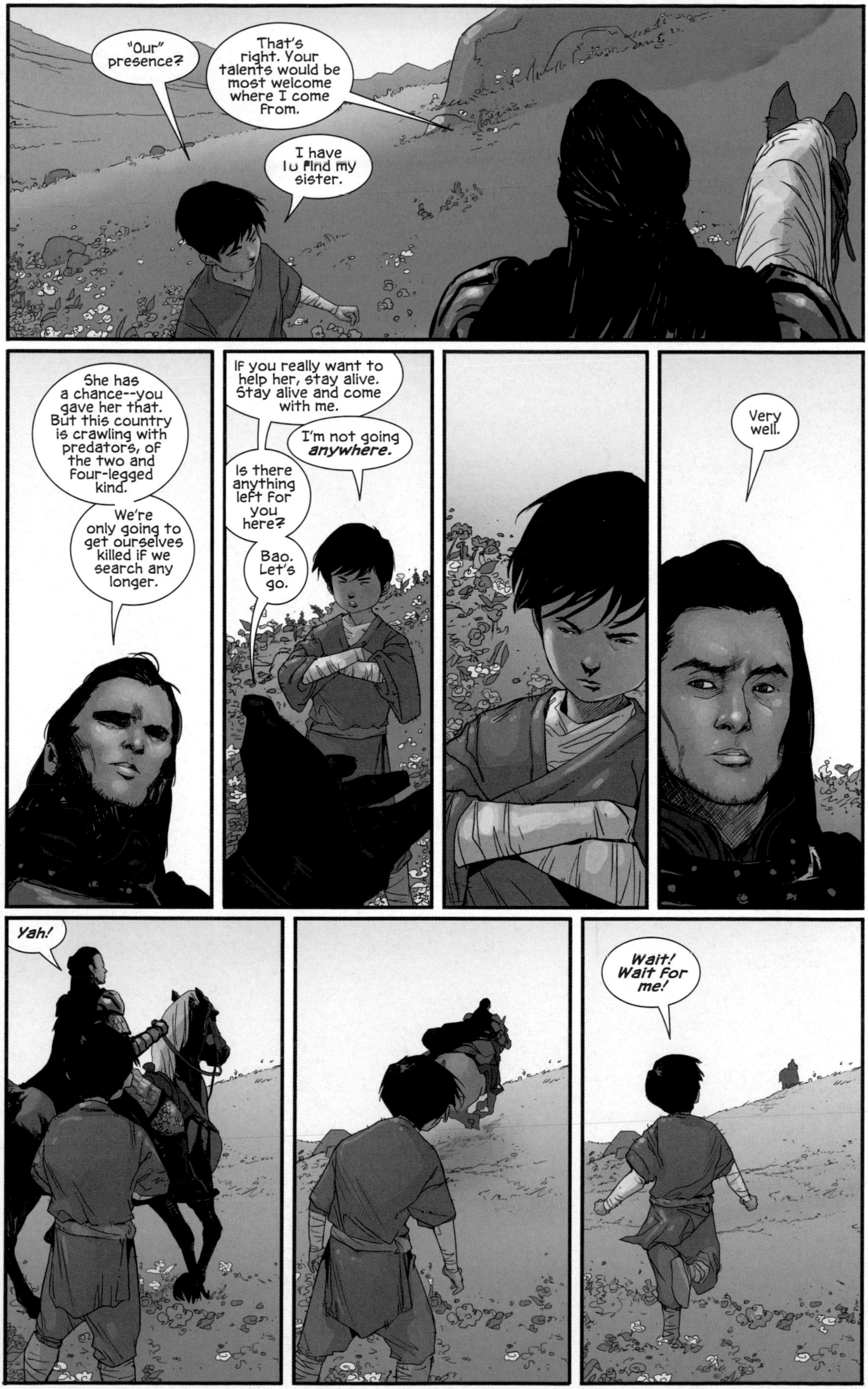
"Our" presence?
That's right. Your talents would be most welcome where I come from.
I have to find my sister.
She has a chance--you gave her that. But this country is crawling with predators, of the two and four-legged kind.
We're only going to get ourselves killed if we search any longer.
If you really want to help her, stay alive. Stay alive and come with me.
I'm not going *anywhere.*
Is there anything left for you here?
Bao. Let's go.
Very well.
Yah!
Wait! Wait for me!

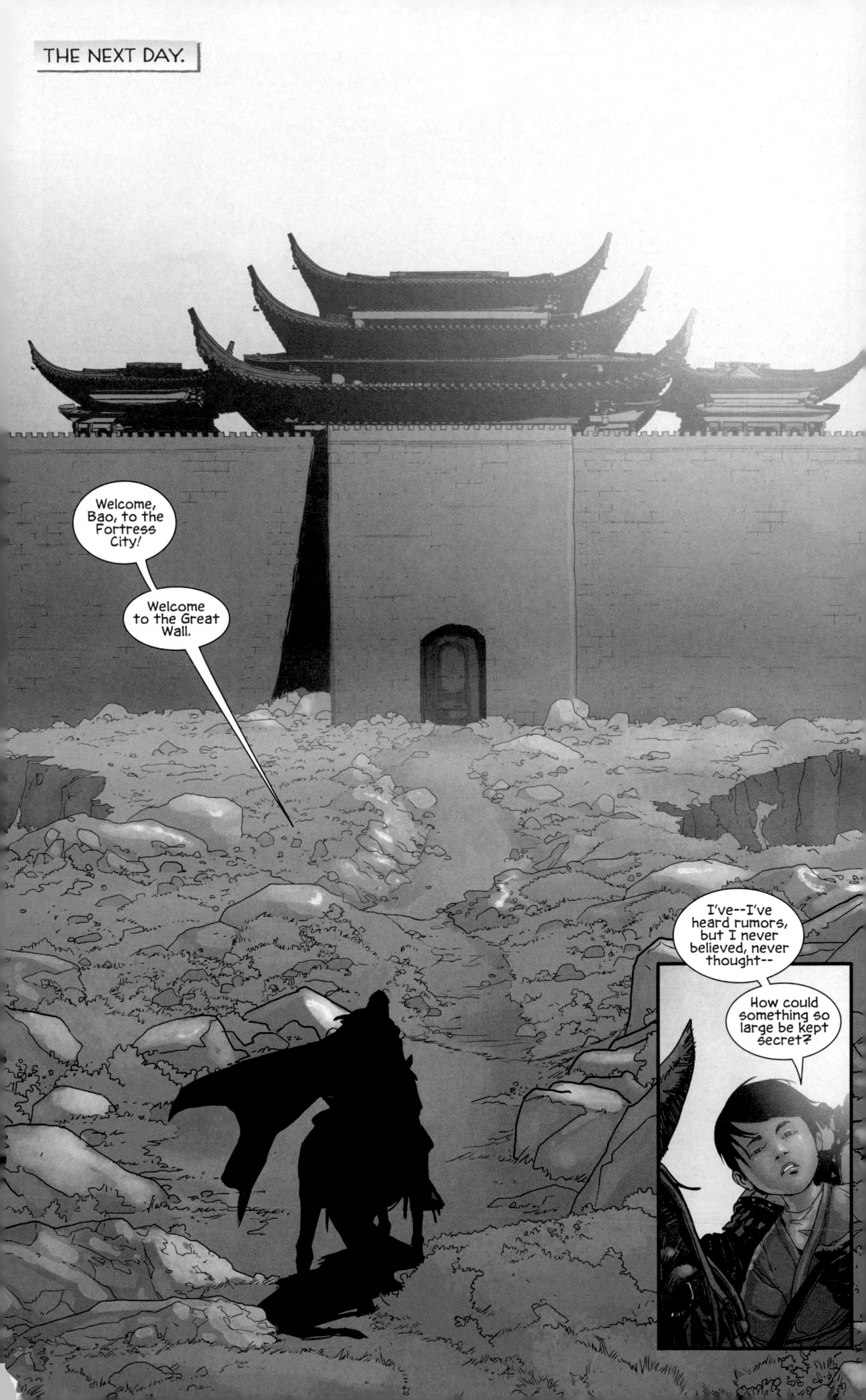
THE NEXT DAY.
Welcome, Bao, to the Fortress City!
Welcome to the Great Wall.
I've--I've heard rumors, but I never believed, never thought--
How could something so large be kept secret?

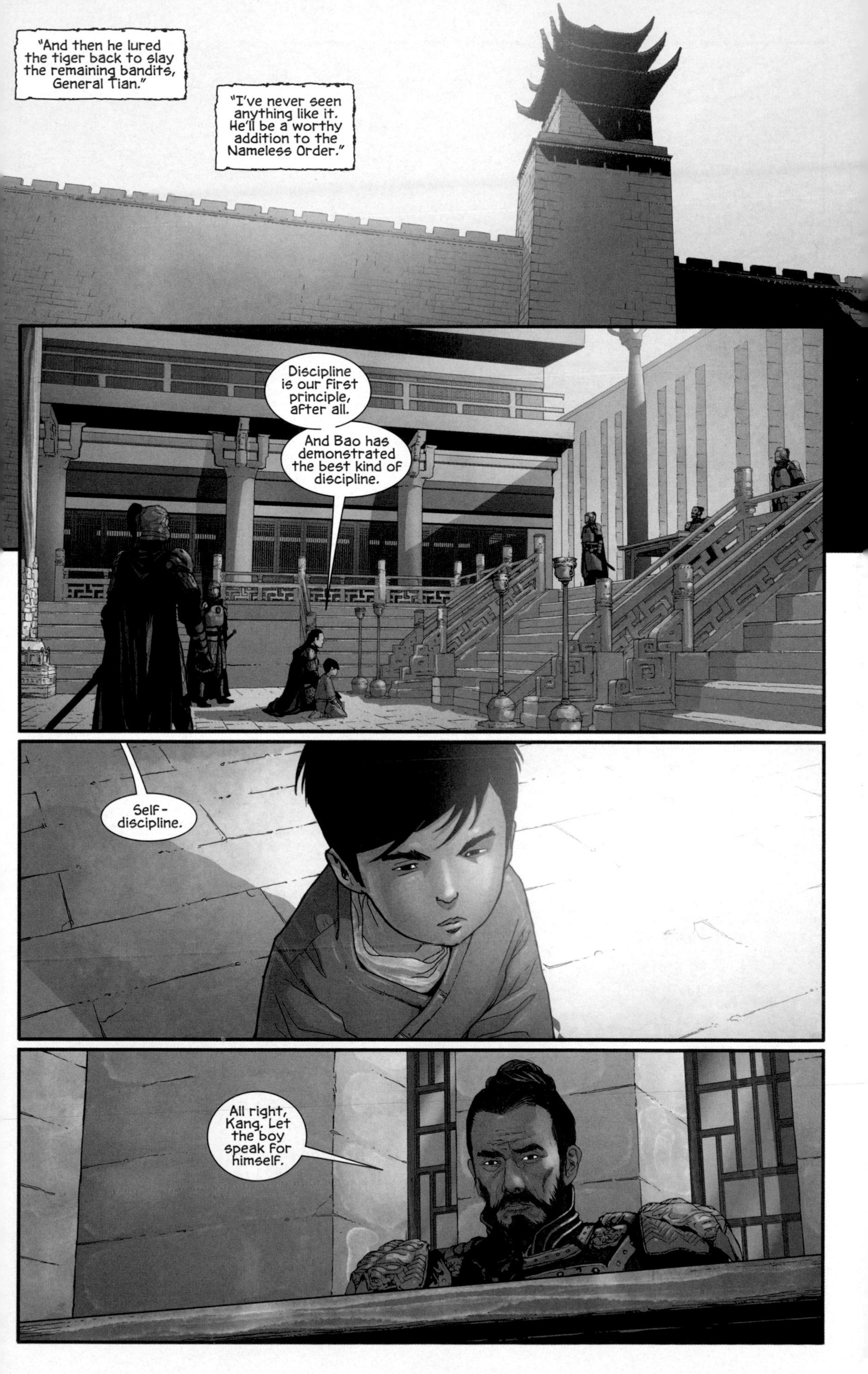
"And then he lured the tiger back to slay the remaining bandits, General Tian."
"I've never seen anything like it. He'll be a worthy addition to the Nameless Order."
Discipline is our first principle, after all.
And Bao has demonstrated the best kind of discipline.
Self-discipline.
All right, Kang. Let the boy speak for himself.

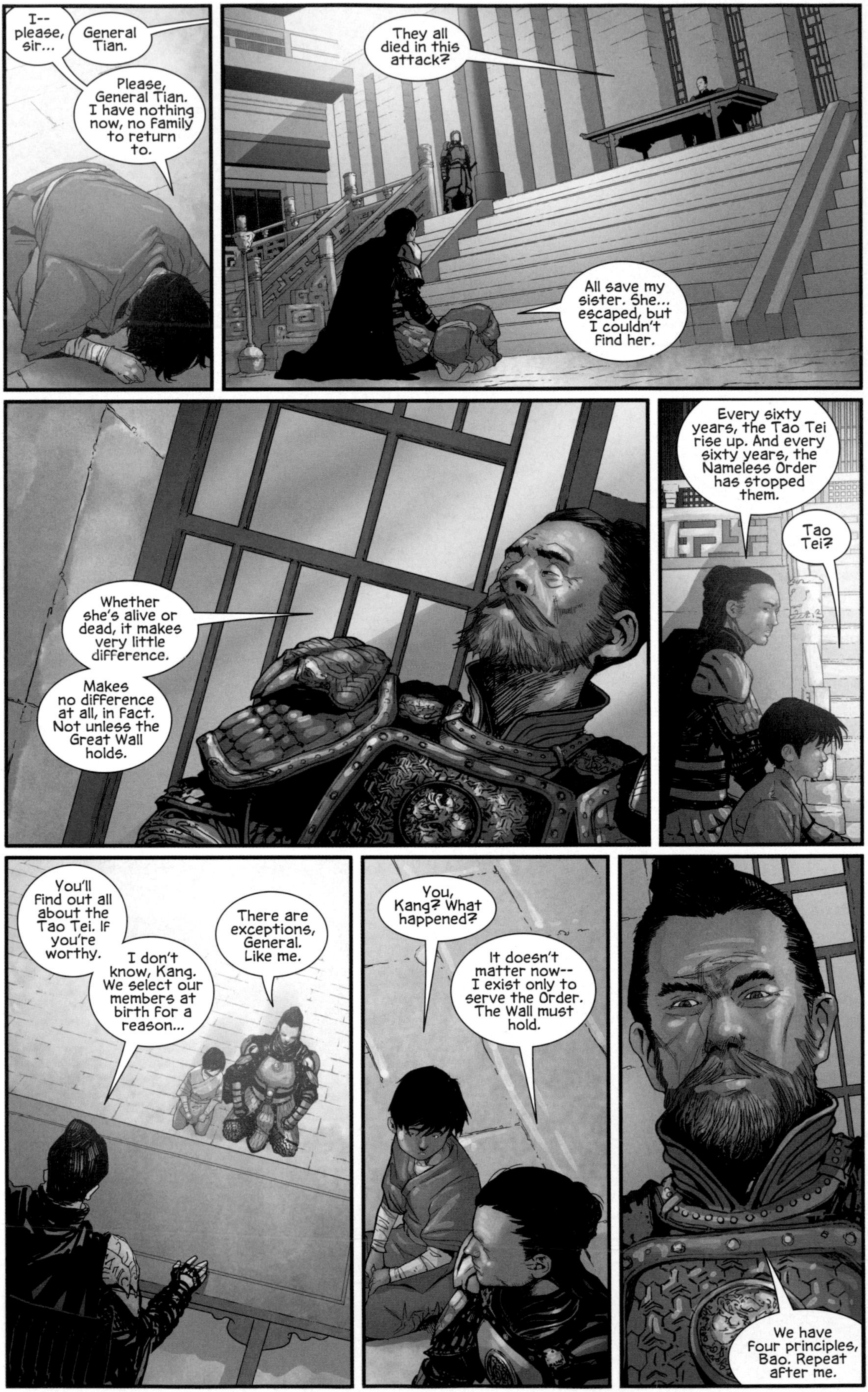
I-- please, sir...
General Tian.
Please, General Tian. I have nothing now, no family to return to.
They all died in this attack?
All save my sister. She... escaped, but I couldn't find her.
Whether she's alive or dead, it makes very little difference.
Makes no difference at all, in fact. Not unless the Great Wall holds.
Every sixty years, the Tao Tei rise up. And every sixty years, the Nameless Order has stopped them.
Tao Tei?
You'll find out all about the Tao Tei. If you're worthy.
I don't know, Kang. We select our members at birth for a reason...
There are exceptions, General. Like me.
You, Kang? What happened?
It doesn't matter now-- I exist only to serve the Order. The Wall must hold.
We have four principles, Bao. Repeat after me.

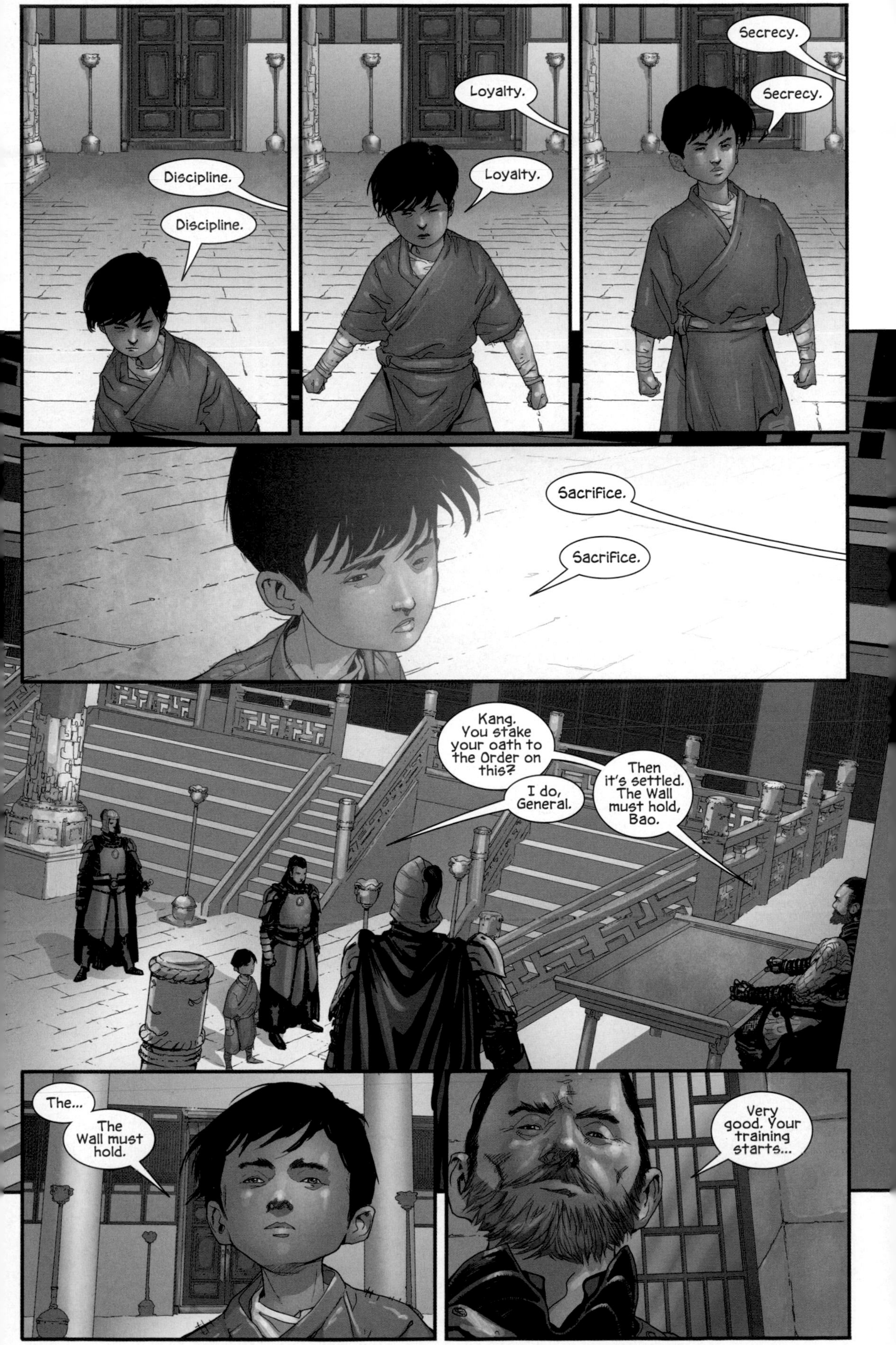
Discipline.
Discipline.
Loyalty.
Loyalty.
Secrecy.
Secrecy.
Sacrifice.
Sacrifice.
Kang. You stake your oath to the Order on this?
I do, General.
Then it's settled. The Wall must hold, Bao.
The...
The Wall must hold.
Very good. Your training starts...

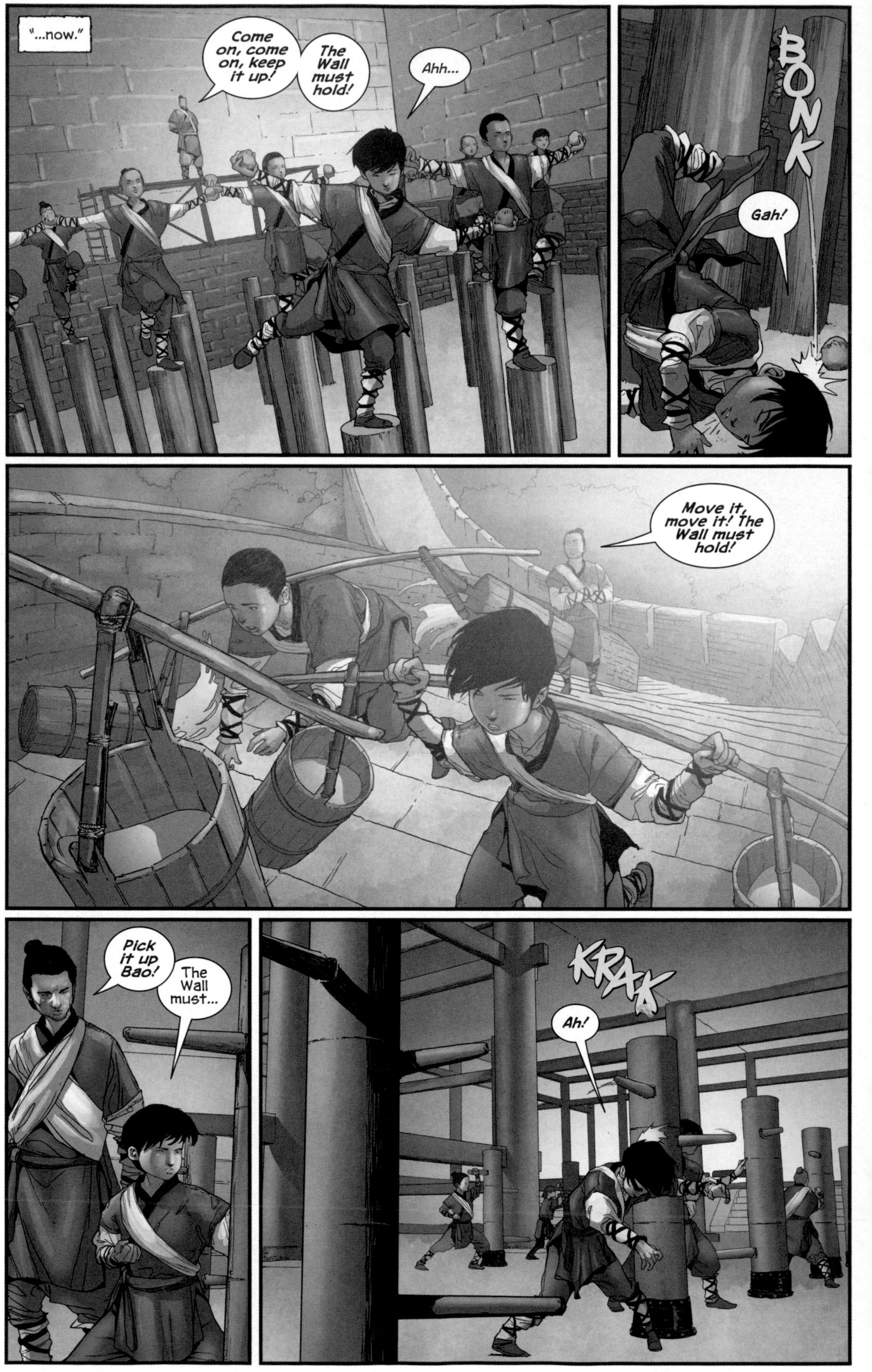
"...now."
Come on, come on, keep it up!
The Wall must hold!
Ahh...
BONK
Gah!
Move it, move it! The Wall must hold!
Pick it up Bao!
The Wall must...
KRAK
Ah!

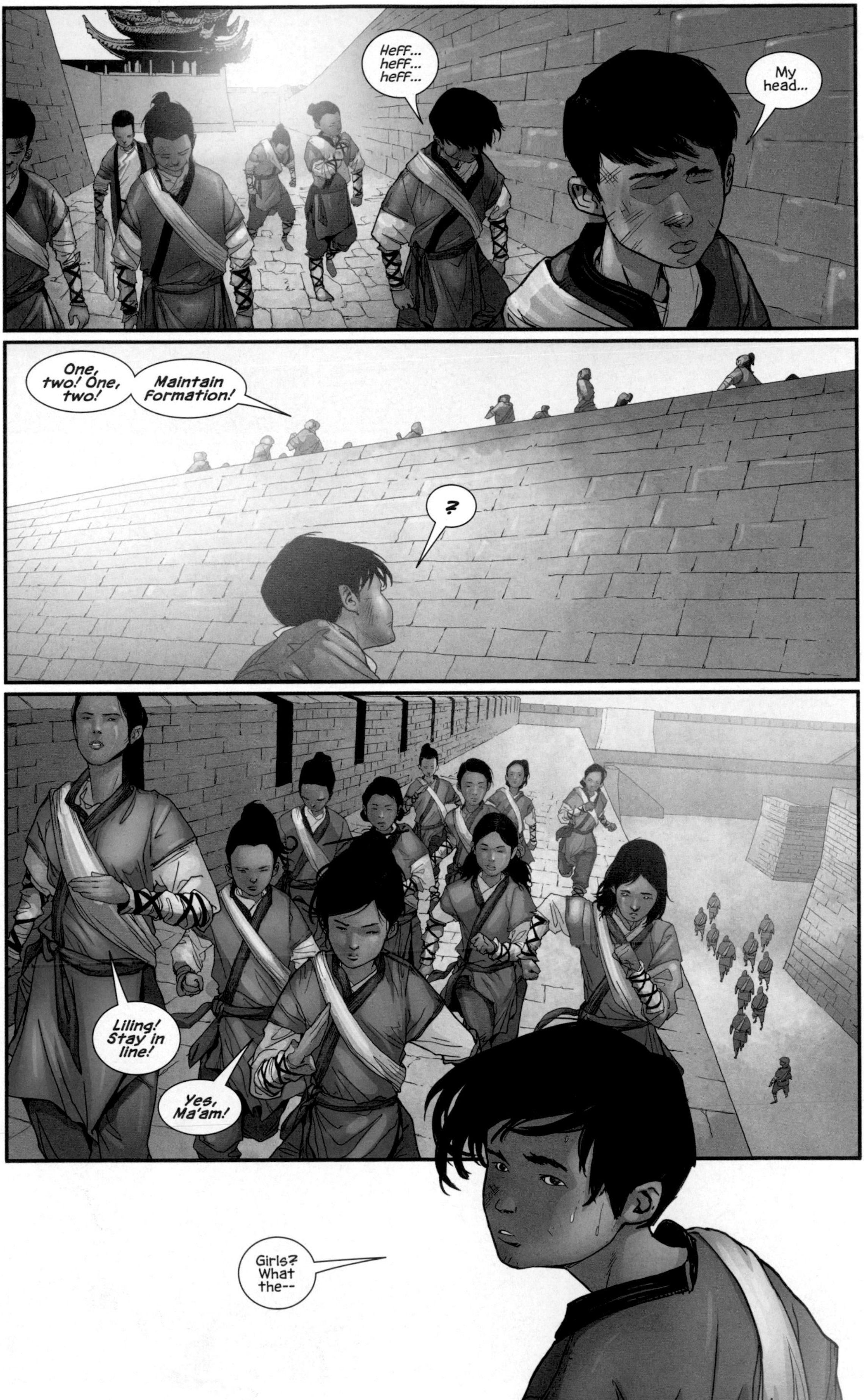
Heff... heff... heff...
My head...
One, two! One, two!
Maintain Formation!
?
Liling! Stay in line!
Yes, Ma'am!
Girls? What the--

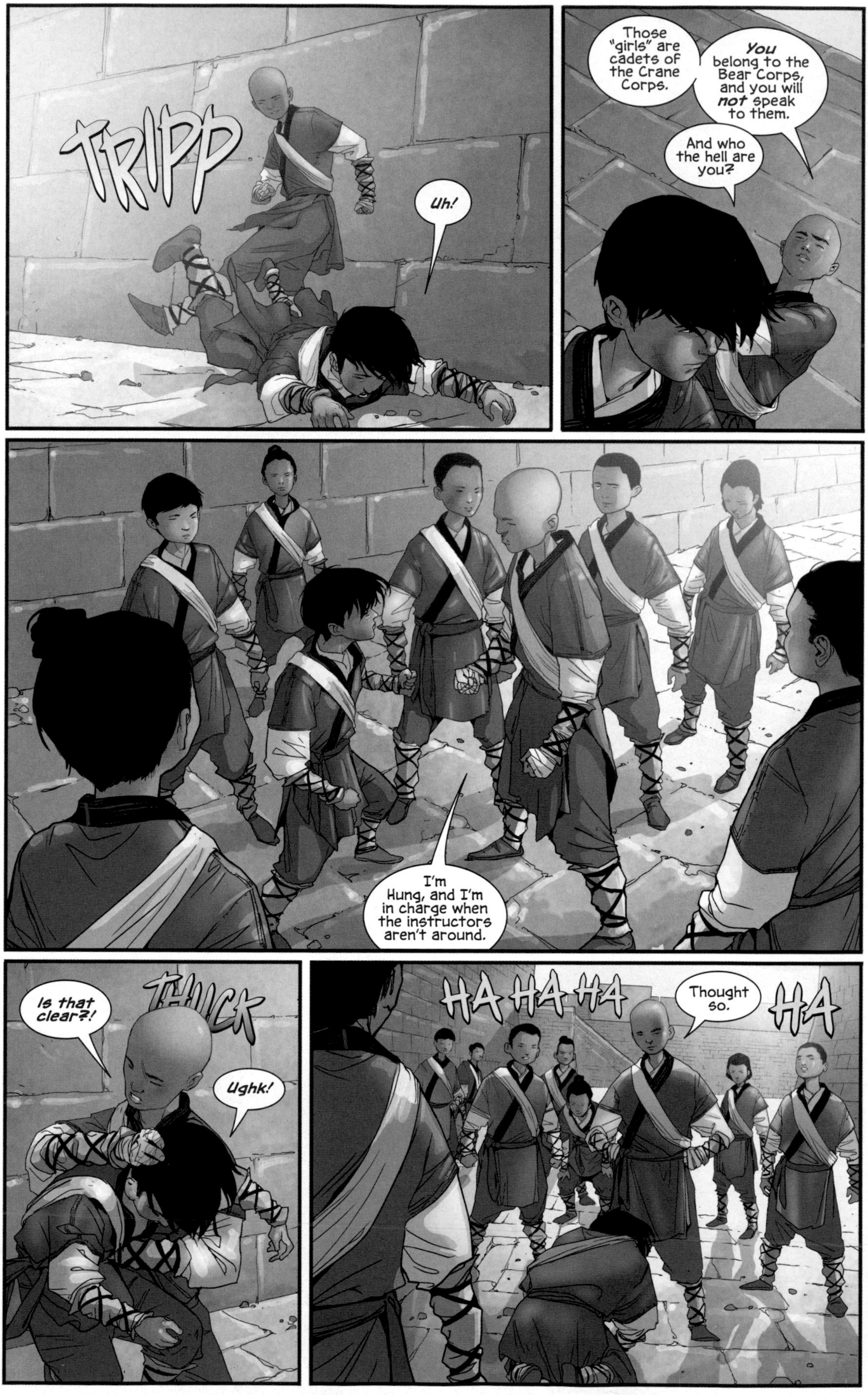
TRIPP
Uh!
Those "girls" are cadets of the Crane Corps.
You belong to the Bear Corps, and you will not speak to them.
And who the hell are you?
I'm Hung, and I'm in charge when the instructors aren't around.
THUCK
Is that clear?!
Ughk!
HA HA HA HA
Thought so.
HA

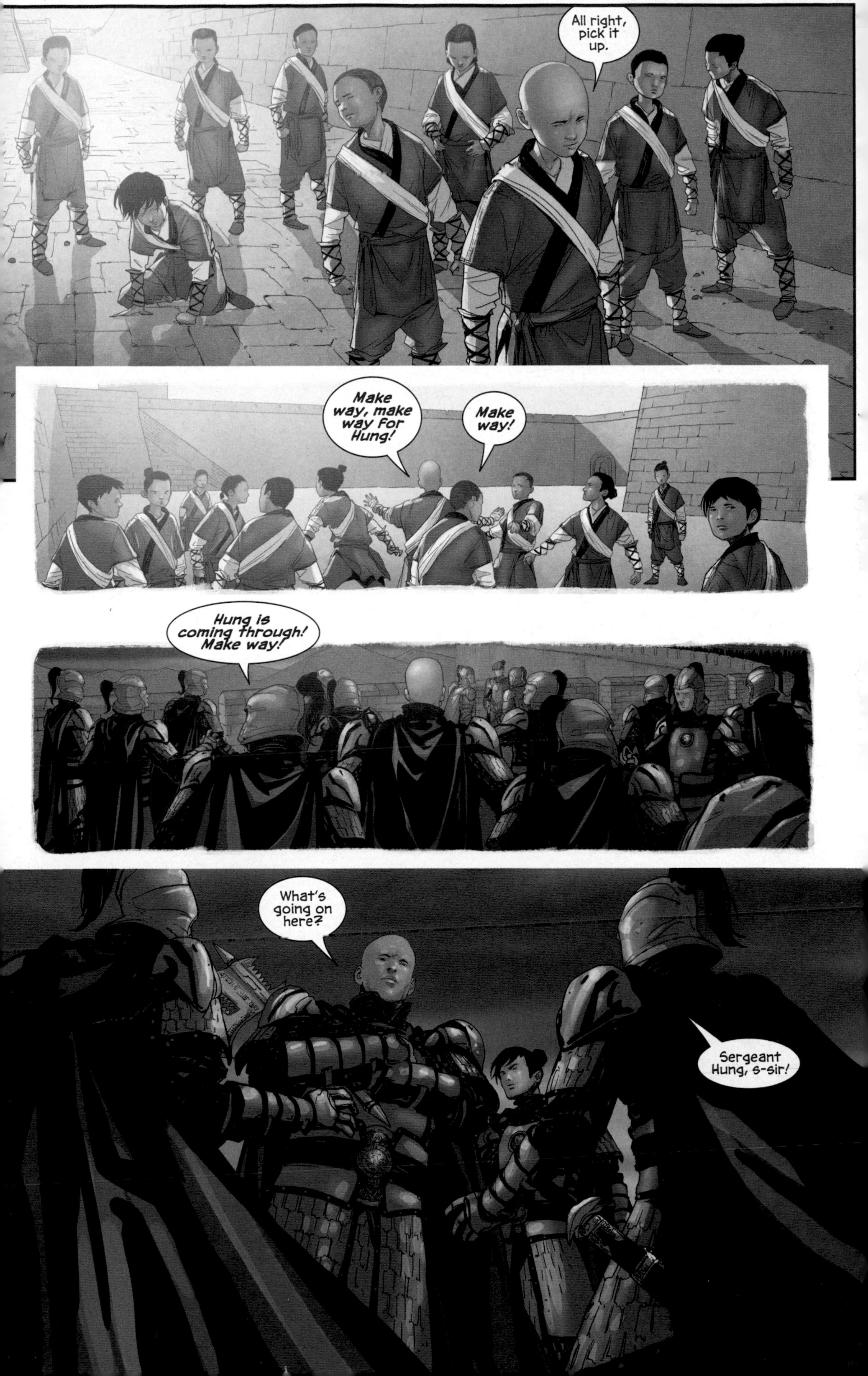

All right, pick it up.
Make way, make way for Hung!
Make way!
Hung is coming through! Make way!
What's going on here?
Sergeant Hung, s-sir!

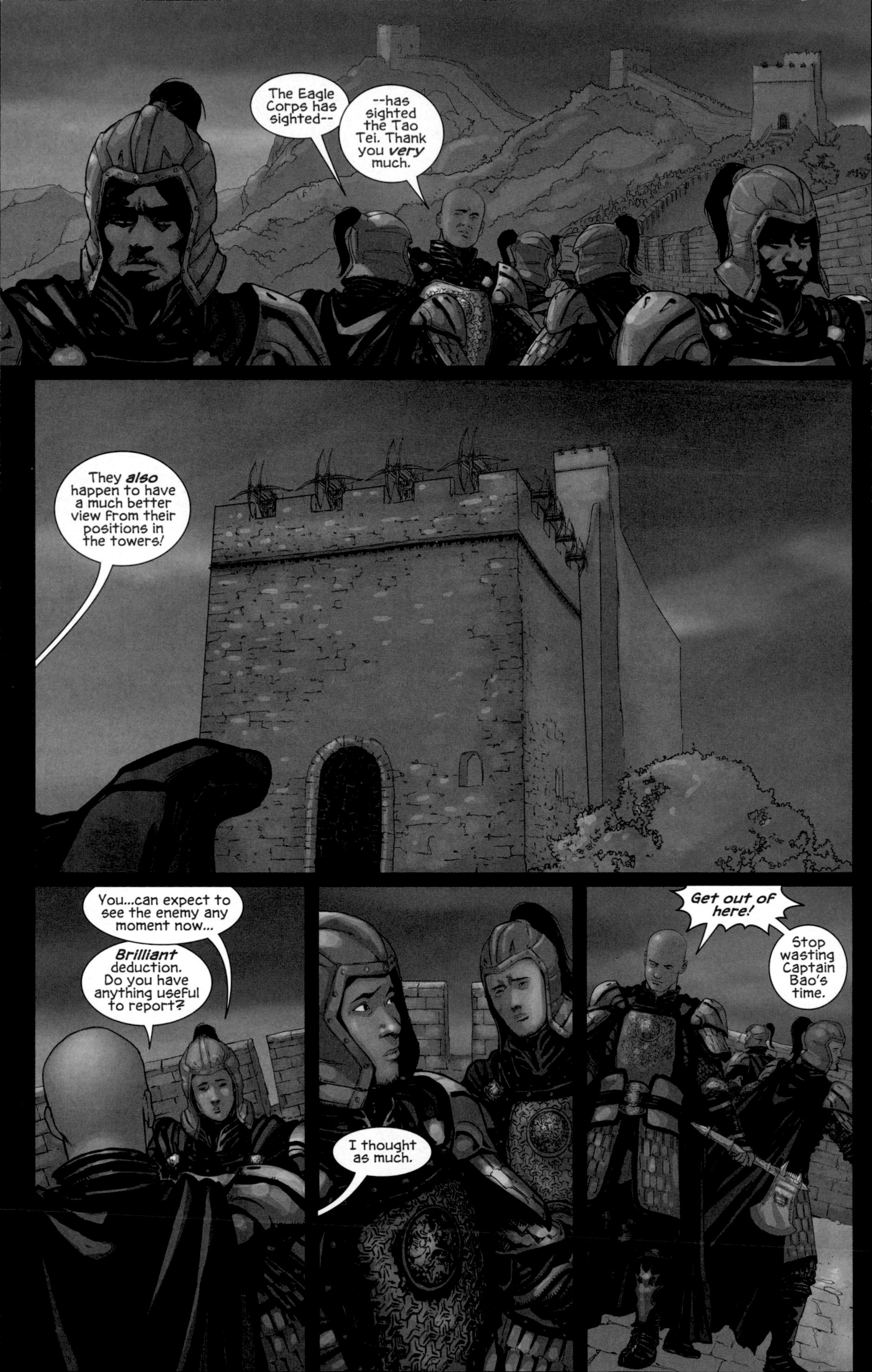
The Eagle Corps has sighted--
--has sighted the Tao Tei. Thank you *very* much.
They *also* happen to have a much better view from their positions in the towers!
You...can expect to see the enemy any moment now...
Brilliant deduction. Do you have anything useful to report?
I thought as much.
Get out of here!
Stop wasting Captain Bao's time.

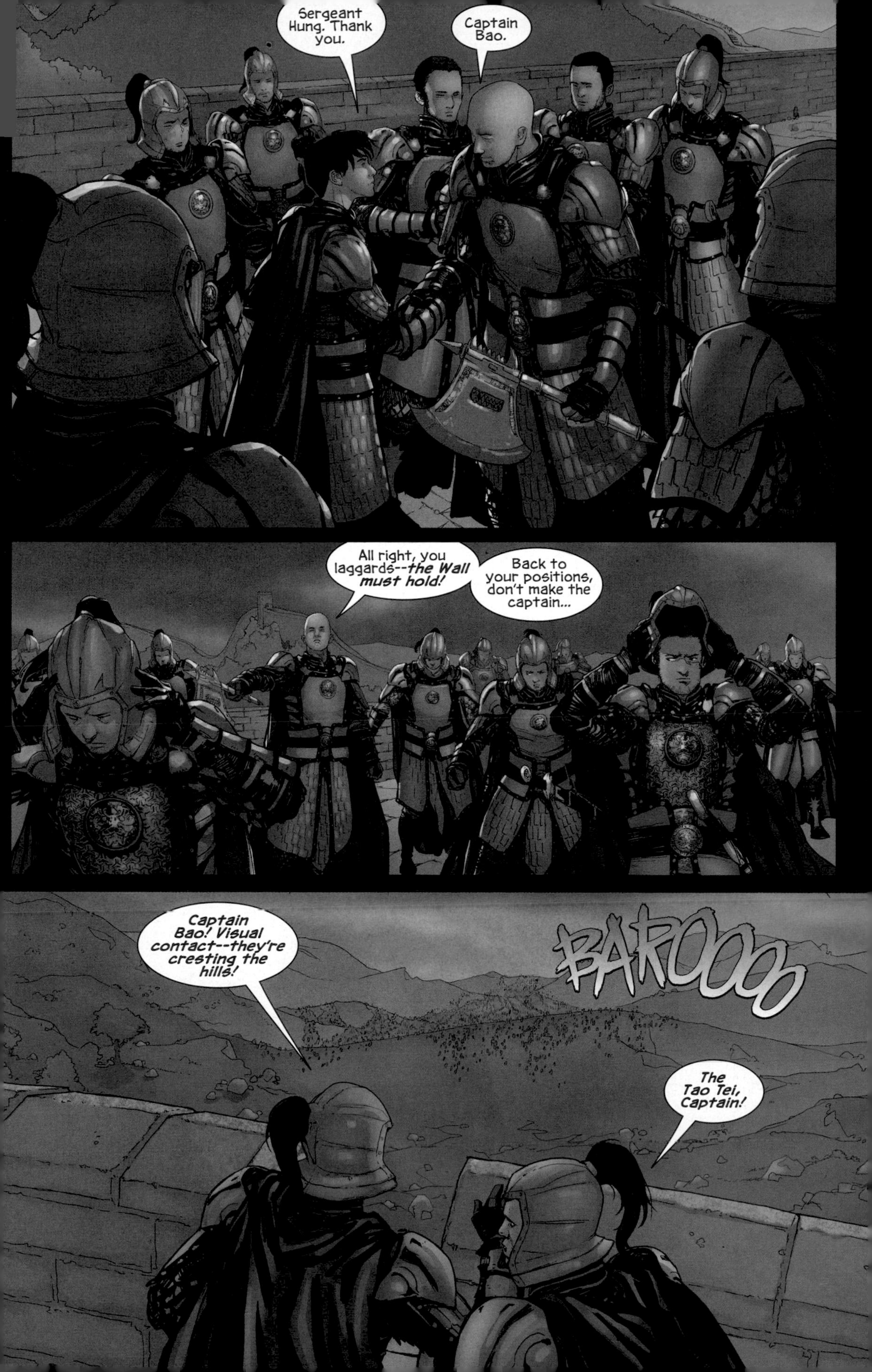

Sergeant Hung. Thank you.
Captain Bao.
All right, you laggards--*the Wall must hold!*
Back to your positions, don't make the captain...
Captain Bao! Visual contact--they're cresting the hills!
BAROOOO
The Tao Tei, Captain!

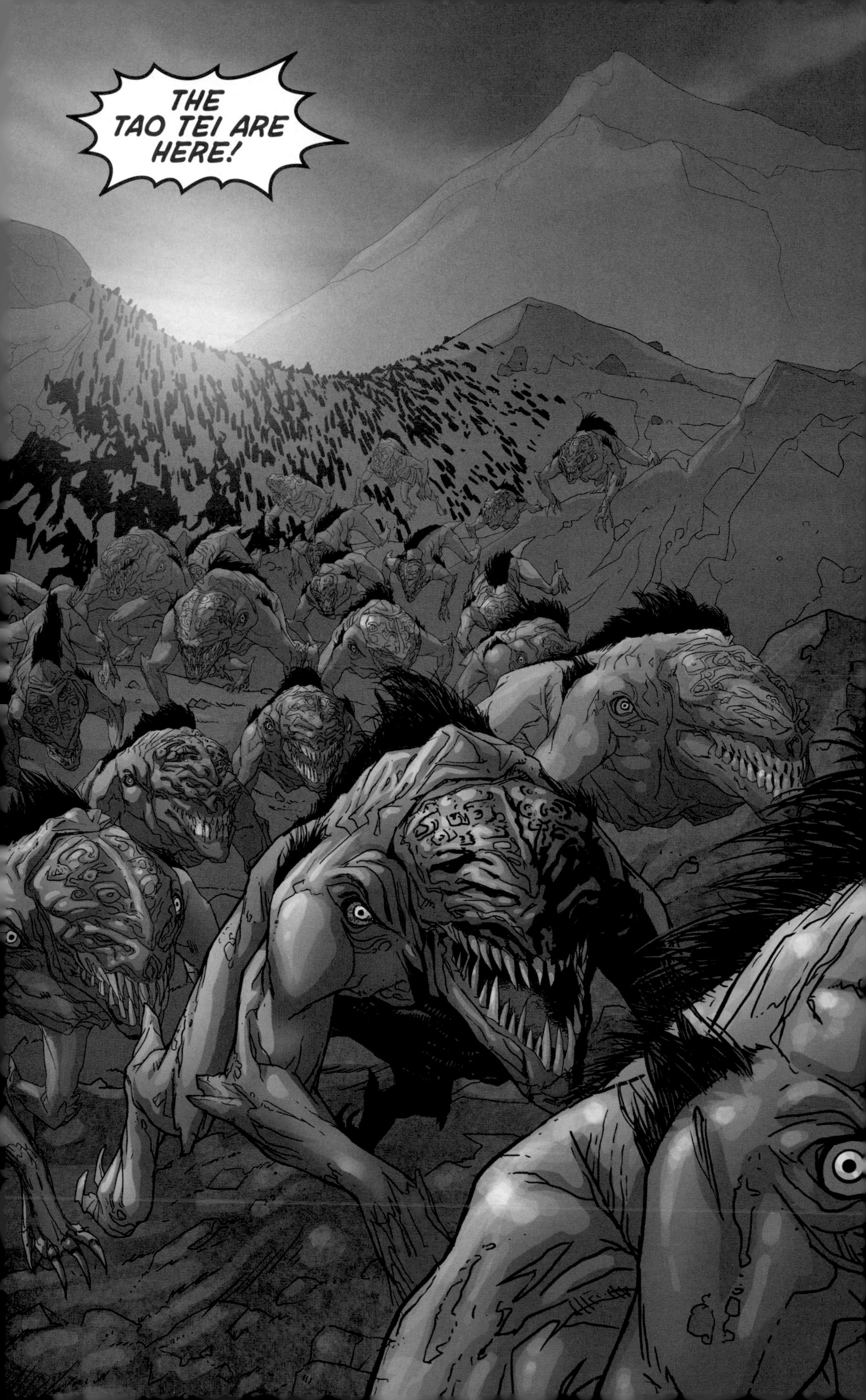
THE TAO TEI ARE HERE!

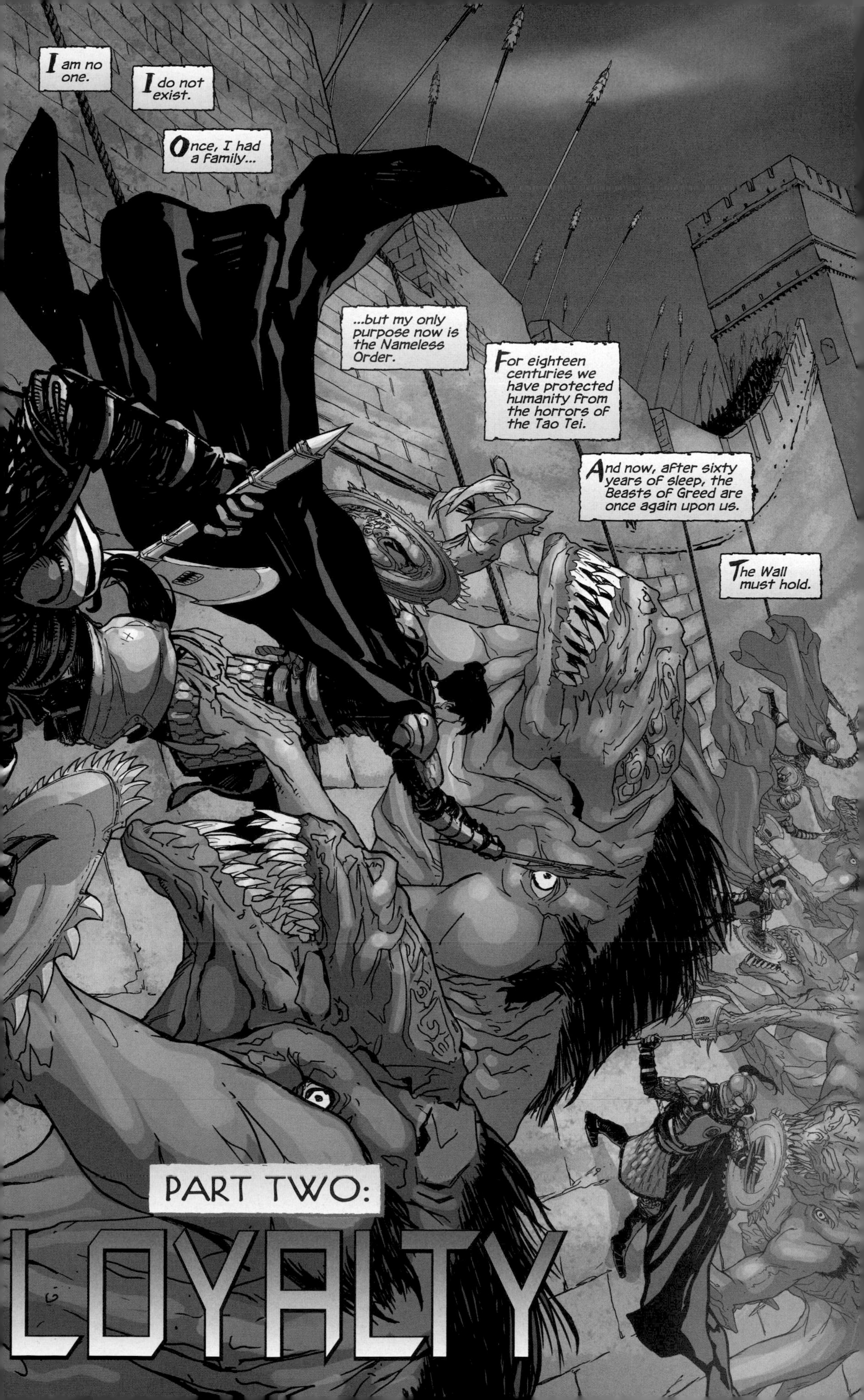
I am no one.
I do not exist.
Once, I had a family...
...but my only purpose now is the Nameless Order.
For eighteen centuries we have protected humanity from the horrors of the Tao Tei.
And now, after sixty years of sleep, the Beasts of Greed are once again upon us.
The Wall must hold.
PART TWO:
LOYALTY

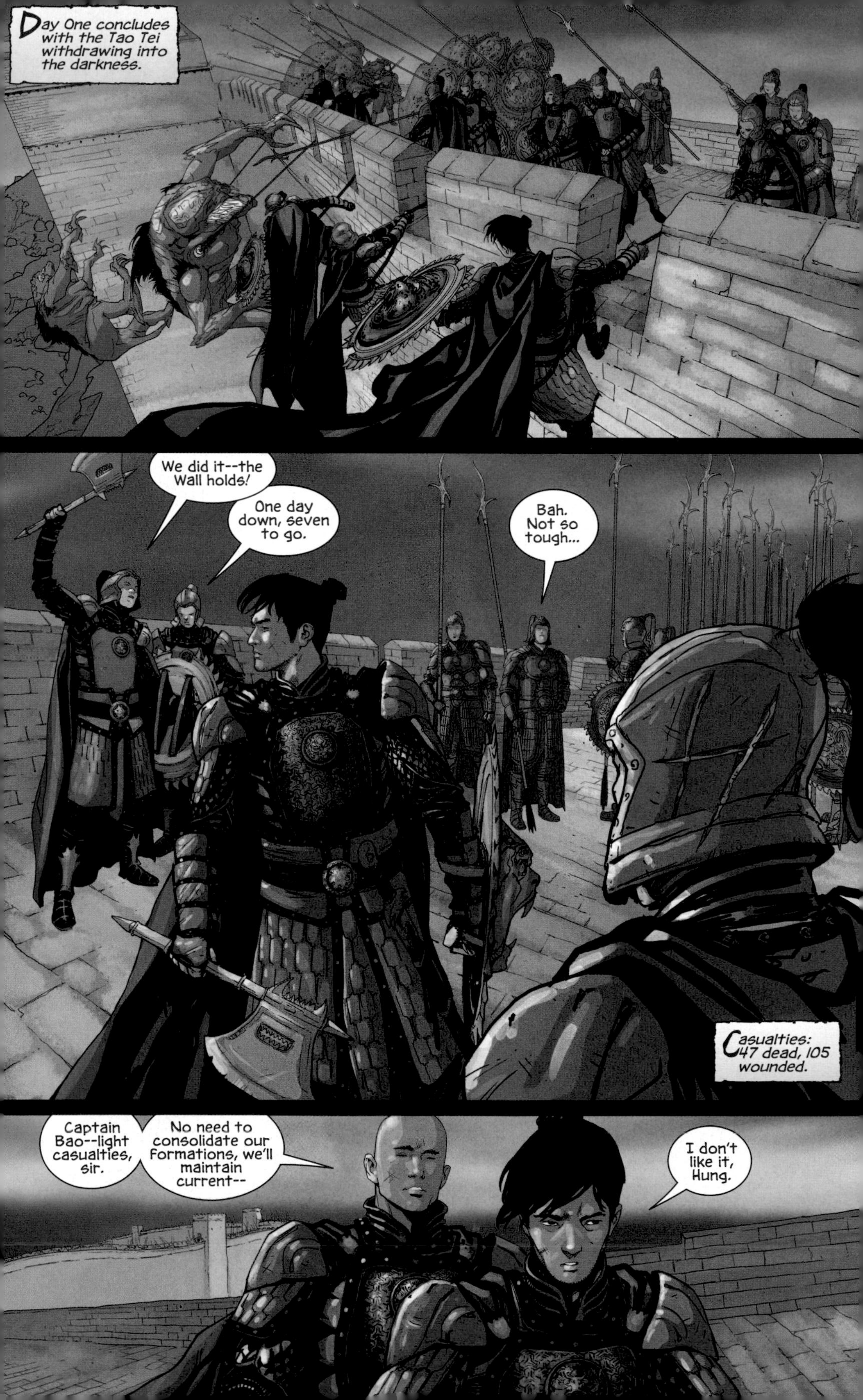
Day One concludes with the Tao Tei withdrawing into the darkness.
We did it--the Wall holds!
One day down, seven to go.
Bah. Not so tough...
Casualties: 47 dead, 105 wounded.
Captain Bao--light casualties, sir.
No need to consolidate our formations, we'll maintain current--
I don't like it, Hung.

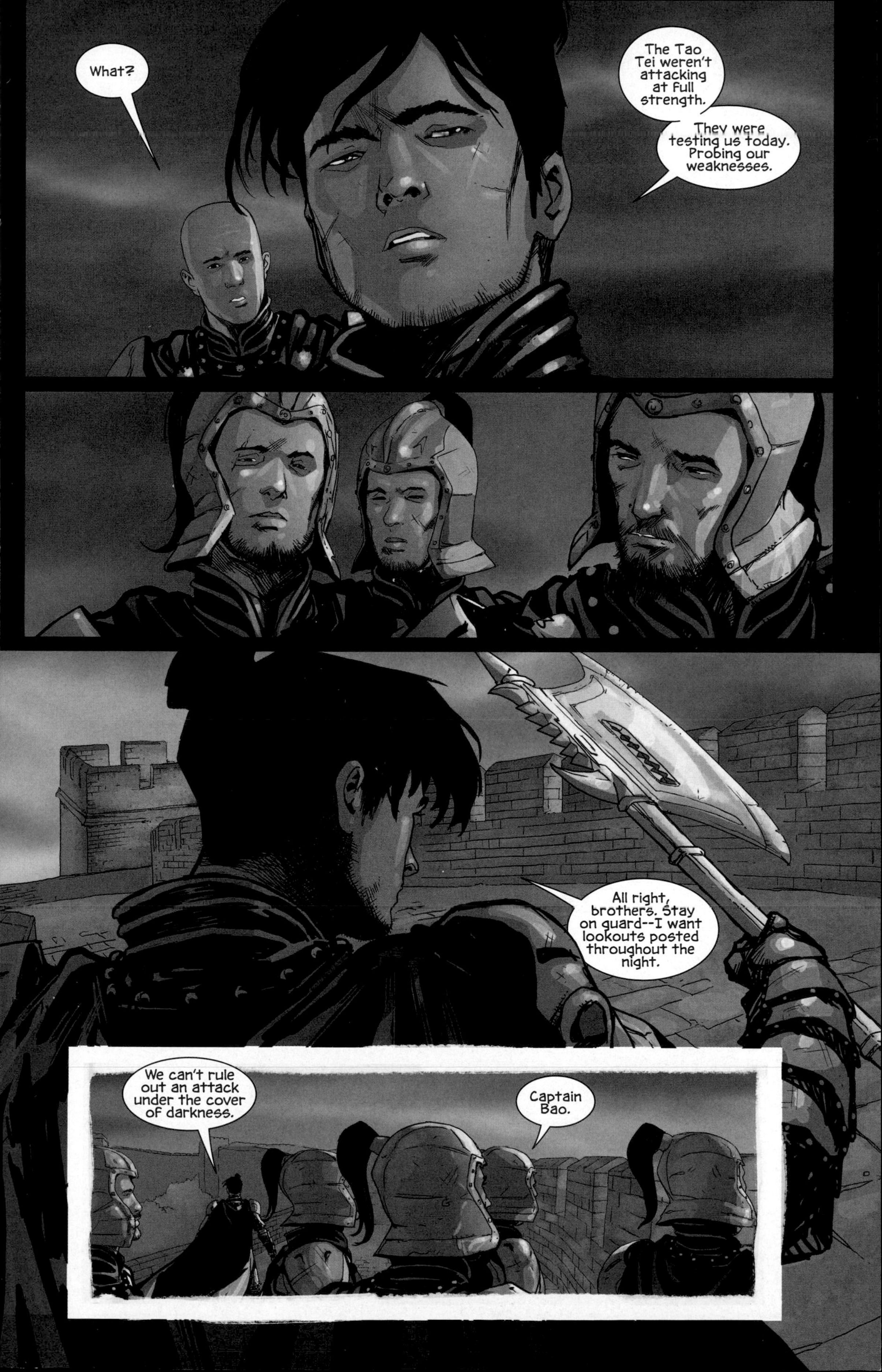
What?
The Tao Tei weren't attacking at full strength.
They were testing us today. Probing our weaknesses.
All right, brothers. Stay on guard--I want lookouts posted throughout the night.
We can't rule out an attack under the cover of darkness.
Captain Bao.

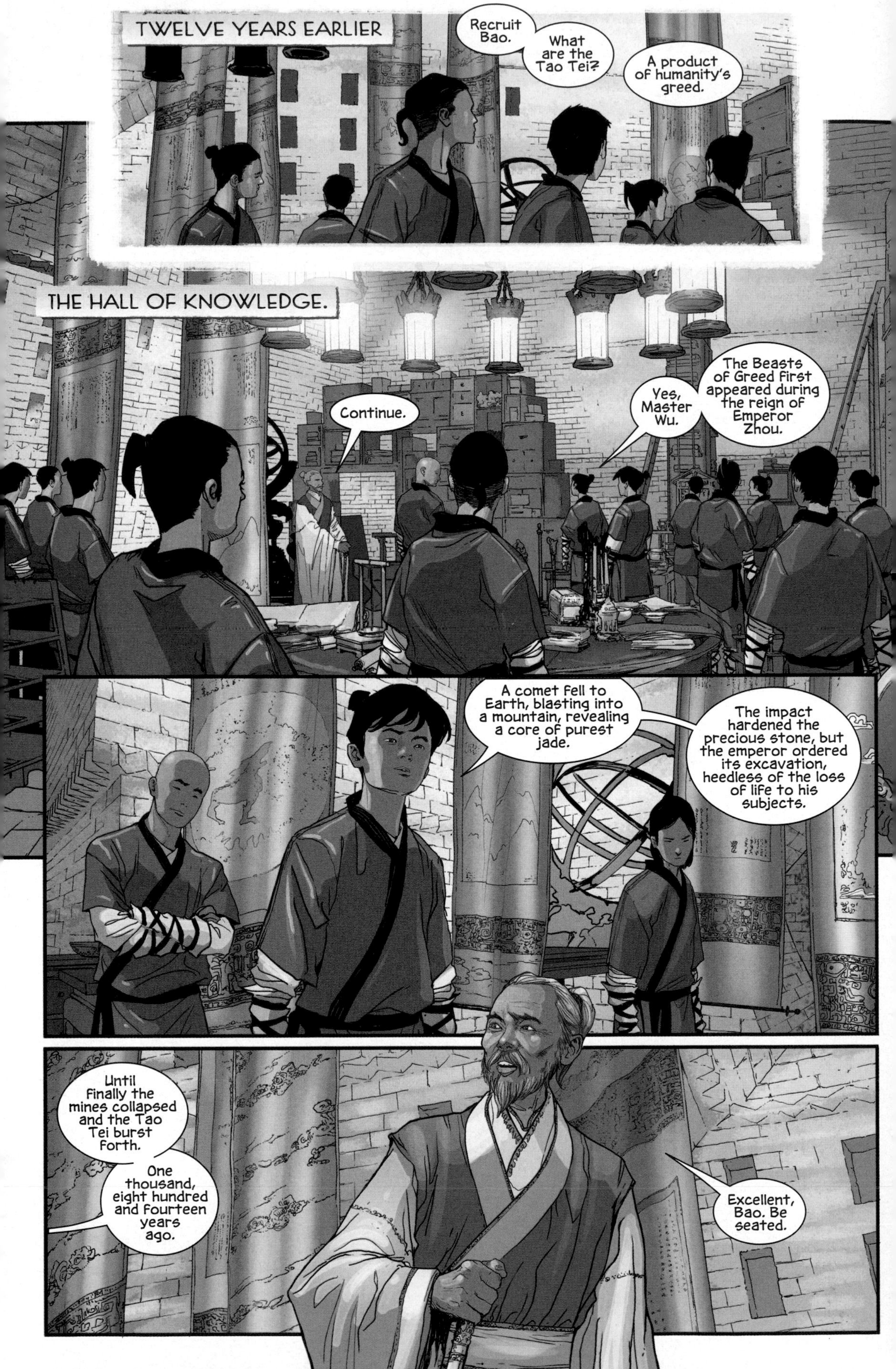
TWELVE YEARS EARLIER
Recruit Bao.
What are the Tao Tei?
A product of humanity's greed.
THE HALL OF KNOWLEDGE.
Continue.
Yes, Master Wu.
The Beasts of Greed first appeared during the reign of Emperor Zhou.
A comet fell to Earth, blasting into a mountain, revealing a core of purest jade.
The impact hardened the precious stone, but the emperor ordered its excavation, heedless of the loss of life to his subjects.
Until finally the mines collapsed and the Tao Tei burst forth.
One thousand, eight hundred and fourteen years ago.
Excellent, Bao. Be seated.

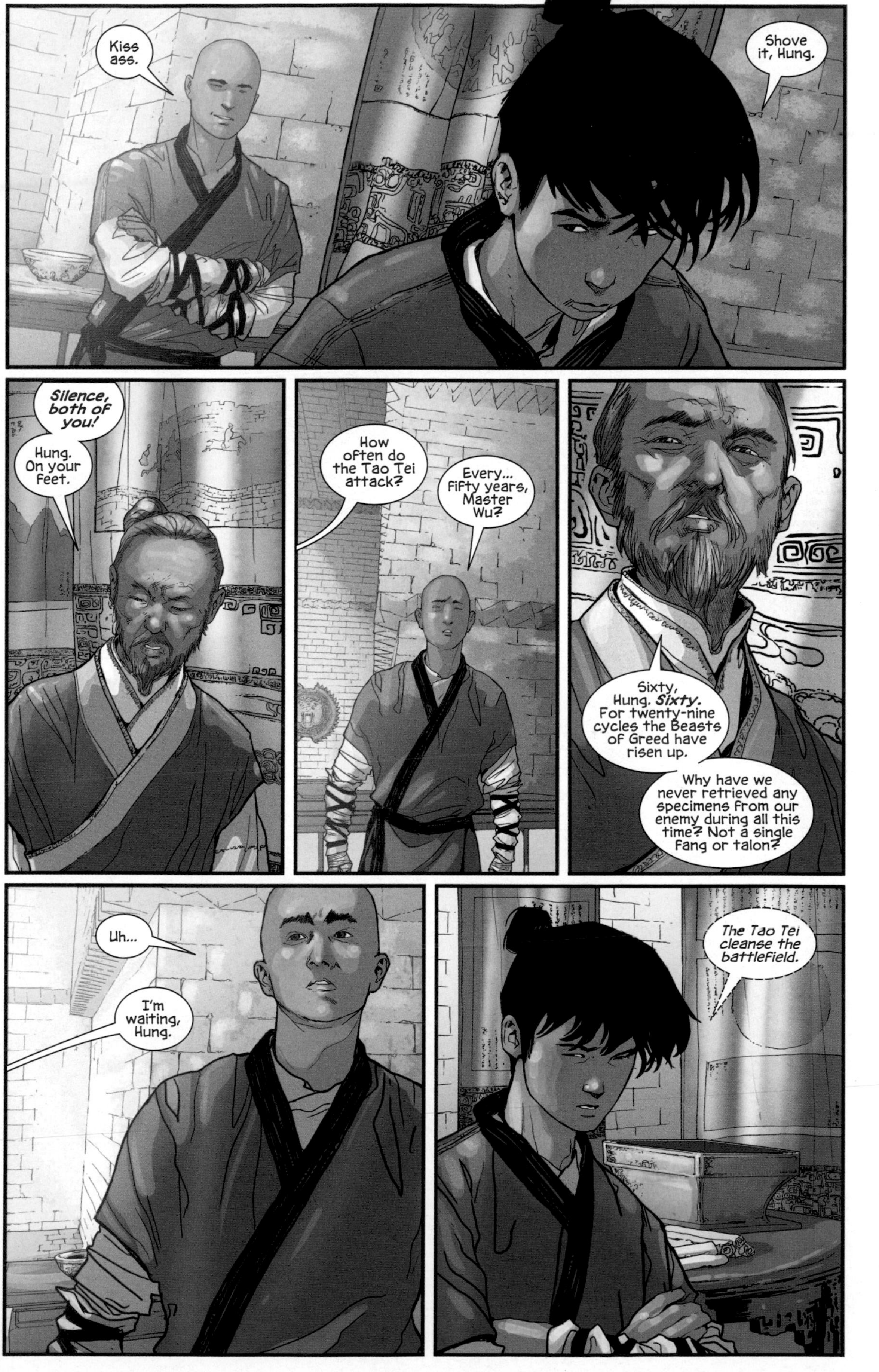
Kiss ass.
Shove it, Hung.
Silence, both of you!
Hung. On your feet.
How often do the Tao Tei attack?
Every... fifty years, Master Wu?
Sixty, Hung. Sixty. For twenty-nine cycles the Beasts of Greed have risen up.
Why have we never retrieved any specimens from our enemy during all this time? Not a single fang or talon?
Uh...
I'm waiting, Hung.
The Tao Tei cleanse the battlefield.

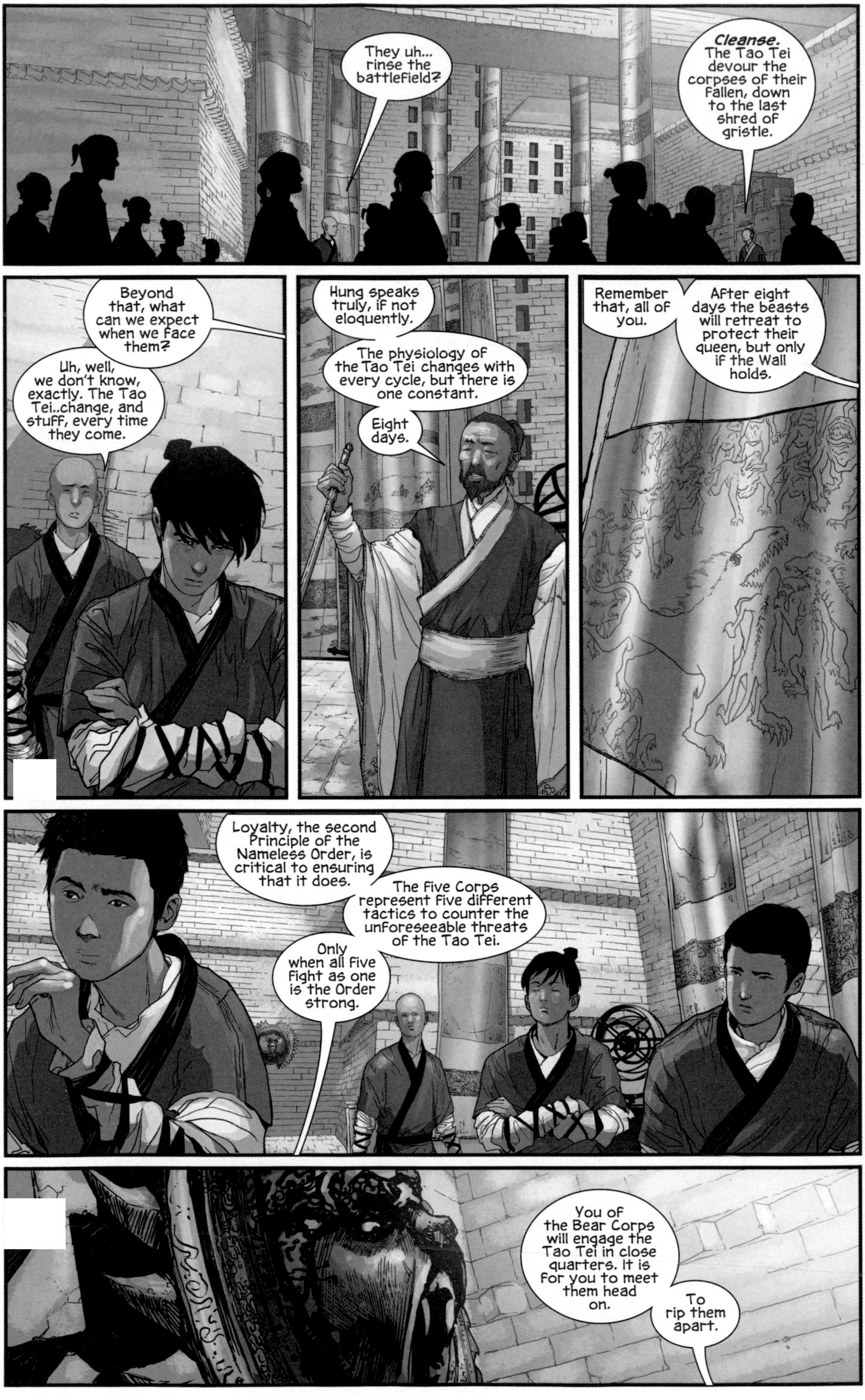
They uh... rinse the battlefield?
Cleanse. The Tao Tei devour the corpses of their fallen, down to the last shred of gristle.
Beyond that, what can we expect when we face them?
Uh, well, we don't know, exactly. The Tao Tei..change, and stuff, every time they come.
Hung speaks truly, if not eloquently.
The physiology of the Tao Tei changes with every cycle, but there is one constant.
Eight days.
Remember that, all of you.
After eight days the beasts will retreat to protect their queen, but only if the Wall holds.
Loyalty, the second Principle of the Nameless Order, is critical to ensuring that it does.
The Five Corps represent five different tactics to counter the unforeseeable threats of the Tao Tei.
Only when all five fight as one is the Order strong.
You of the Bear Corps will engage the Tao Tei in close quarters. It is for you to meet them head on.
To rip them apart.

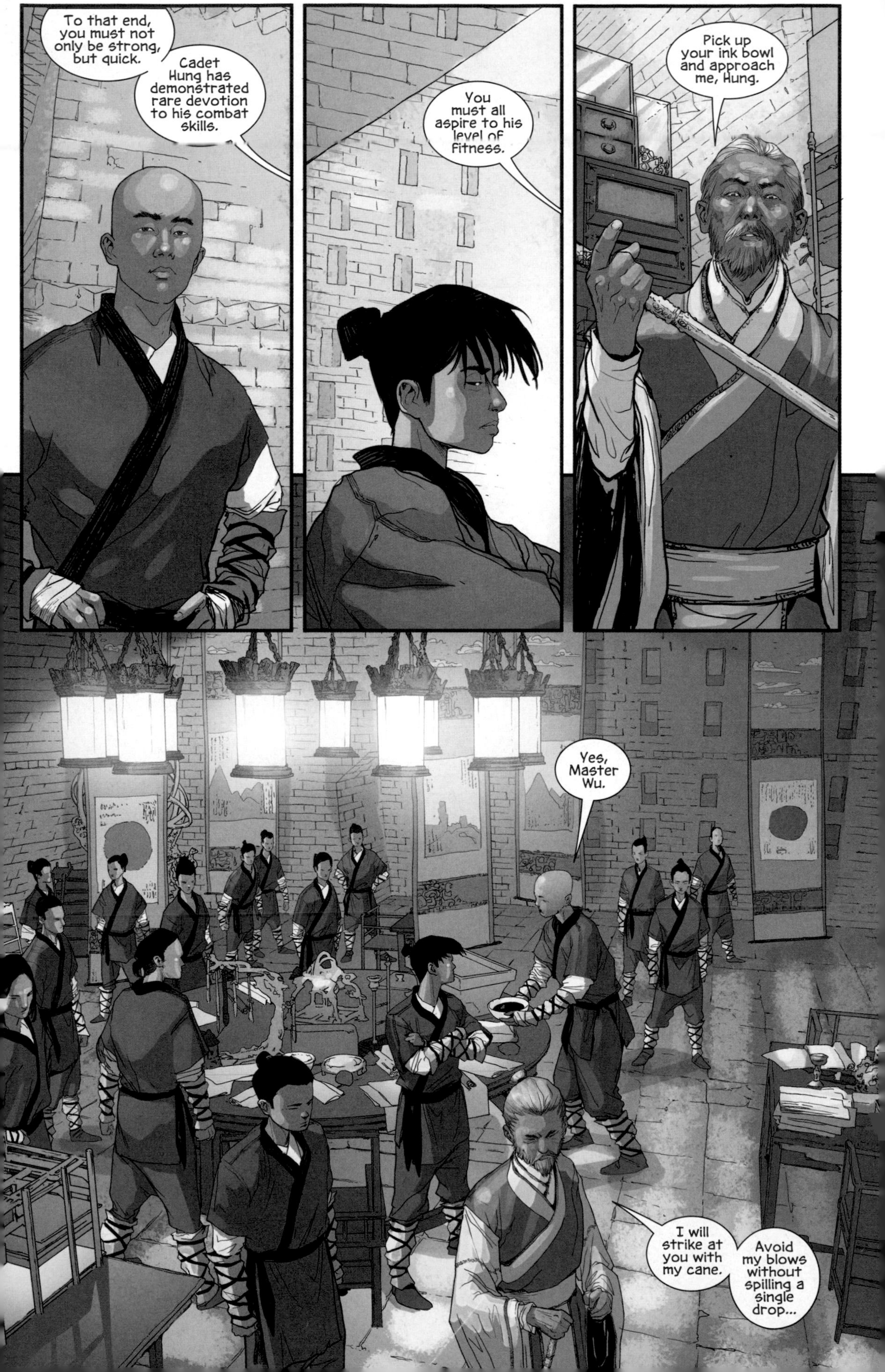
To that end, you must not only be strong, but quick.
Cadet Hung has demonstrated rare devotion to his combat skills.
You must all aspire to his level of fitness.
Pick up your ink bowl and approach me, Hung.
Yes, Master Wu.
I will strike at you with my cane.
Avoid my blows without spilling a single drop...

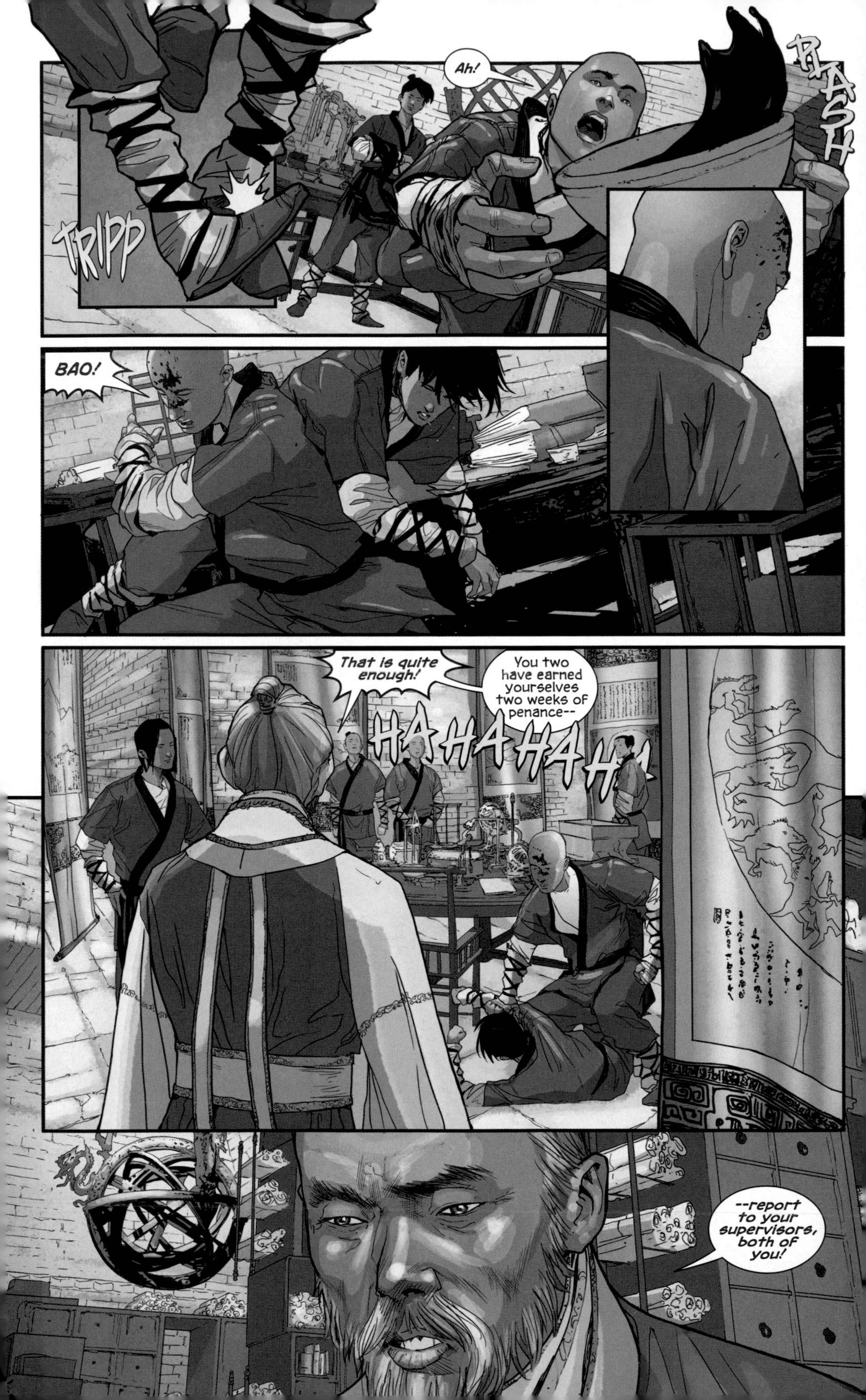
Ah!
RASH
TRIPP
BAO!
That is quite enough!
You two have earned yourselves two weeks of penance--
HAHAHAHA
--report to your supervisors, both of you!

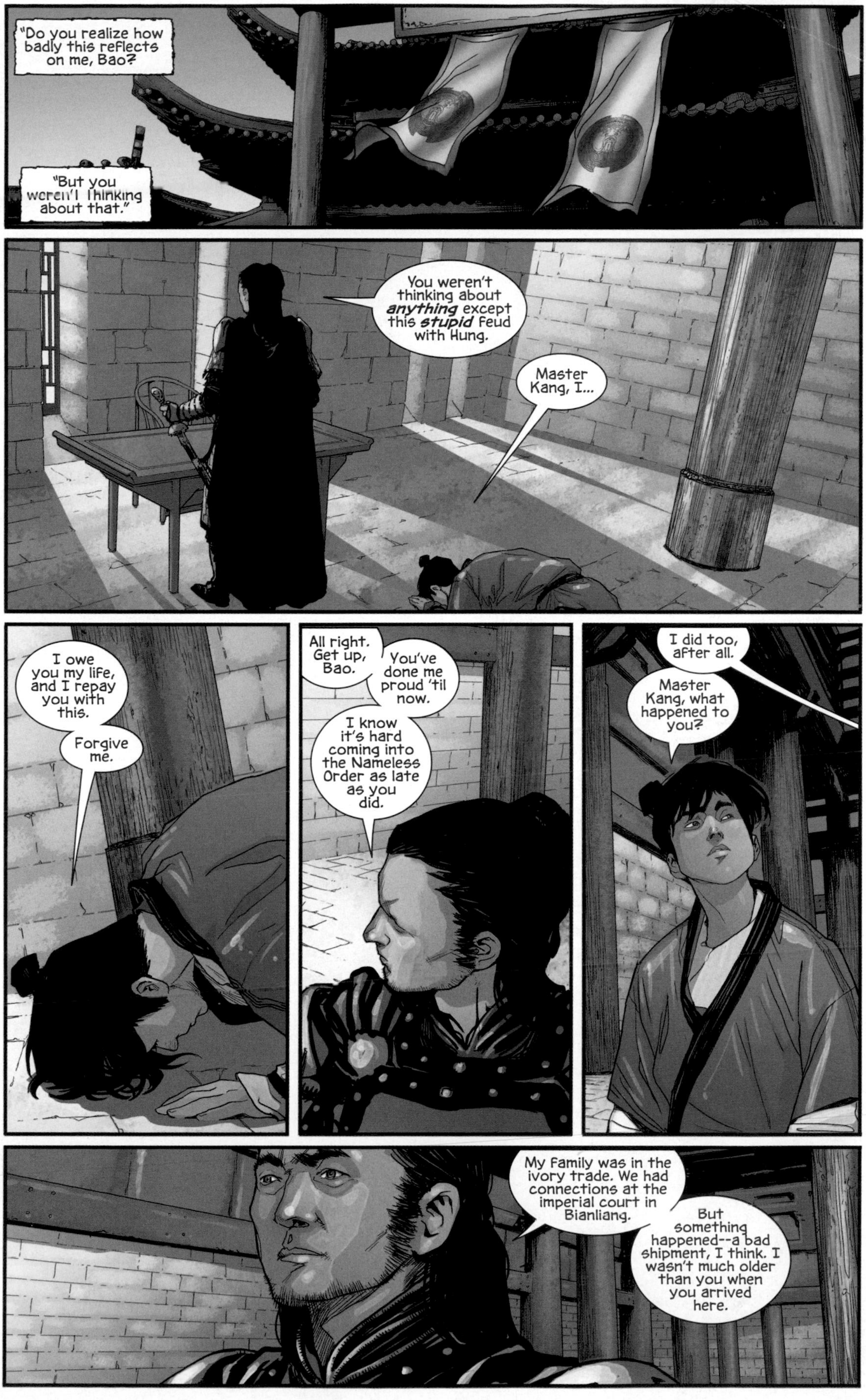
"Do you realize how badly this reflects on me, Bao?
"But you weren't thinking about that."
You weren't thinking about anything except this stupid feud with Hung.
Master Kang, I...
I owe you my life, and I repay you with this.
Forgive me.
All right. Get up, Bao.
You've done me proud 'til now.
I know it's hard coming into the Nameless Order as late as you did.
I did too, after all.
Master Kang, what happened to you?
My family was in the ivory trade. We had connections at the imperial court in Bianliang.
But something happened--a bad shipment, I think. I wasn't much older than you when you arrived here.

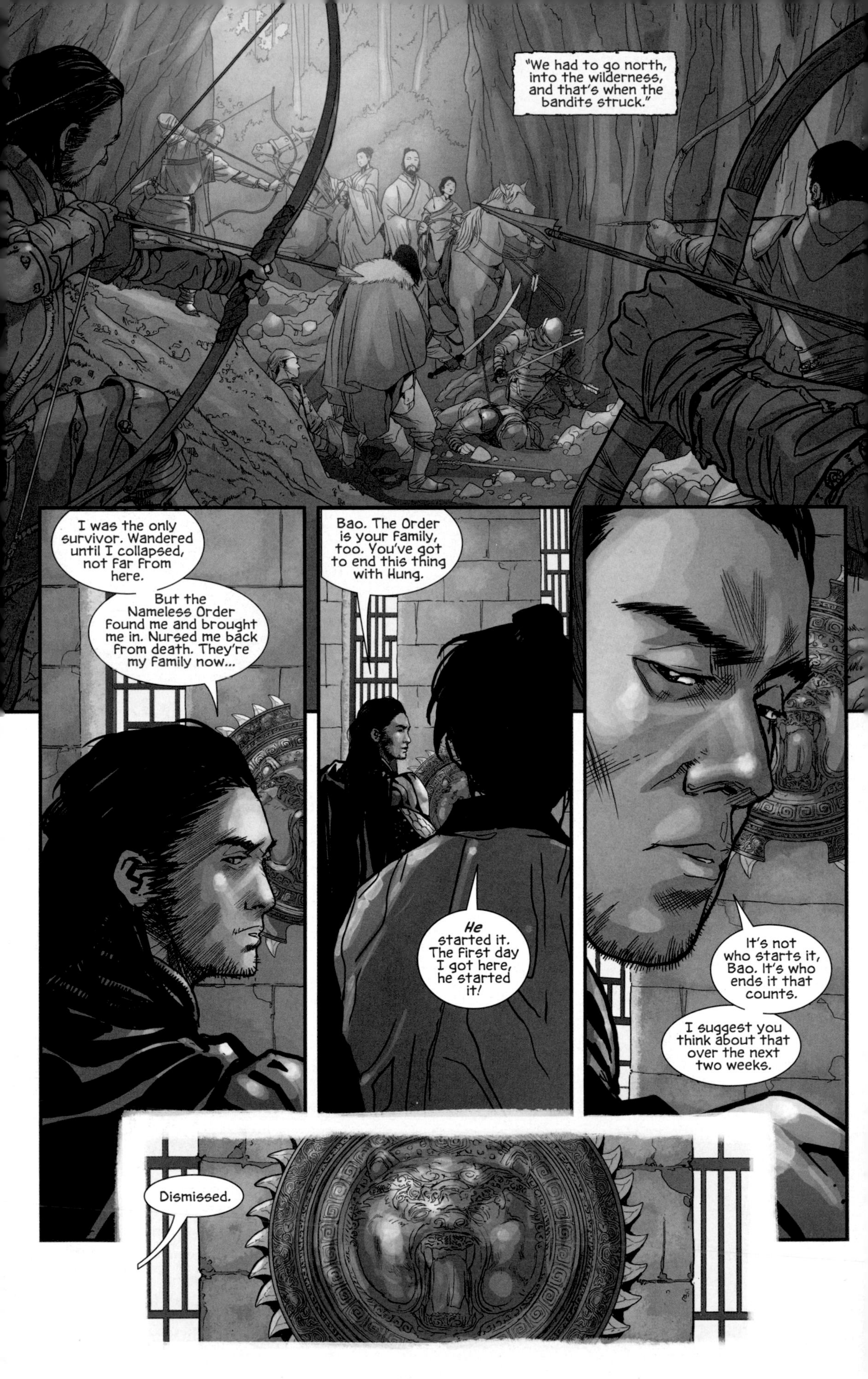
"We had to go north, into the wilderness, and that's when the bandits struck."
I was the only survivor. Wandered until I collapsed, not far from here.
But the Nameless Order found me and brought me in. Nursed me back from death. They're my family now...
Bao. The Order is your family, too. You've got to end this thing with Hung.
He started it. The first day I got here, he started it!
It's not who starts it, Bao. It's who ends it that counts.
I suggest you think about that over the next two weeks.
Dismissed.

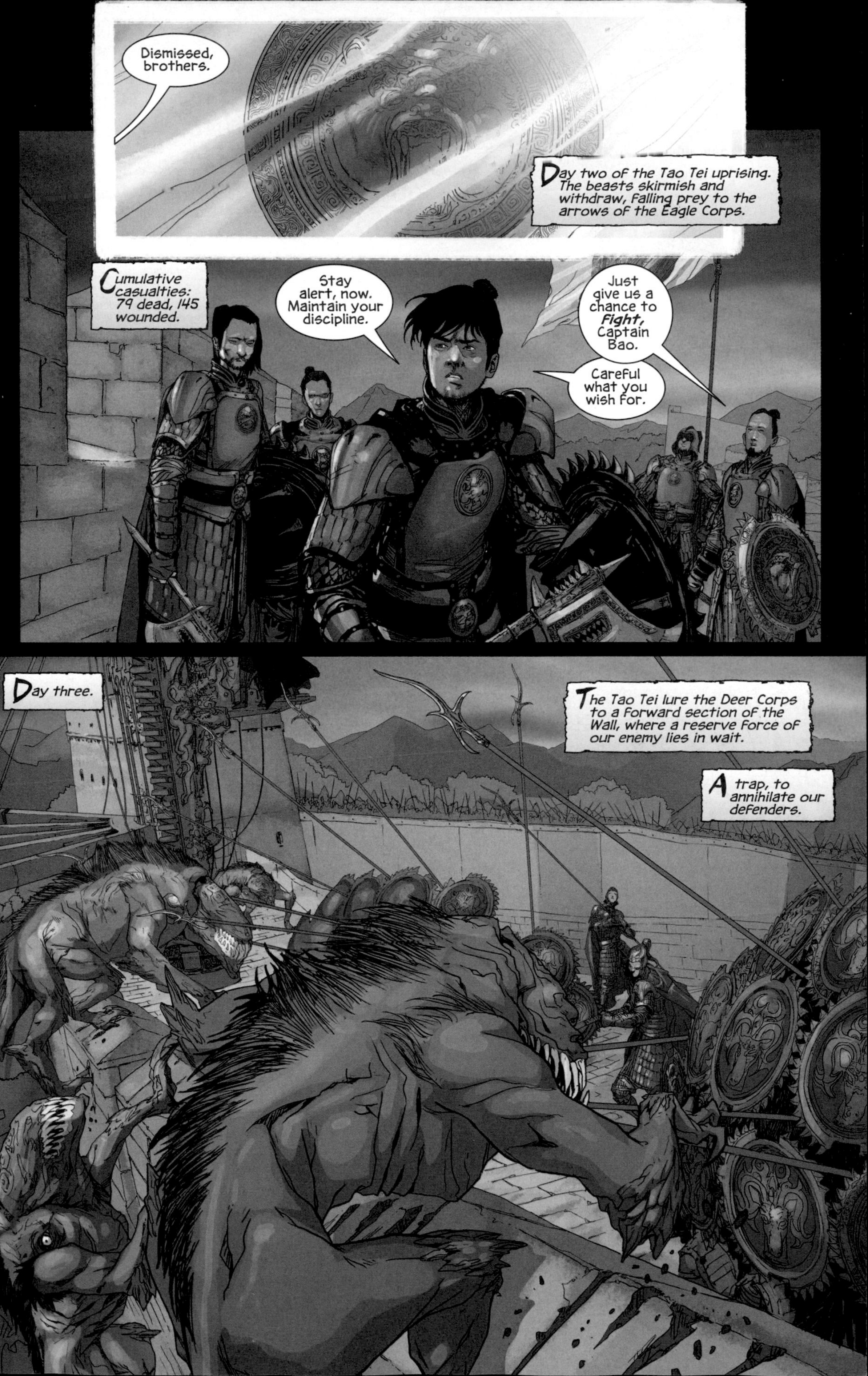
Dismissed, brothers.
Day two of the Tao Tei uprising. The beasts skirmish and withdraw, falling prey to the arrows of the Eagle Corps.
Cumulative casualties: 79 dead, 145 wounded.
Stay alert, now. Maintain your discipline.
Just give us a chance to Fight, Captain Bao.
Careful what you wish for.
Day three.
The Tao Tei lure the Deer Corps to a forward section of the Wall, where a reserve force of our enemy lies in wait.
A trap, to annihilate our defenders.

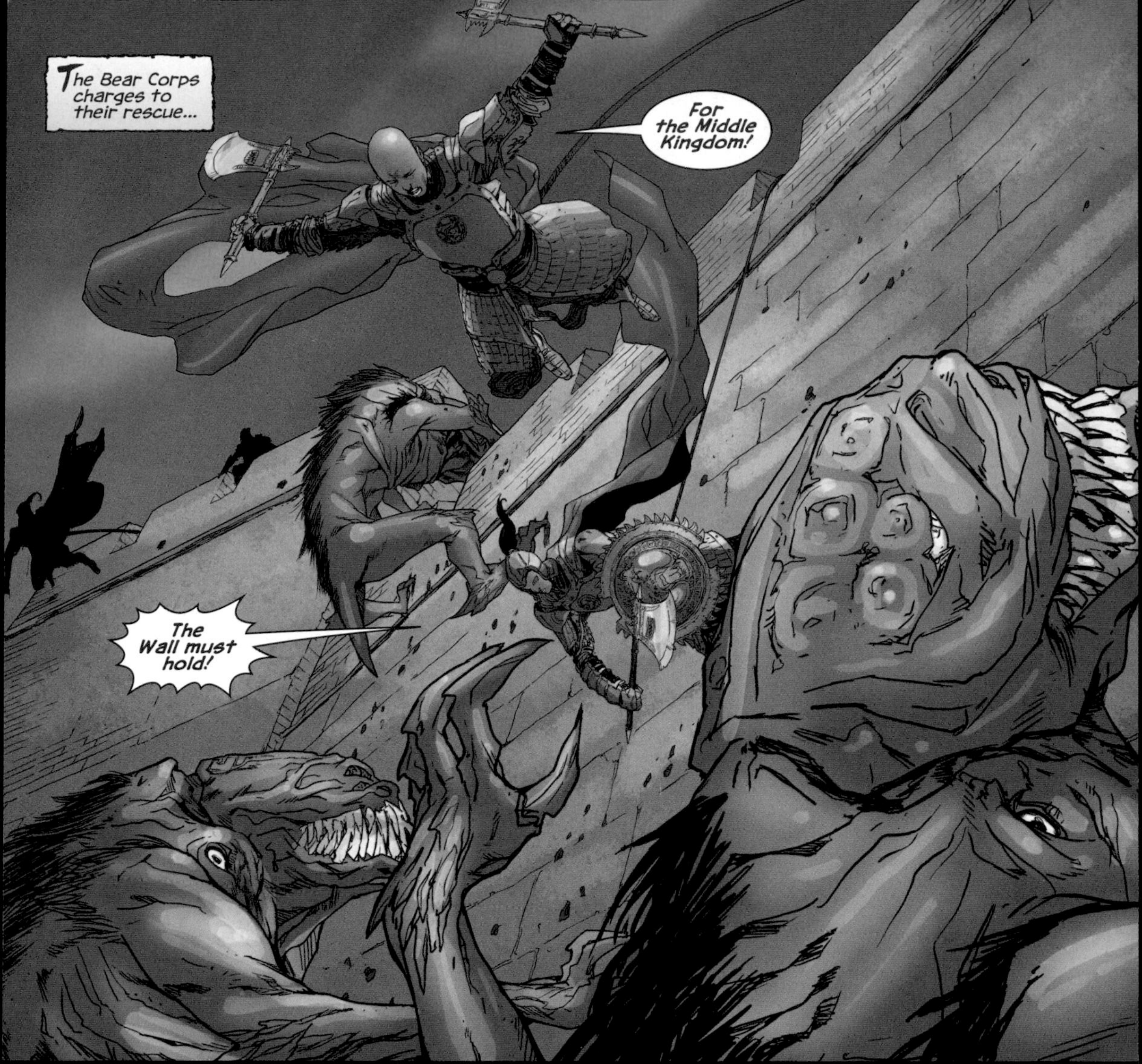
The Bear Corps charges to their rescue...
For the Middle Kingdom!
The Wall must hold!

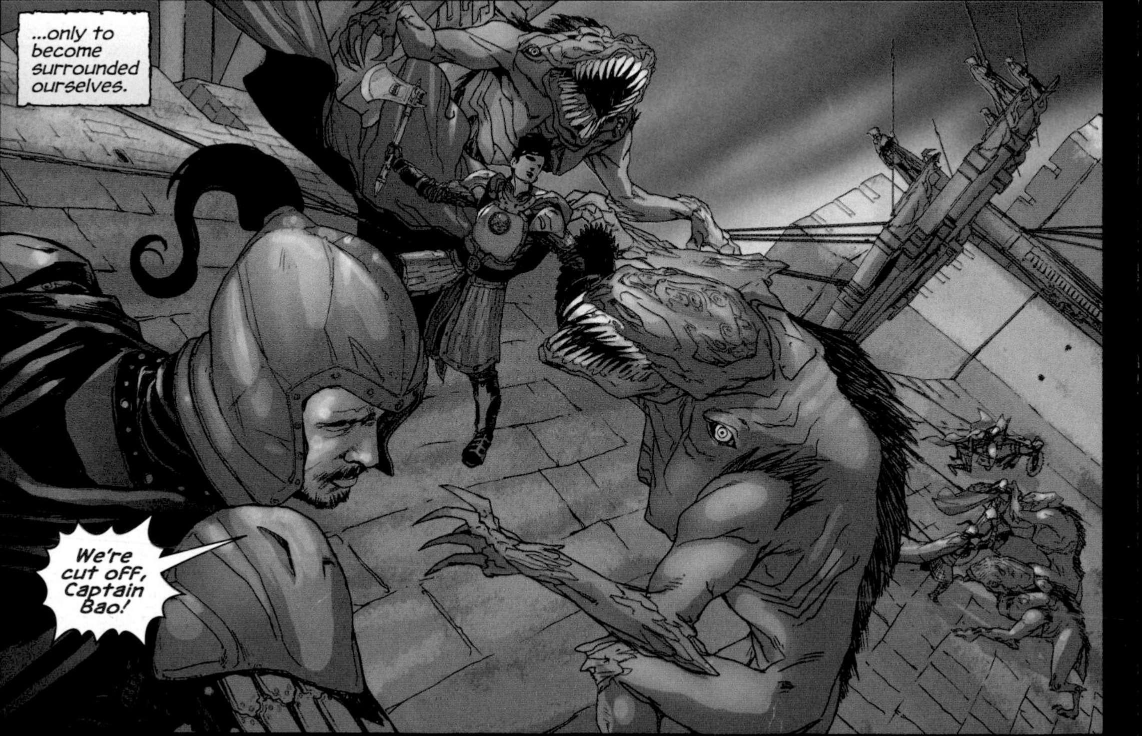
...only to become surrounded ourselves.
We're cut off, Captain Bao!

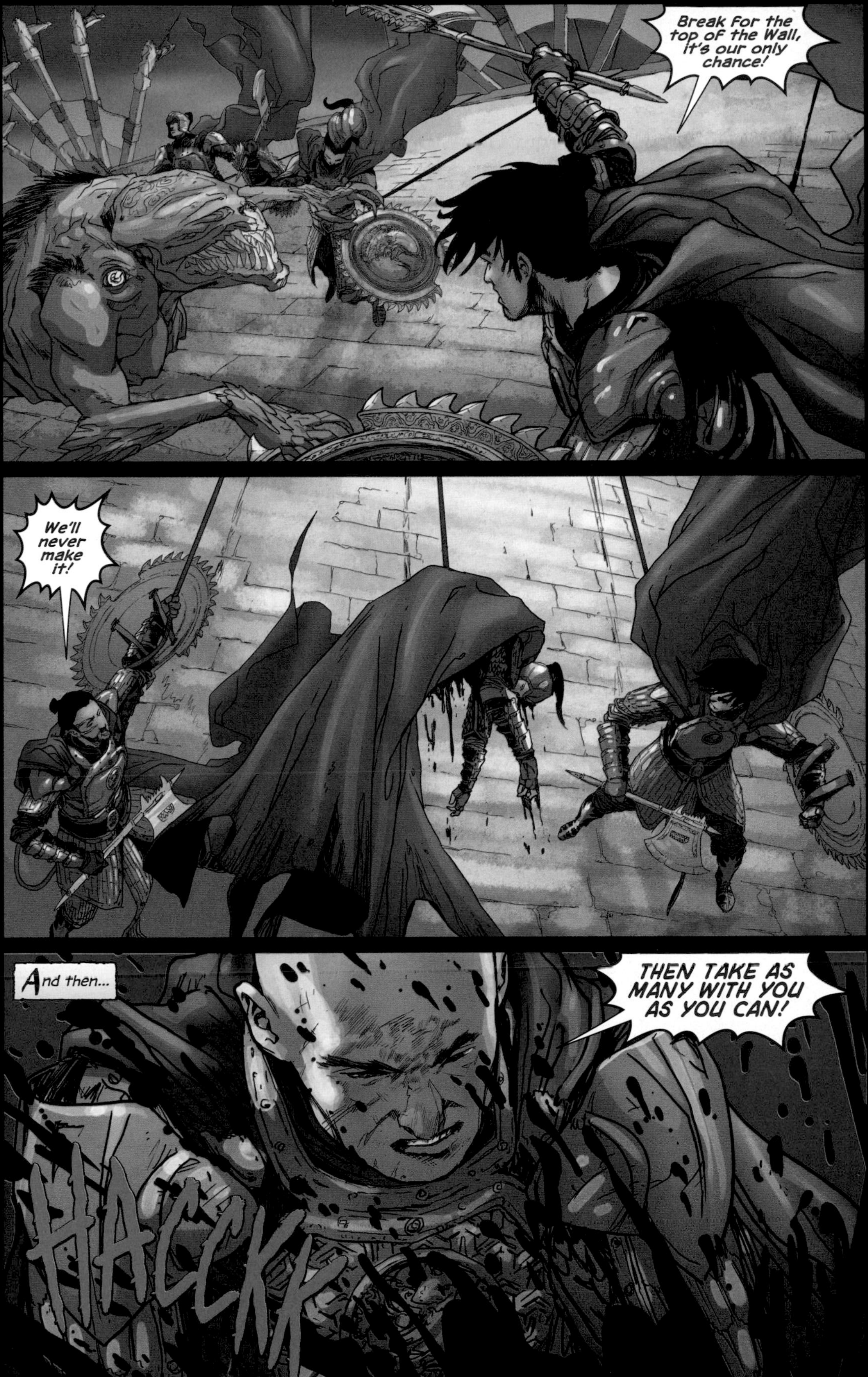
Break for the top of the Wall, it's our only chance!
We'll never make it!
And then...
THEN TAKE AS MANY WITH YOU AS YOU CAN!
HACCKK

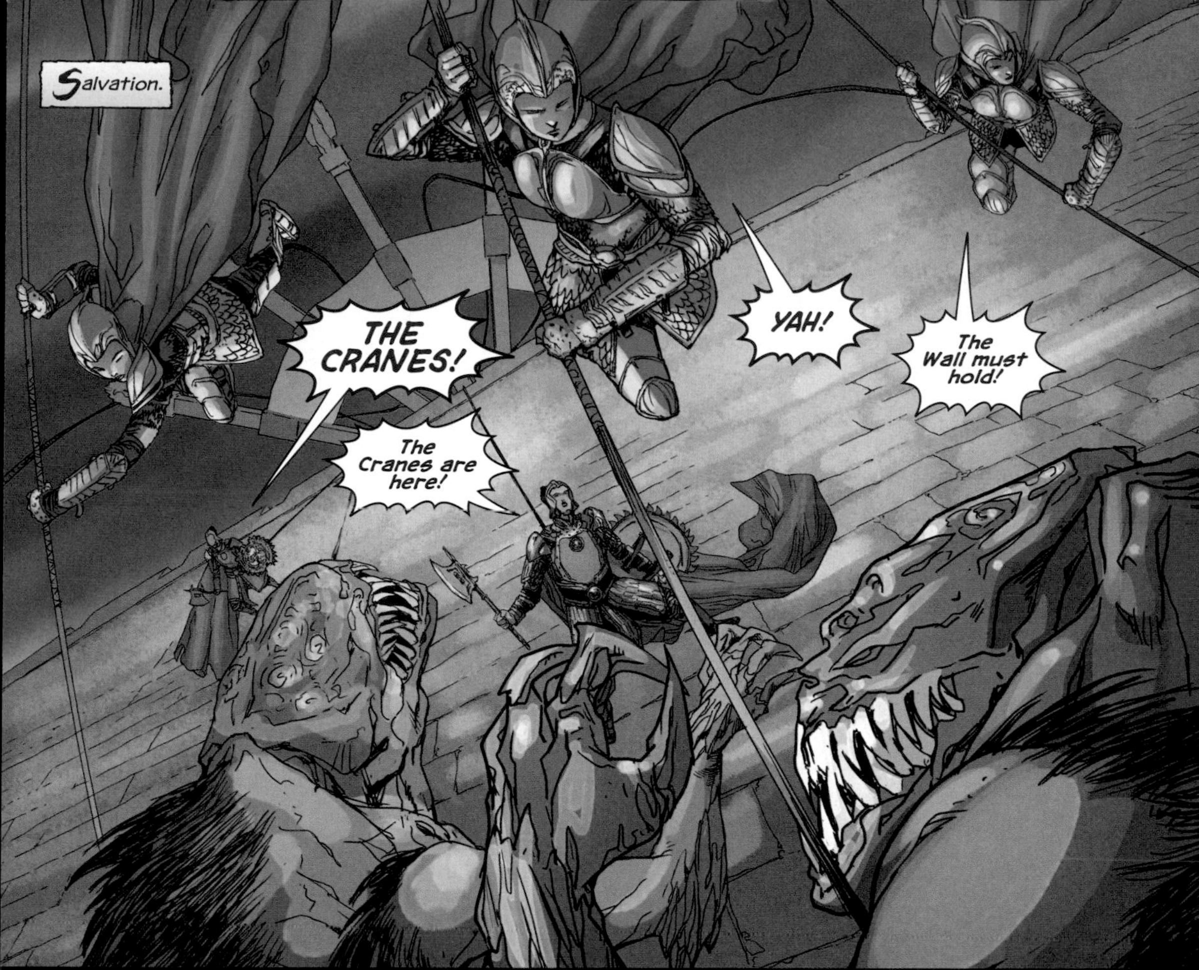
Salvation.
THE CRANES!
The Cranes are here!
YAH!
The Wall must hold!

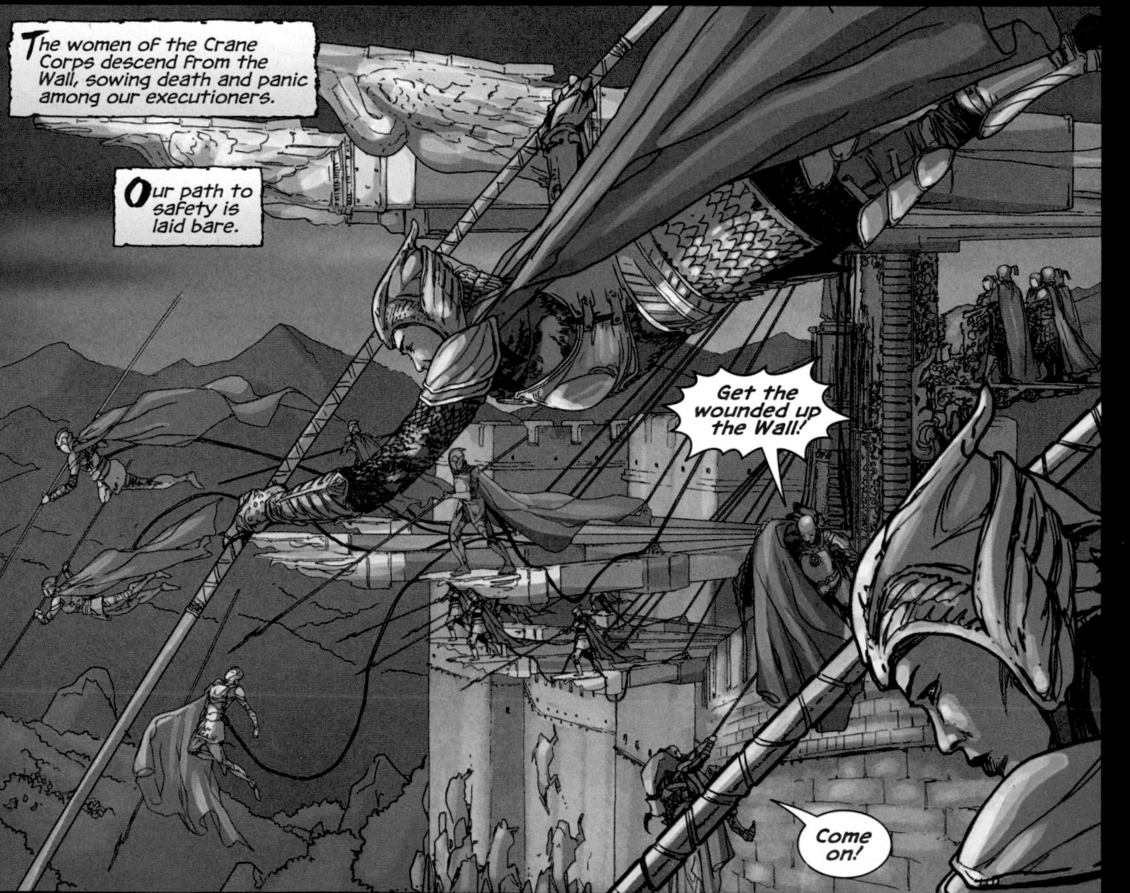
The women of the Crane Corps descend from the Wall, sowing death and panic among our executioners.
Our path to safety is laid bare.
Get the wounded up the Wall!
Come on!

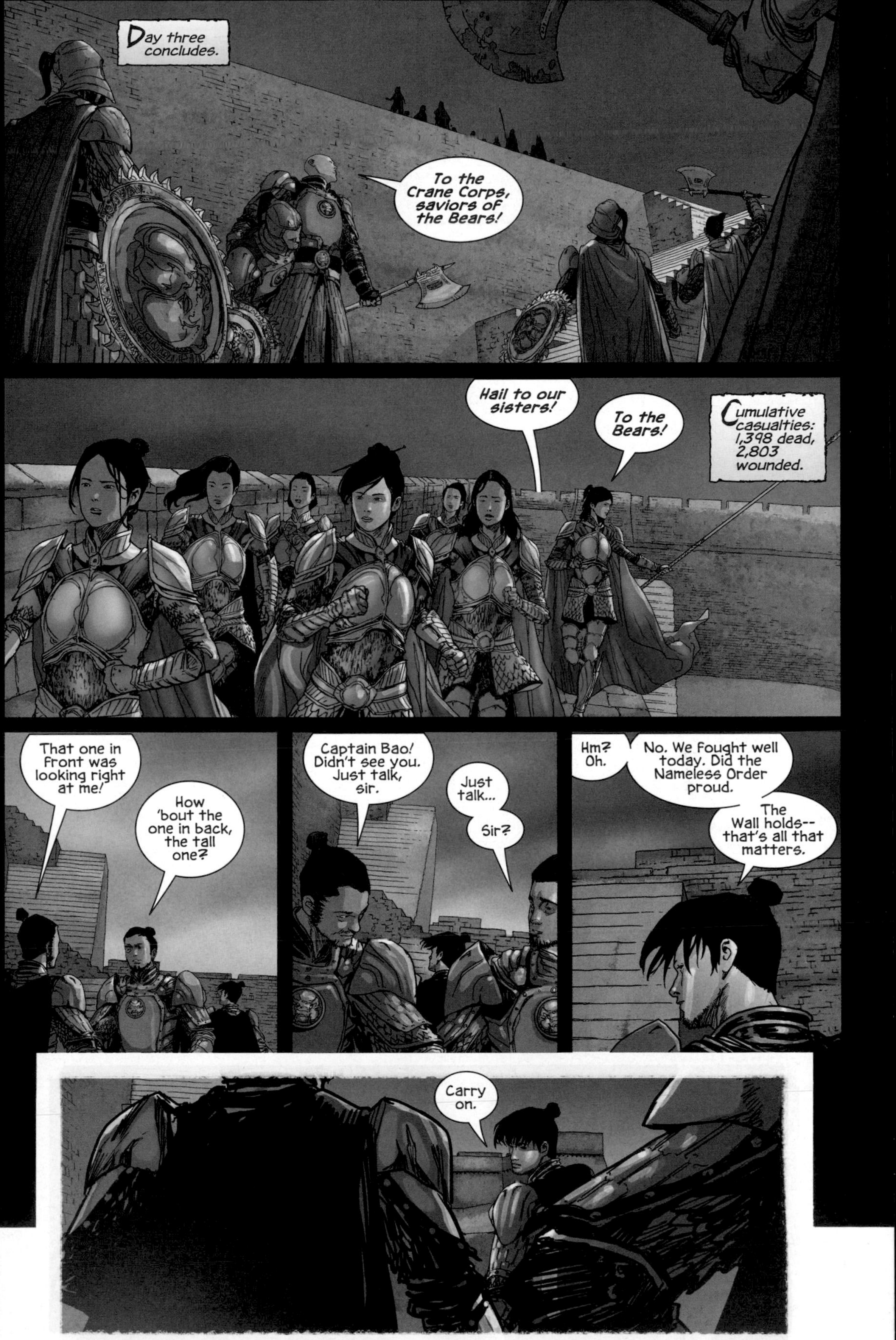
Day three concludes.
To the Crane Corps, saviors of the Bears!
Hail to our sisters!
To the Bears!
Cumulative casualties: 1,398 dead, 2,803 wounded.
That one in front was looking right at me!
How 'bout the one in back, the tall one?
Captain Bao! Didn't see you. Just talk, sir.
Just talk...
Sir?
Hm? Oh.
No. We fought well today. Did the Nameless Order proud.
The Wall holds--that's all that matters.
Carry on.

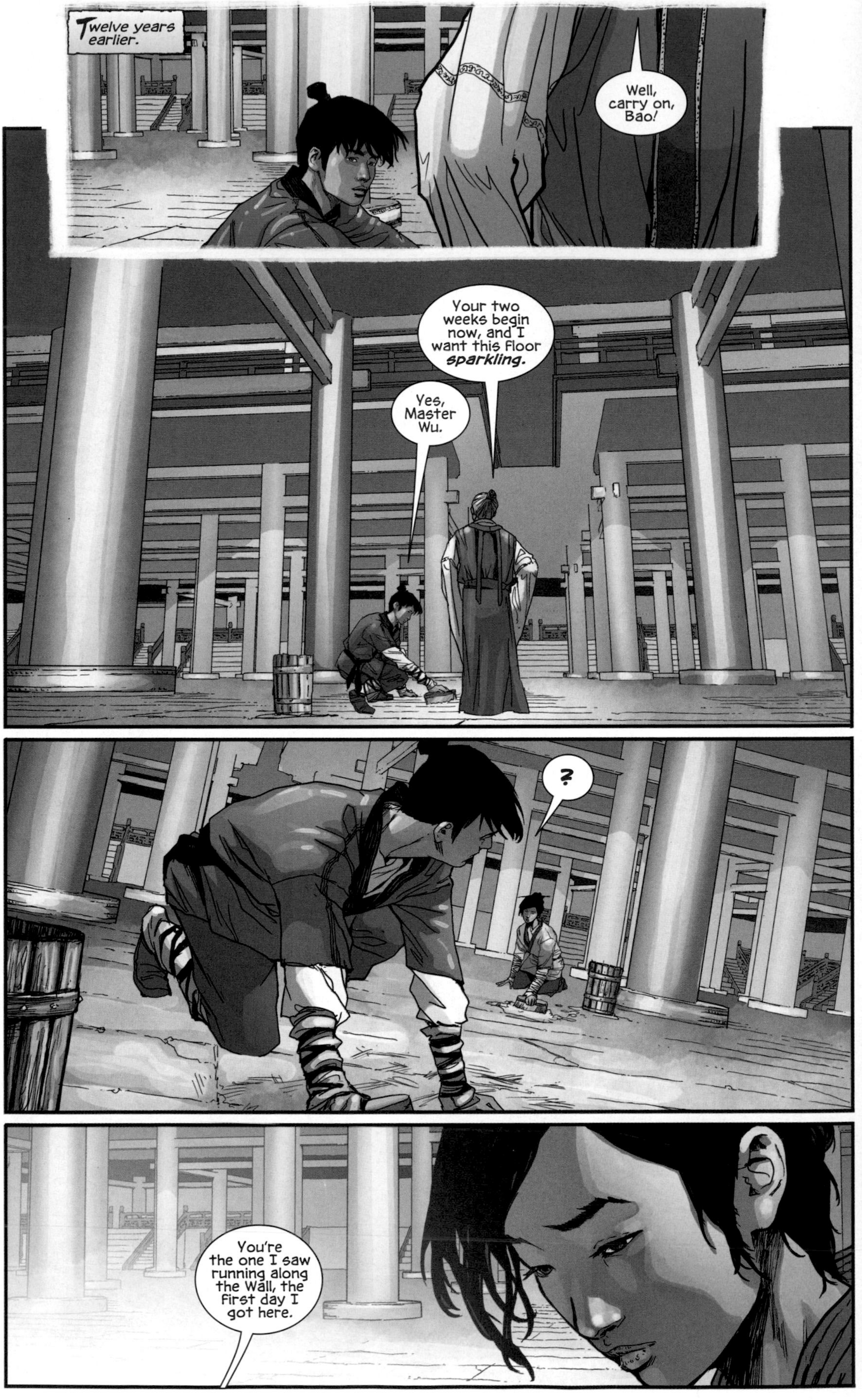
Twelve years earlier.
Well, carry on, Bao!
Your two weeks begin now, and I want this floor *sparkling.*
Yes, Master Wu.
?
You're the one I saw running along the Wall, the first day I got here.

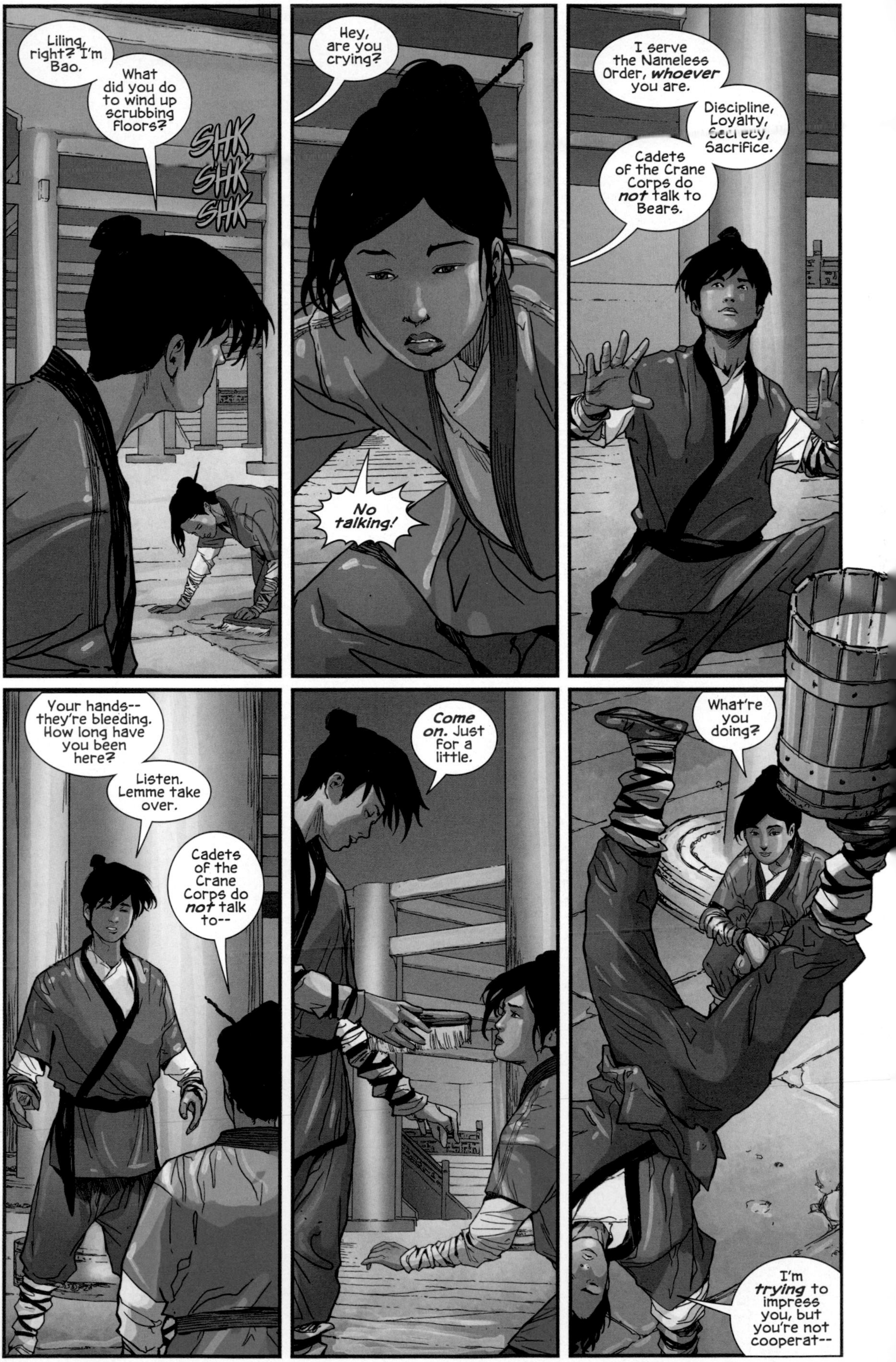
Liling, right? I'm Bao.
What did you do to wind up scrubbing floors?
SHK SHK SHK
Hey, are you crying?
No talking!
I serve the Nameless Order, *whoever* you are.
Discipline, Loyalty, Secrecy, Sacrifice.
Cadets of the Crane Corps do *not* talk to Bears.
Your hands-- they're bleeding. How long have you been here?
Listen. Lemme take over.
Cadets of the Crane Corps do *not* talk to--
Come on. Just for a little.
What're you doing?
I'm *trying* to impress you, but you're not cooperat--

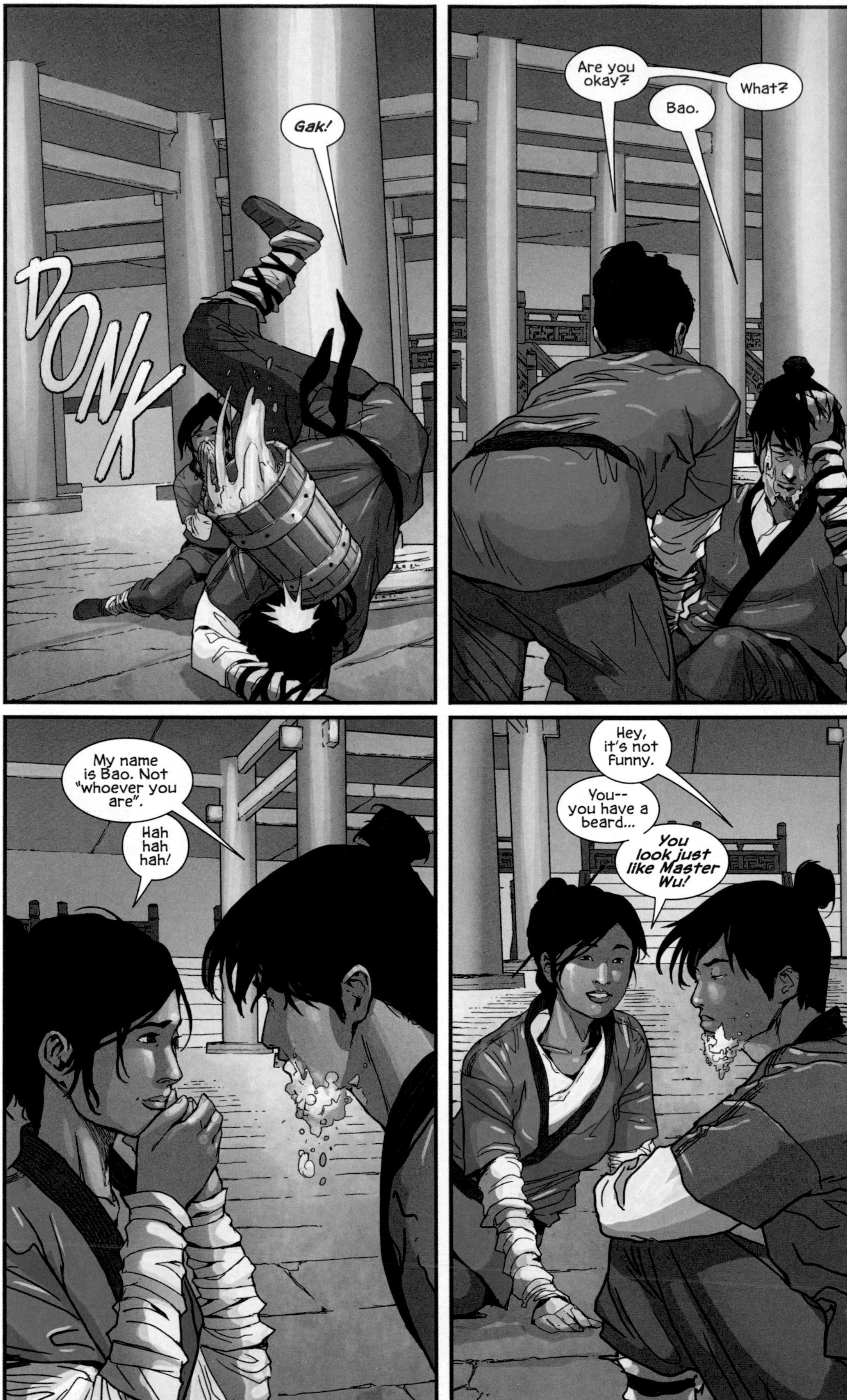

DONK
Gak!
Are you okay?
Bao.
What?
My name is Bao. Not "whoever you are".
Hah hah hah!
Hey, it's not funny.
You-- you have a beard...
You look just like Master Wu!

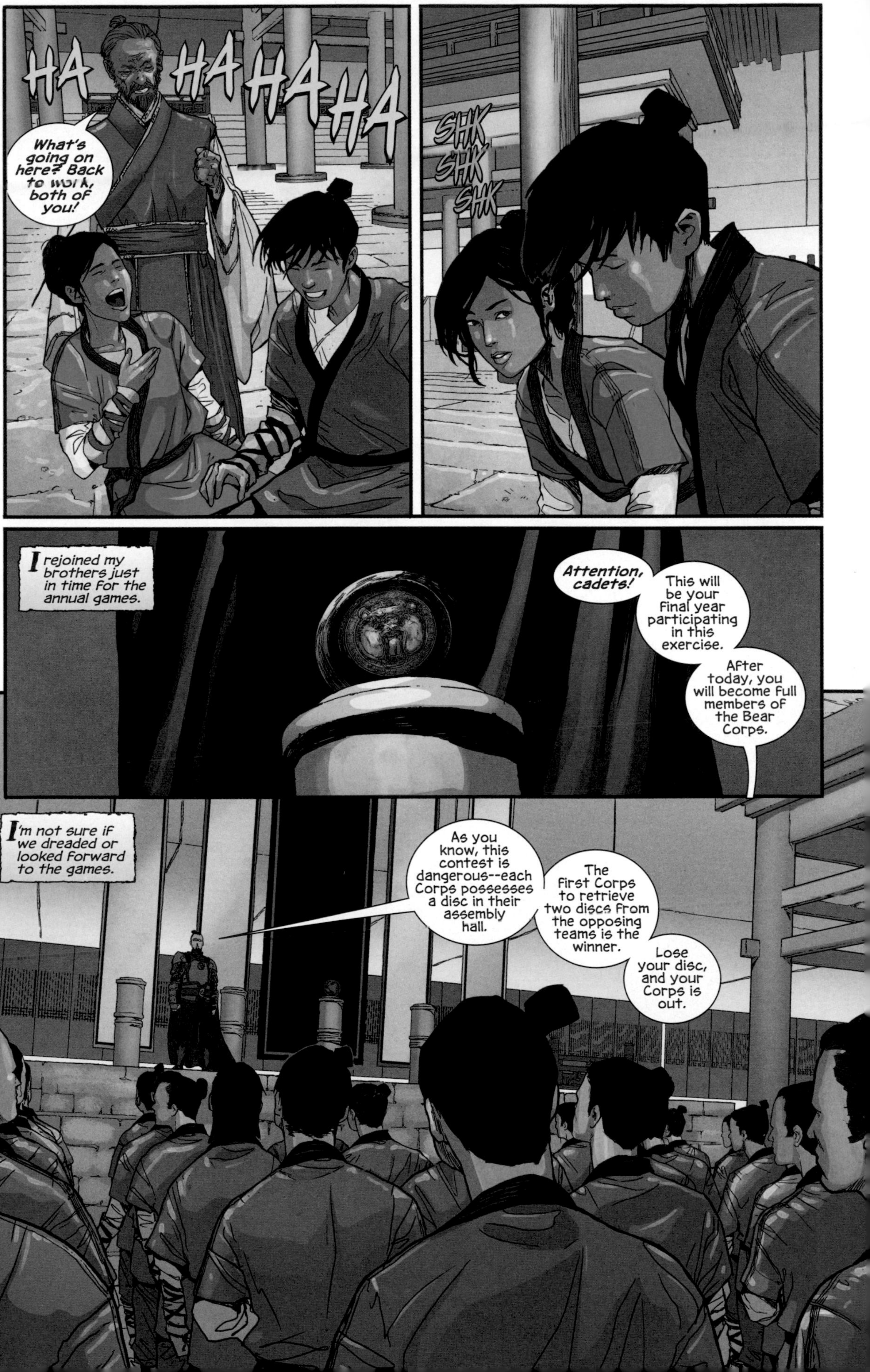
HA HAHAHAHA
What's going on here? Back to work, both of you!
SHK SHK SHK
I rejoined my brothers just in time for the annual games.
Attention, cadets!
This will be your final year participating in this exercise.
After today, you will become full members of the Bear Corps.
I'm not sure if we dreaded or looked forward to the games.
As you know, this contest is dangerous--each Corps possesses a disc in their assembly hall.
The first Corps to retrieve two discs from the opposing teams is the winner.
Lose your disc, and your Corps is out.

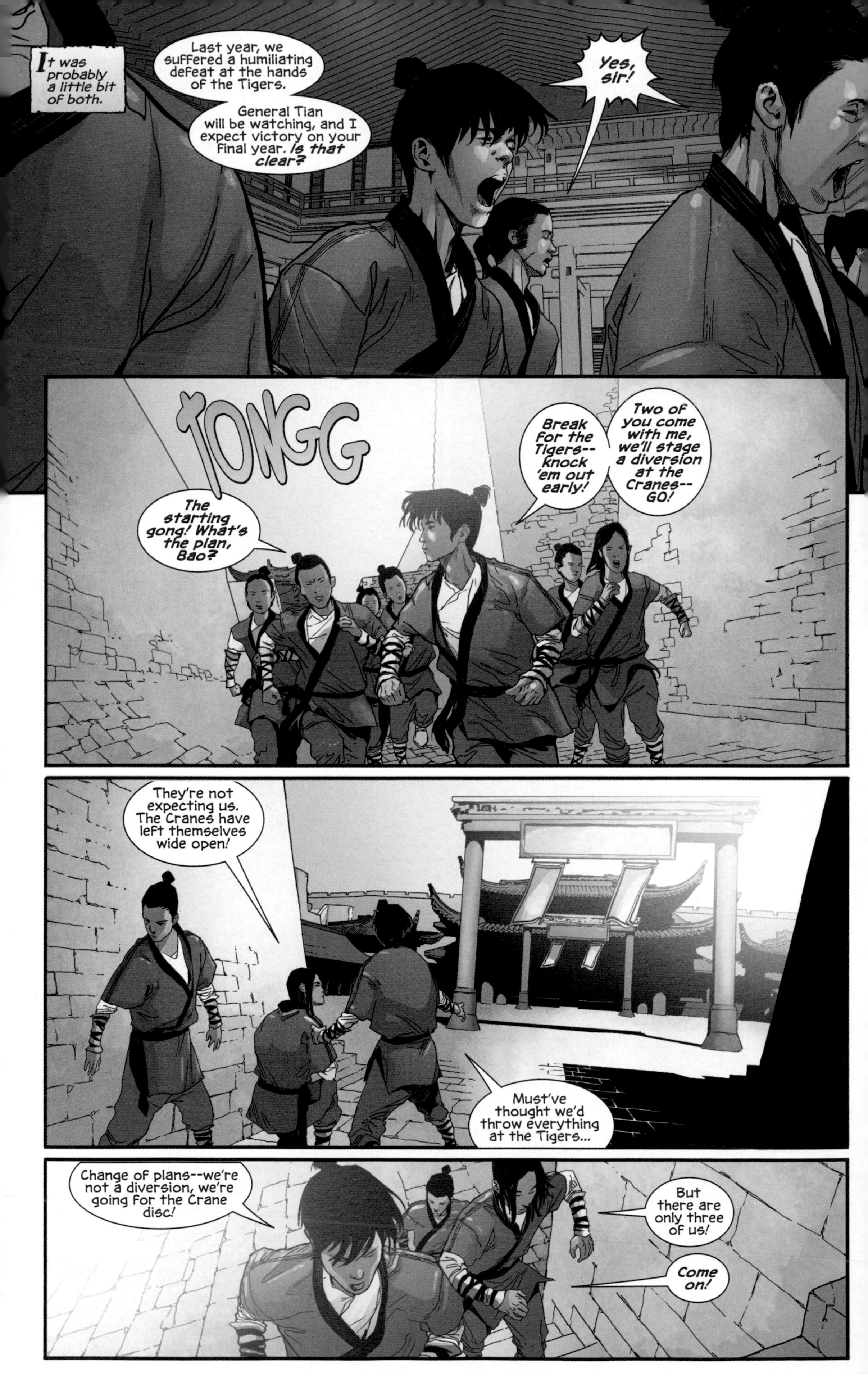
It was probably a little bit of both.
Last year, we suffered a humiliating defeat at the hands of the Tigers.
General Tian will be watching, and I expect victory on your final year. *Is that clear?*
Yes, sir!
TONGG
The starting gong! What's the plan, Bao?
Break for the Tigers--knock 'em out early!
Two of you come with me, we'll stage a diversion at the Cranes--GO!
They're not expecting us. The Cranes have left themselves wide open!
Must've thought we'd throw everything at the Tigers...
Change of plans--we're not a diversion, we're going for the Crane disc!
But there are only three of us!
Come on!

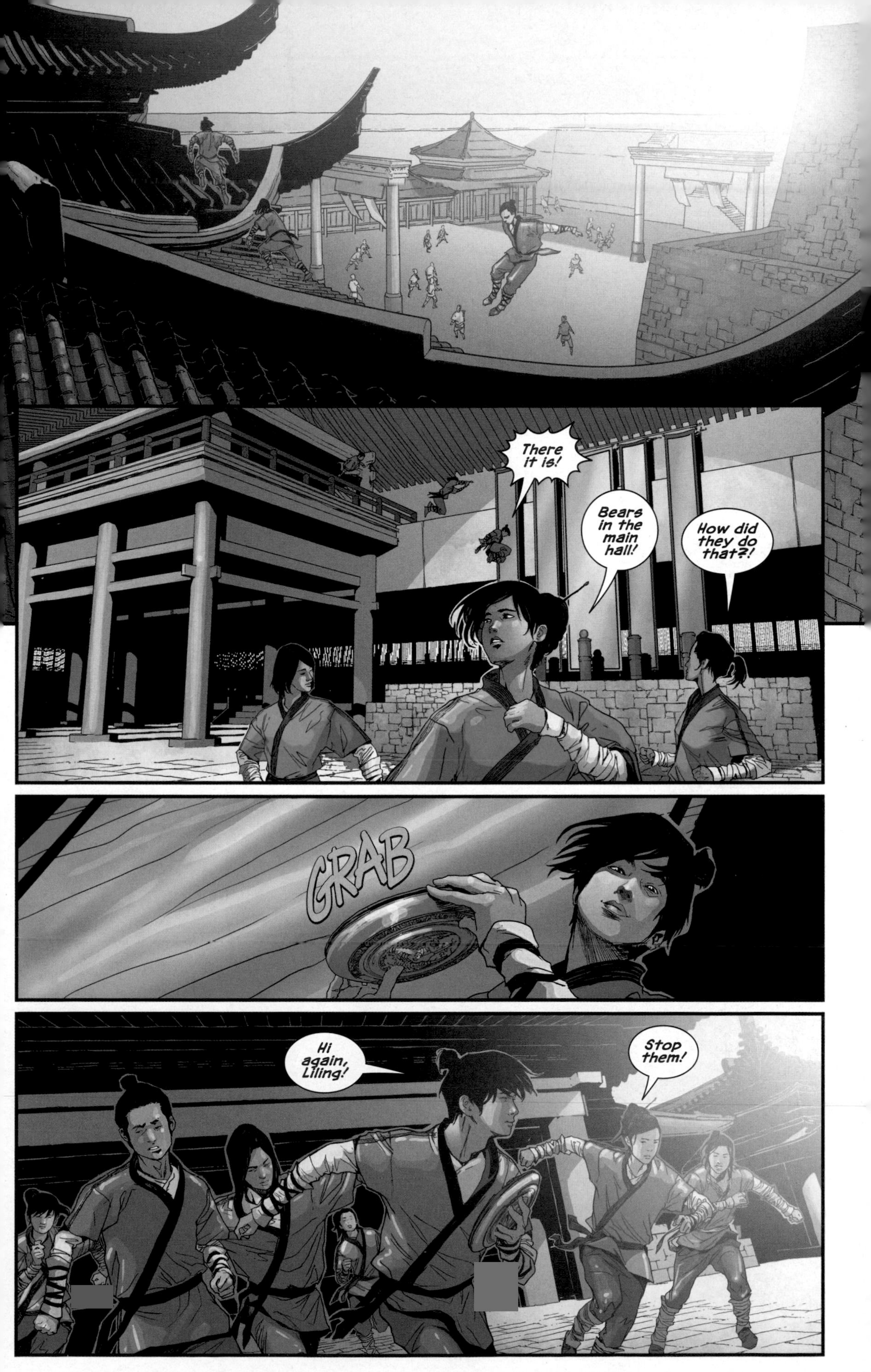
There it is!
Bears in the main hall!
How did they do that?!
GRAB
Hi again, Liling!
Stop them!

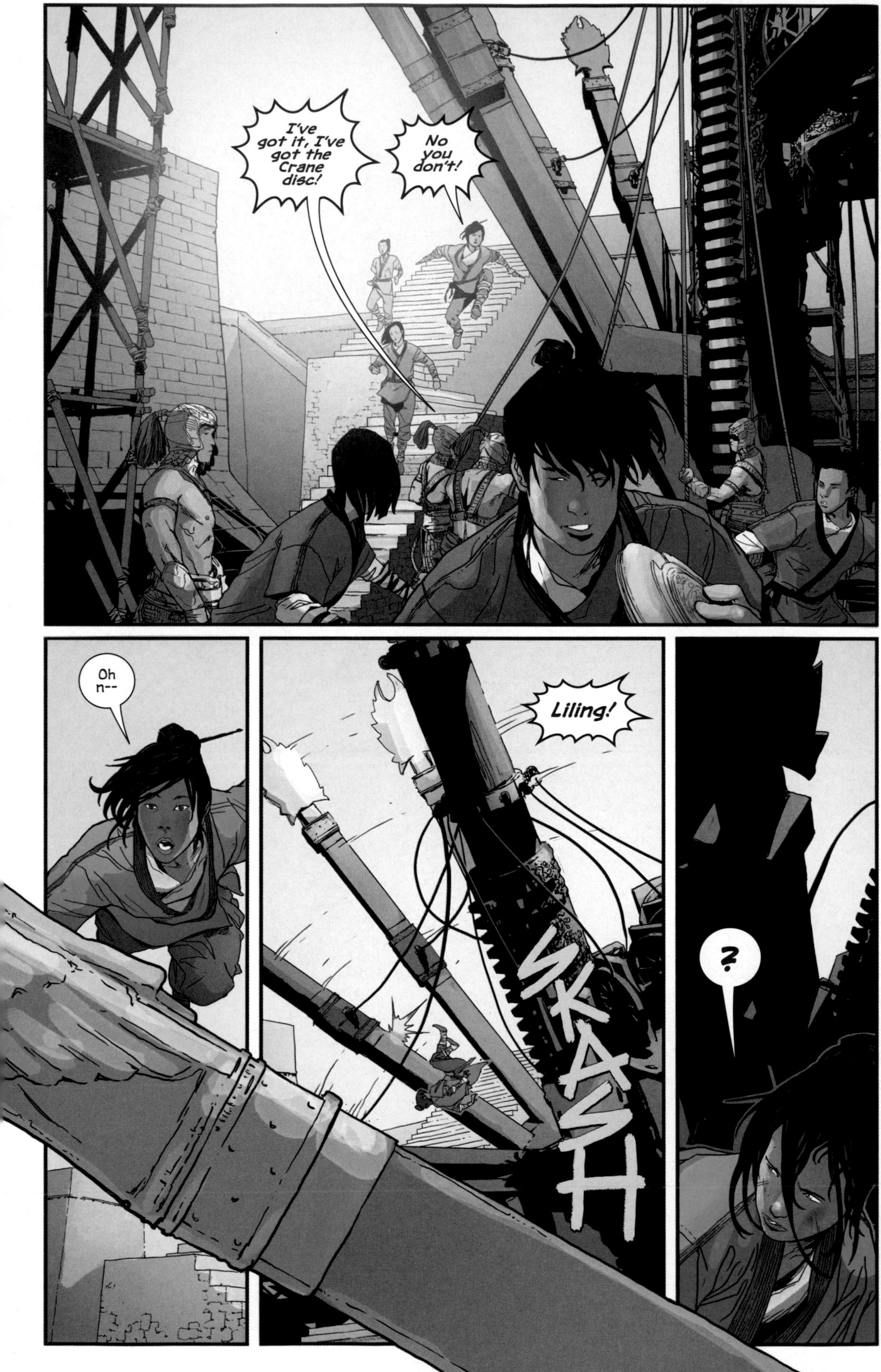
I've got it, I've got the Crane disc!
No you don't!
Oh n--
Liling!
SKASH
?

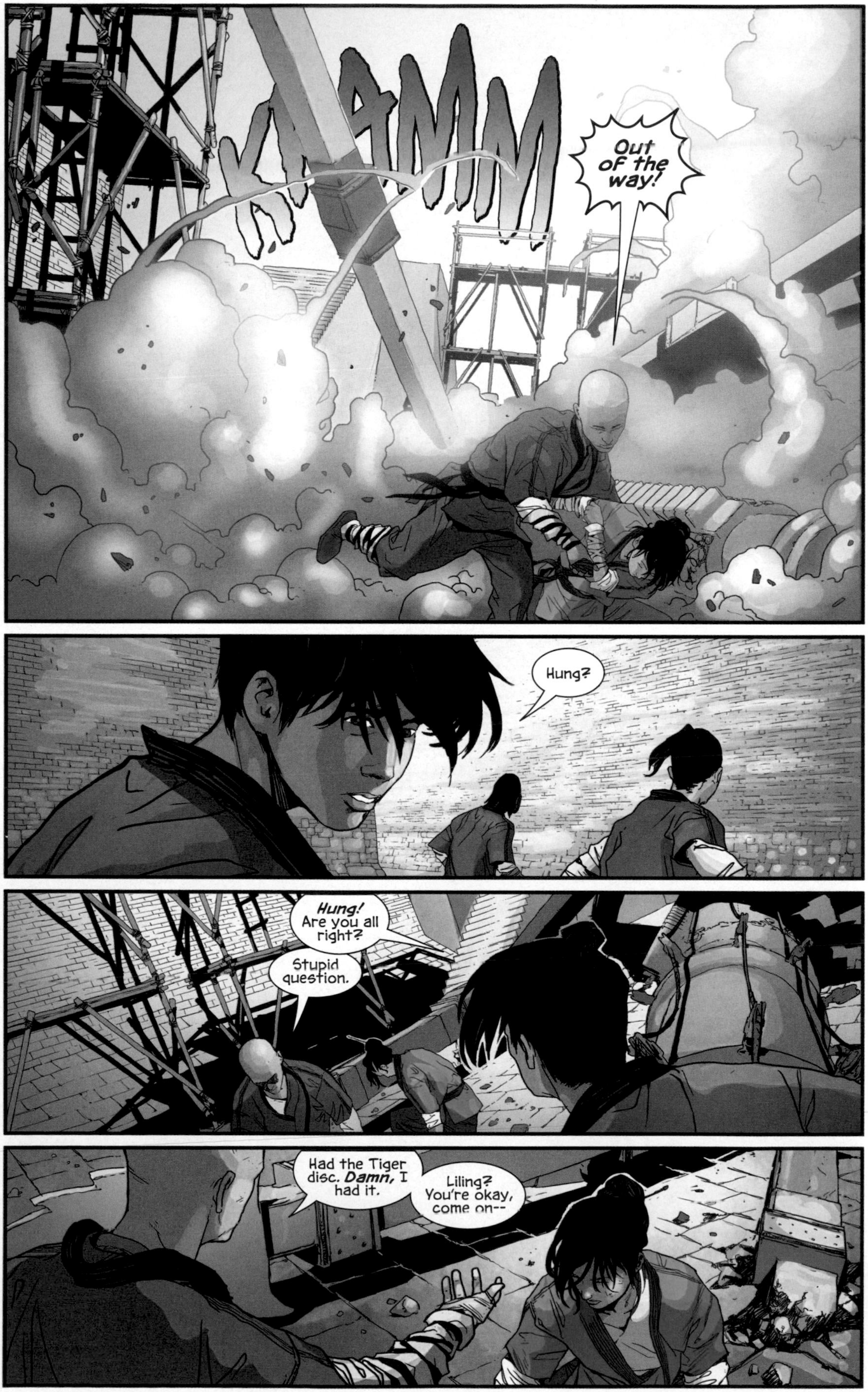

Out of the way!
Hung?
Hung! Are you all right?
Stupid question.
Had the Tiger disc. Damn, I had it.
Liling? You're okay, come on--

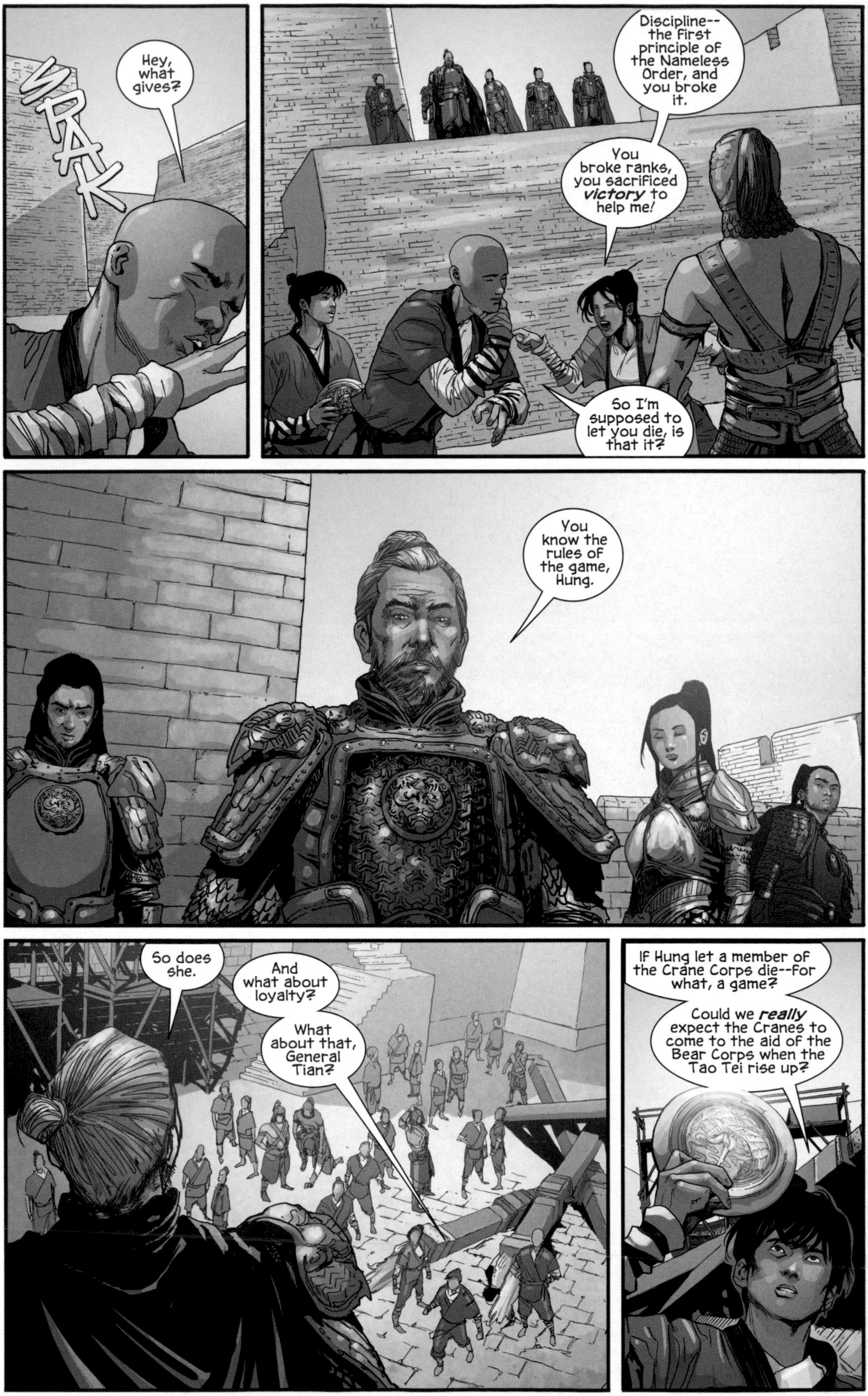
SPAK
Hey, what gives?
Discipline--the first principle of the Nameless Order, and you broke it.
You broke ranks, you sacrificed *victory* to help me!
So I'm supposed to let you die, is that it?
You know the rules of the game, Hung.
So does she.
And what about loyalty?
What about that, General Tian?
If Hung let a member of the Crane Corps die--for what, a game?
Could we *really* expect the Cranes to come to the aid of the Bear Corps when the Tao Tei rise up?

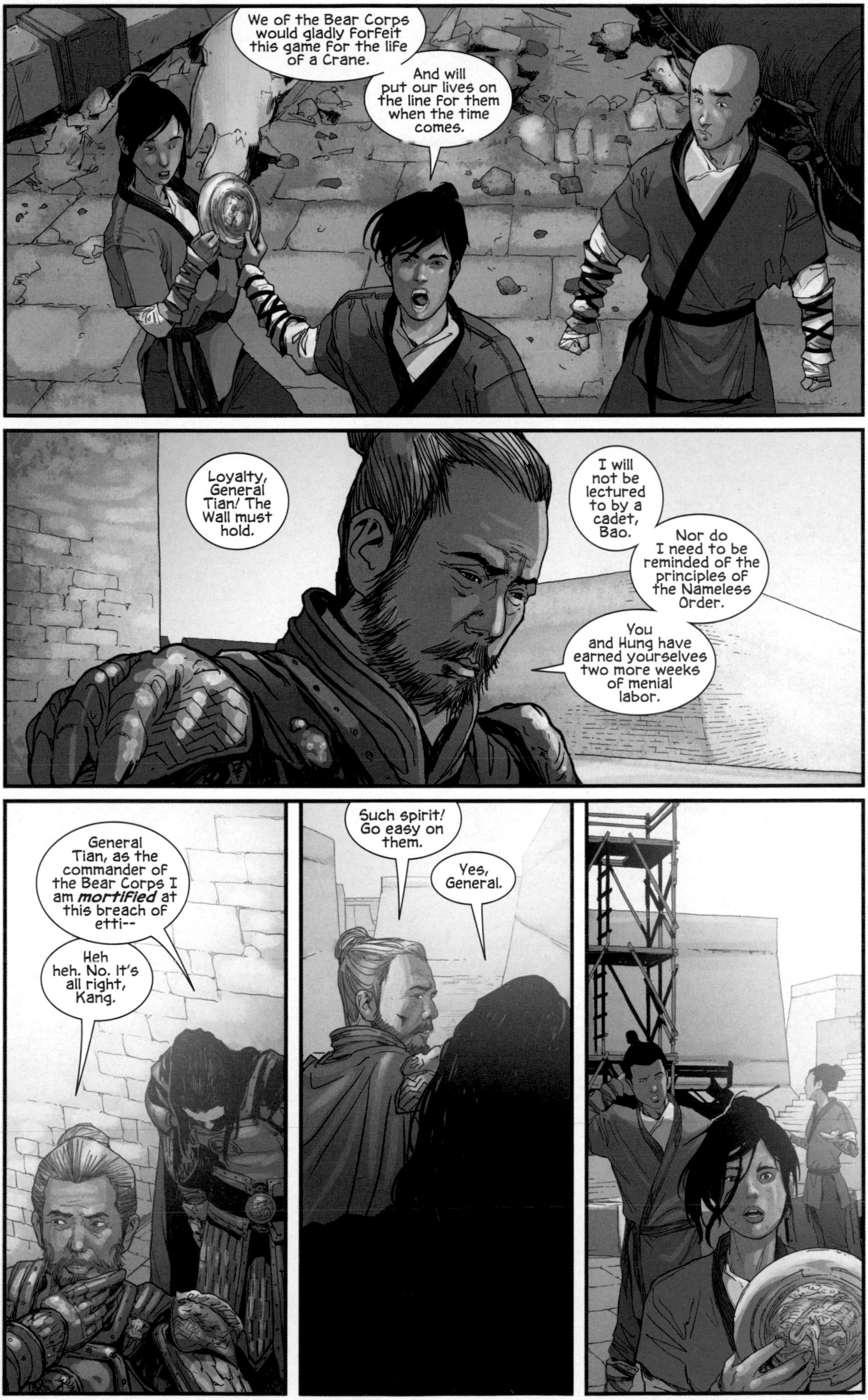
We of the Bear Corps would gladly forfeit this game for the life of a Crane.
And will put our lives on the line for them when the time comes.
Loyalty, General Tian! The Wall must hold.
I will not be lectured to by a cadet, Bao.
Nor do I need to be reminded of the principles of the Nameless Order.
You and Hung have earned yourselves two more weeks of menial labor.
General Tian, as the commander of the Bear Corps I am *mortified* at this breach of etti--
Heh heh. No. It's all right, Kang.
Such spirit! Go easy on them.
Yes, General.

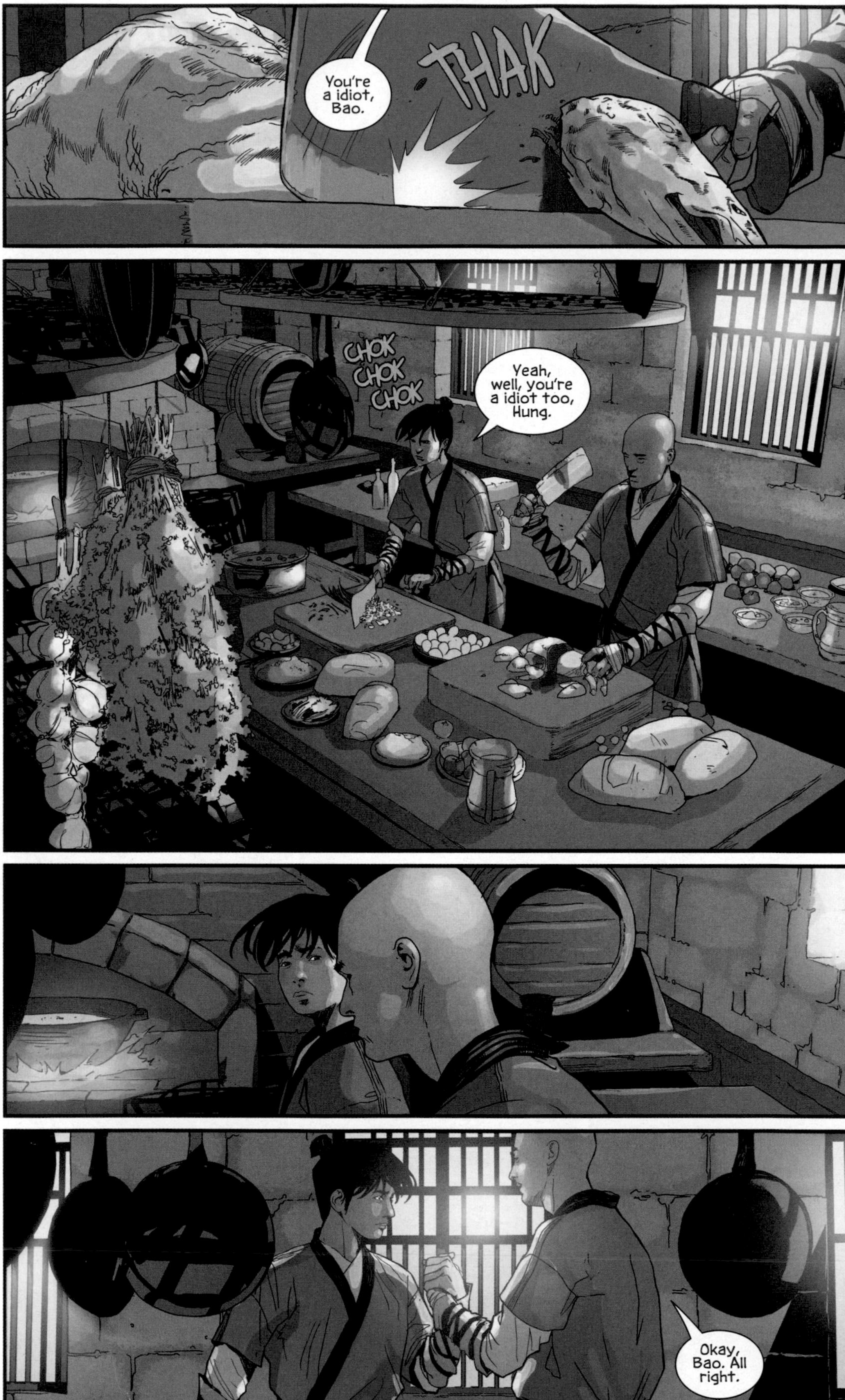
You're a idiot, Bao.
THAK
CHOK CHOK CHOK
Yeah, well, you're a idiot too, Hung.
Okay, Bao. All right.

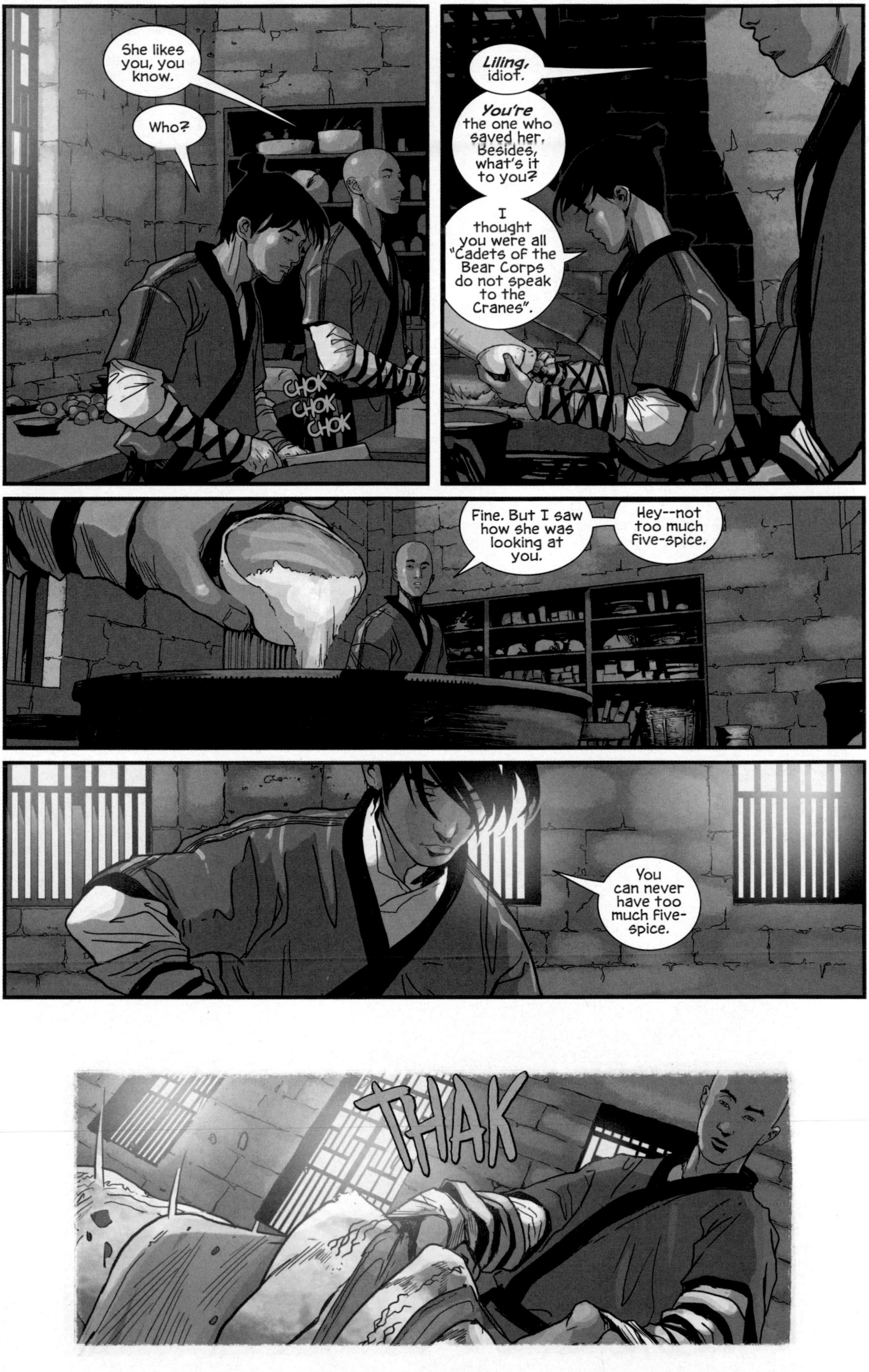
She likes you, you know.
Who?
CHOK CHOK CHOK
Liling, idiot.
You're the one who saved her. Besides, what's it to you?
I thought you were all "Cadets of the Bear Corps do not speak to the Cranes".
Fine. But I saw how she was looking at you.
Hey--not too much five-spice.
You can never have too much five-spice.
THAK

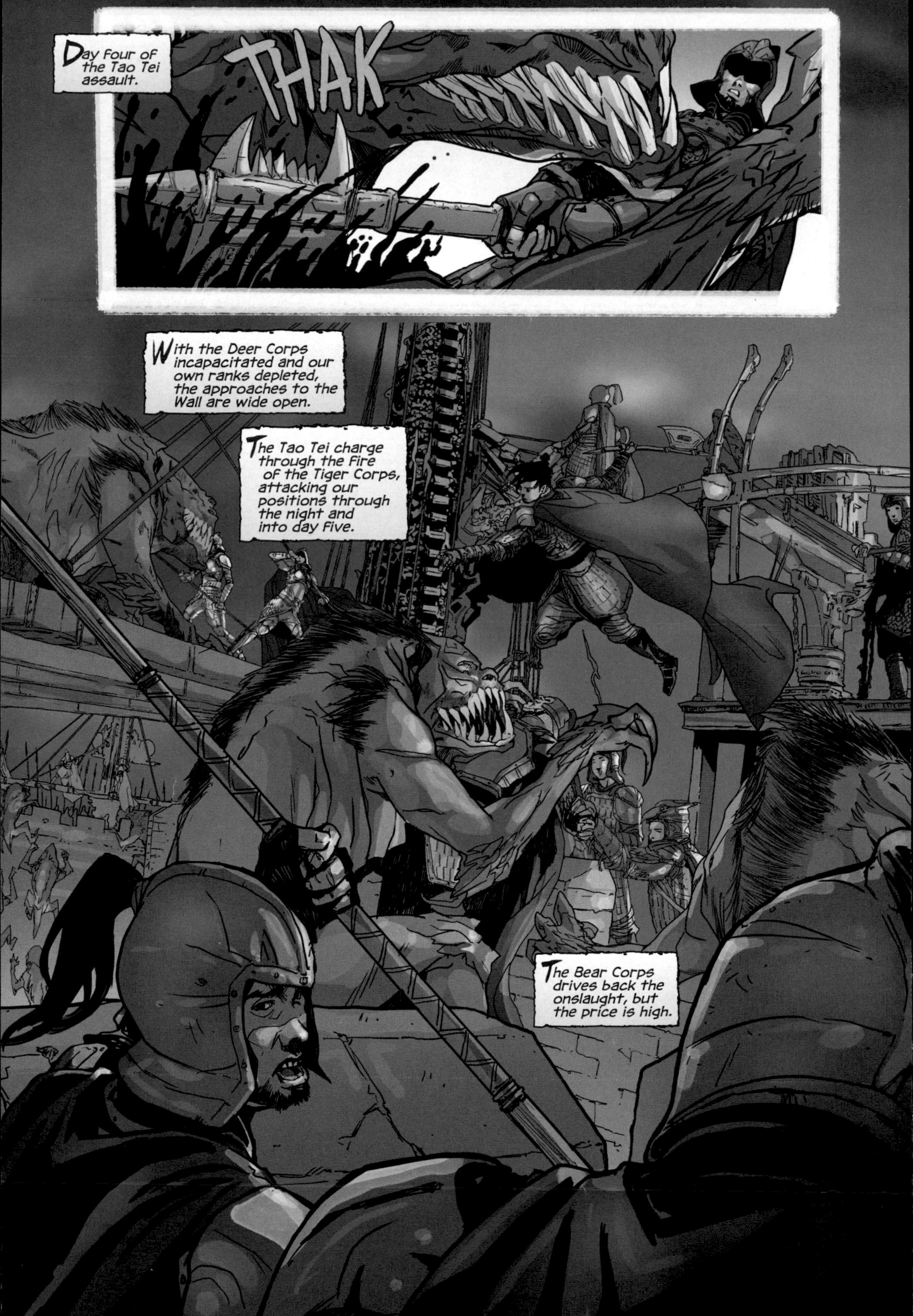
Day four of the Tao Tei assault.
THAK
With the Deer Corps incapacitated and our own ranks depleted, the approaches to the Wall are wide open.
The Tao Tei charge through the Fire of the Tiger Corps, attacking our positions through the night and into day Five.
The Bear Corps drives back the onslaught, but the price is high.

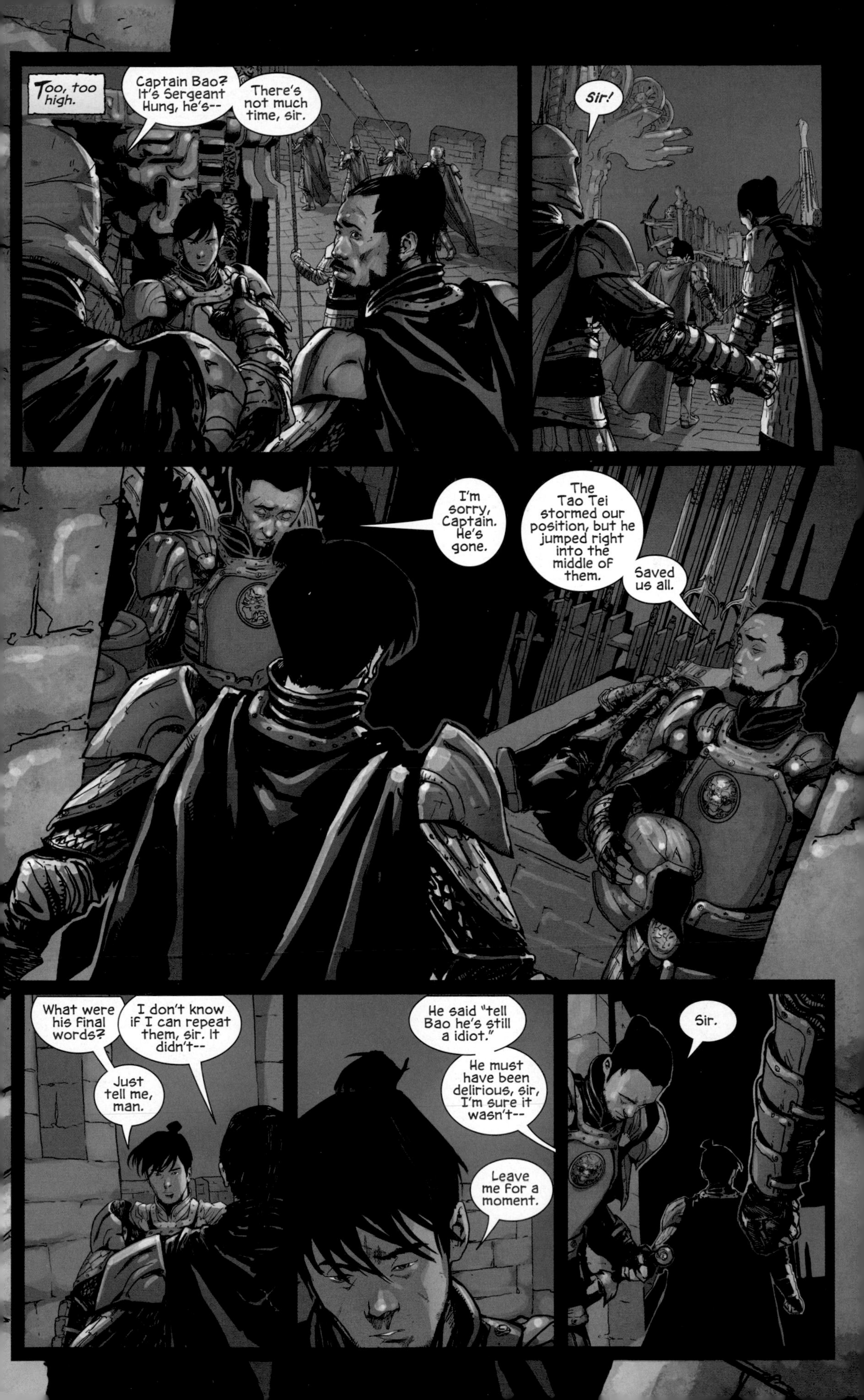

Too, too high.
Captain Bao? It's Sergeant Hung, he's--
There's not much time, sir.
Sir!
I'm sorry, Captain. He's gone.
The Tao Tei stormed our position, but he jumped right into the middle of them.
Saved us all.
What were his final words?
I don't know if I can repeat them, sir. It didn't--
Just tell me, man.
He said "tell Bao he's still a idiot."
He must have been delirious, sir, I'm sure it wasn't--
Leave me for a moment.
Sir.

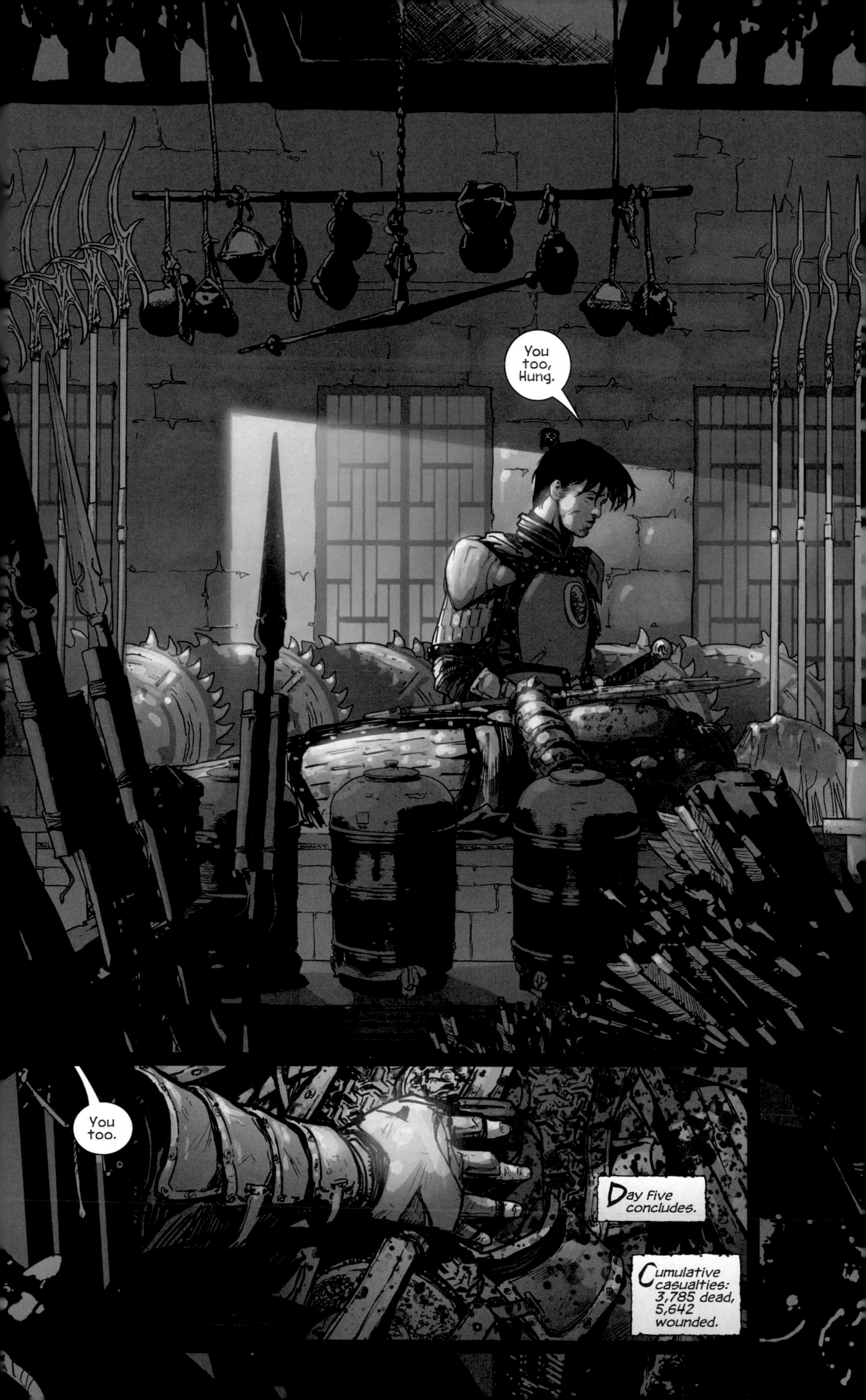
You too, Hung.
You too.
Day Five concludes.
Cumulative casualties: 3,785 dead, 5,642 wounded.

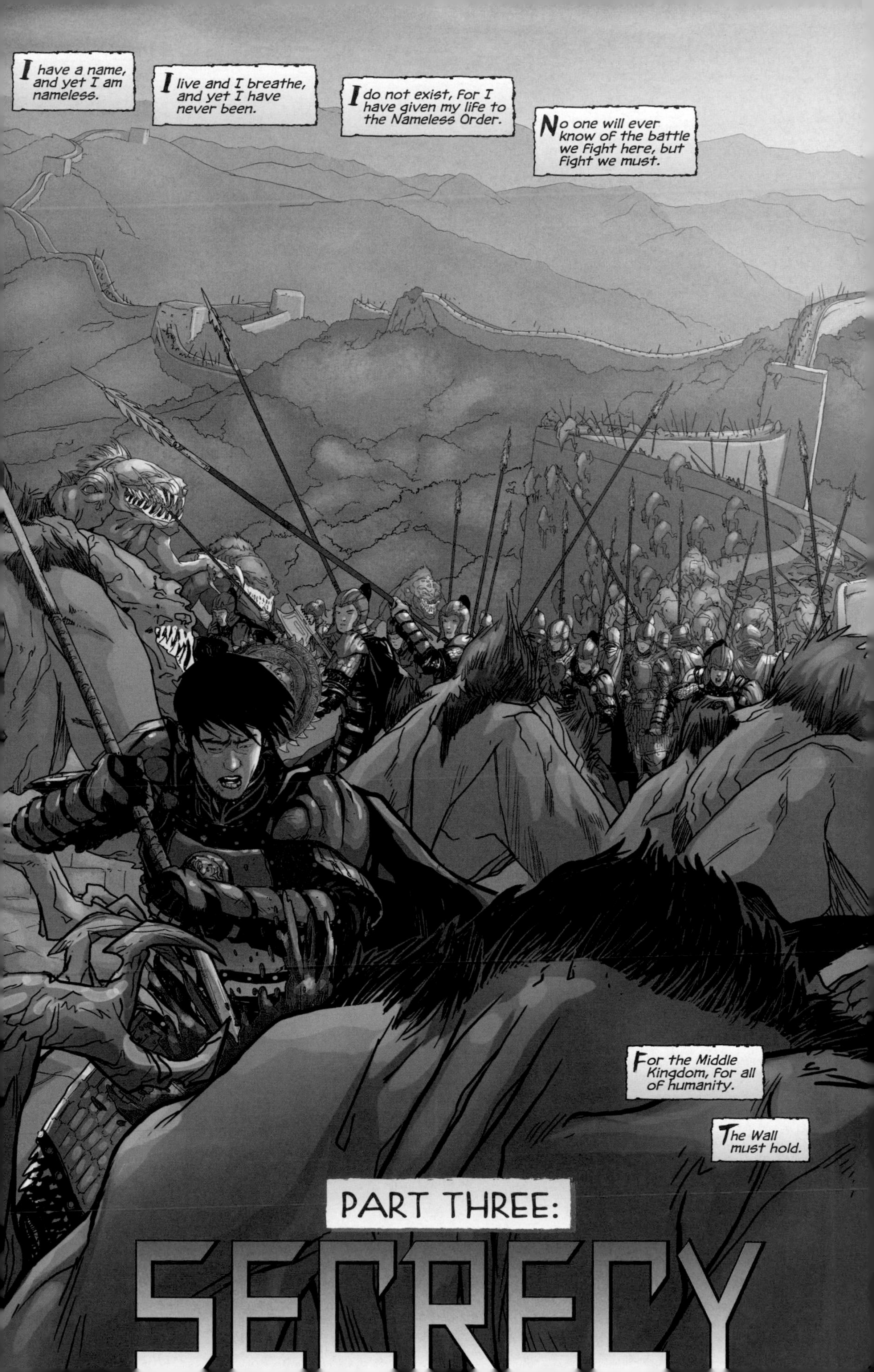
I have a name, and yet I am nameless.
I live and I breathe, and yet I have never been.
I do not exist, for I have given my life to the Nameless Order.
No one will ever know of the battle we fight here, but fight we must.
For the Middle Kingdom, for all of humanity.
The Wall must hold.
PART THREE:
SECRECY

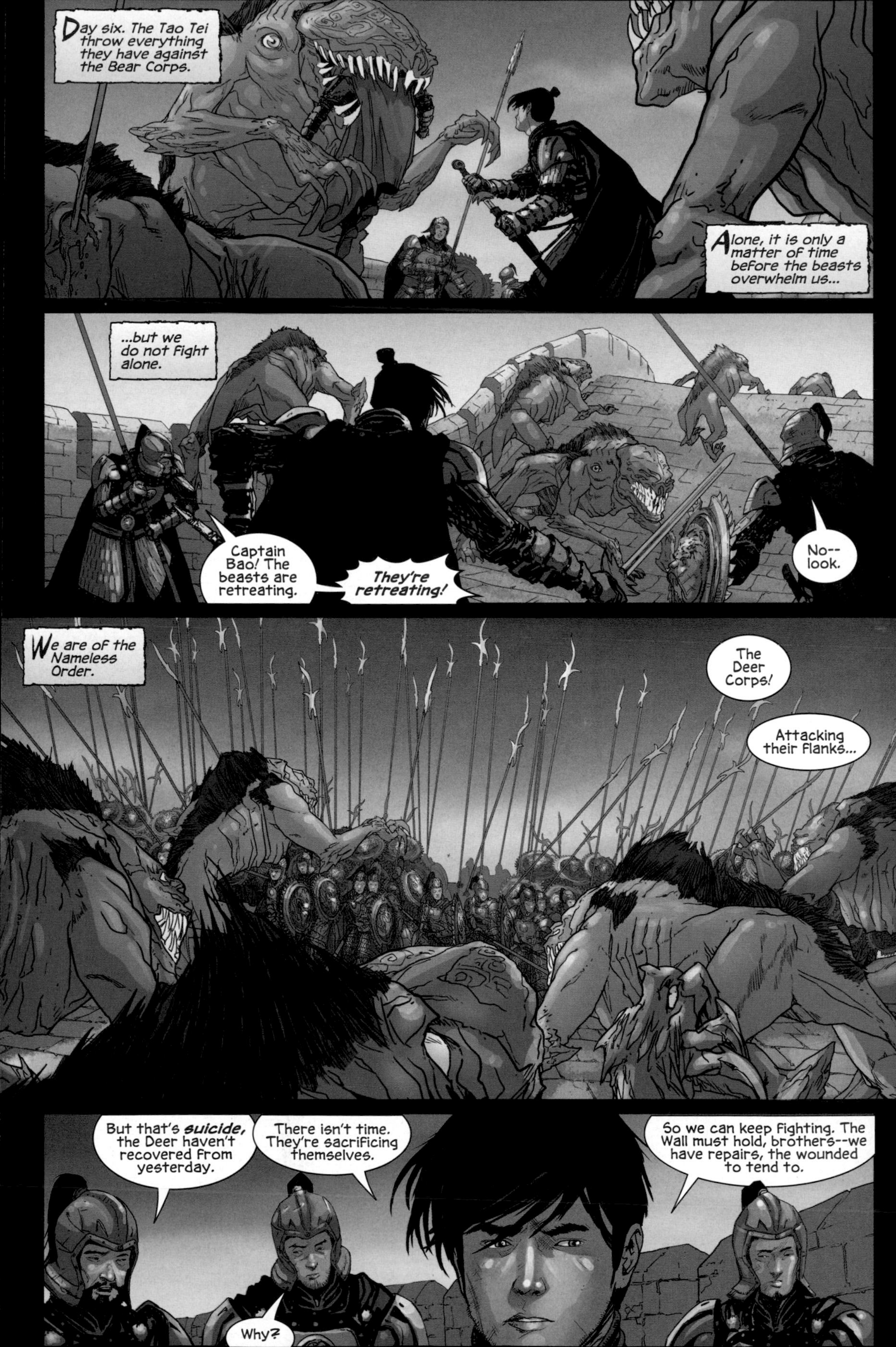
Day six. The Tao Tei throw everything they have against the Bear Corps.
Alone, it is only a matter of time before the beasts overwhelm us...
...but we do not fight alone.
Captain Bao! The beasts are retreating.
They're retreating!
No-- look.
We are of the Nameless Order.
The Deer Corps!
Attacking their flanks...
But that's suicide, the Deer haven't recovered from yesterday.
There isn't time. They're sacrificing themselves.
Why?
So we can keep fighting. The Wall must hold, brothers--we have repairs, the wounded to tend to.

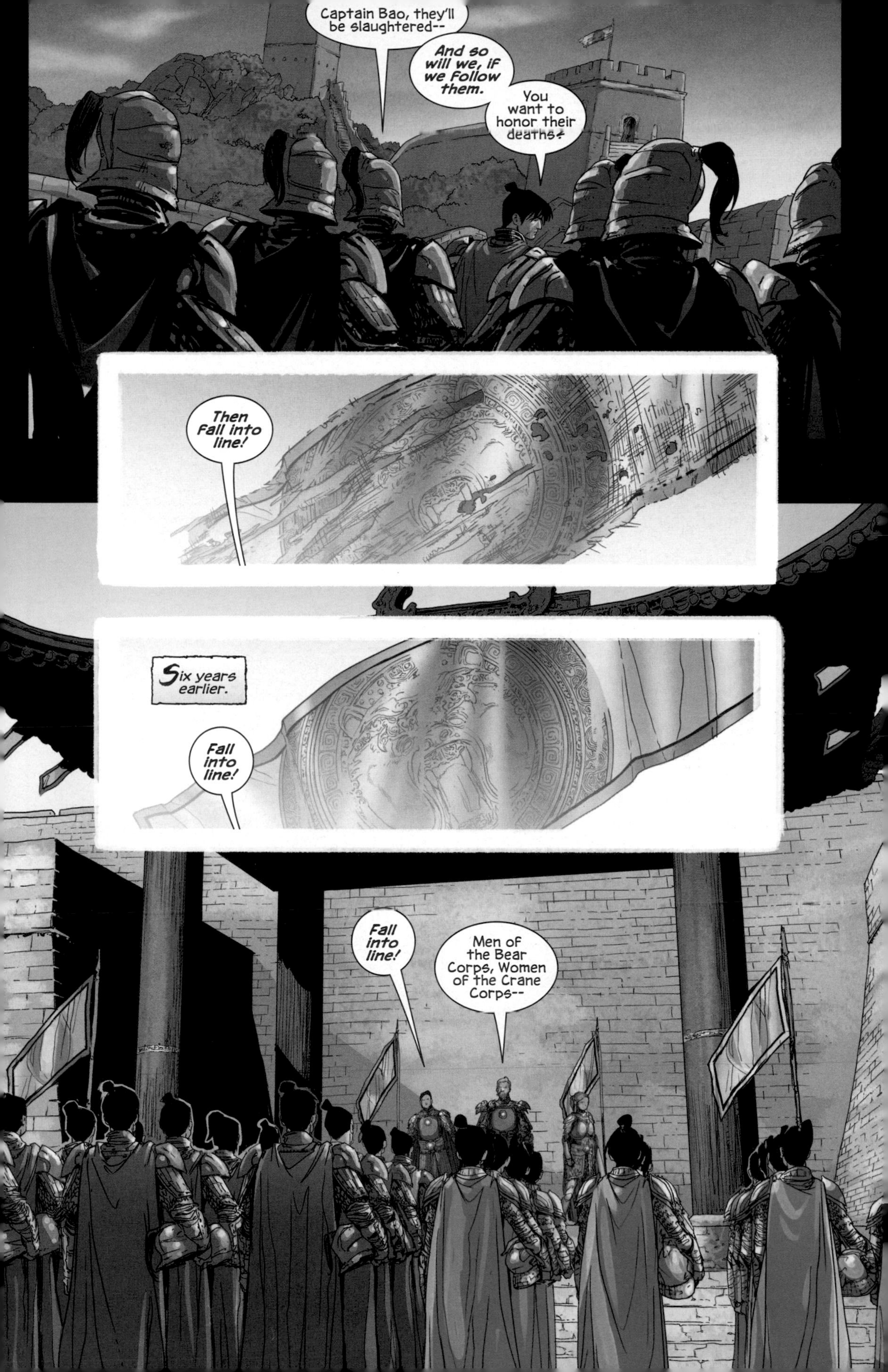

Captain Bao, they'll be slaughtered--
And so will we, if we follow them.
You want to honor their deaths?
Then fall into line!
Six years earlier.
Fall into line!
Fall into line!
Men of the Bear Corps, Women of the Crane Corps--

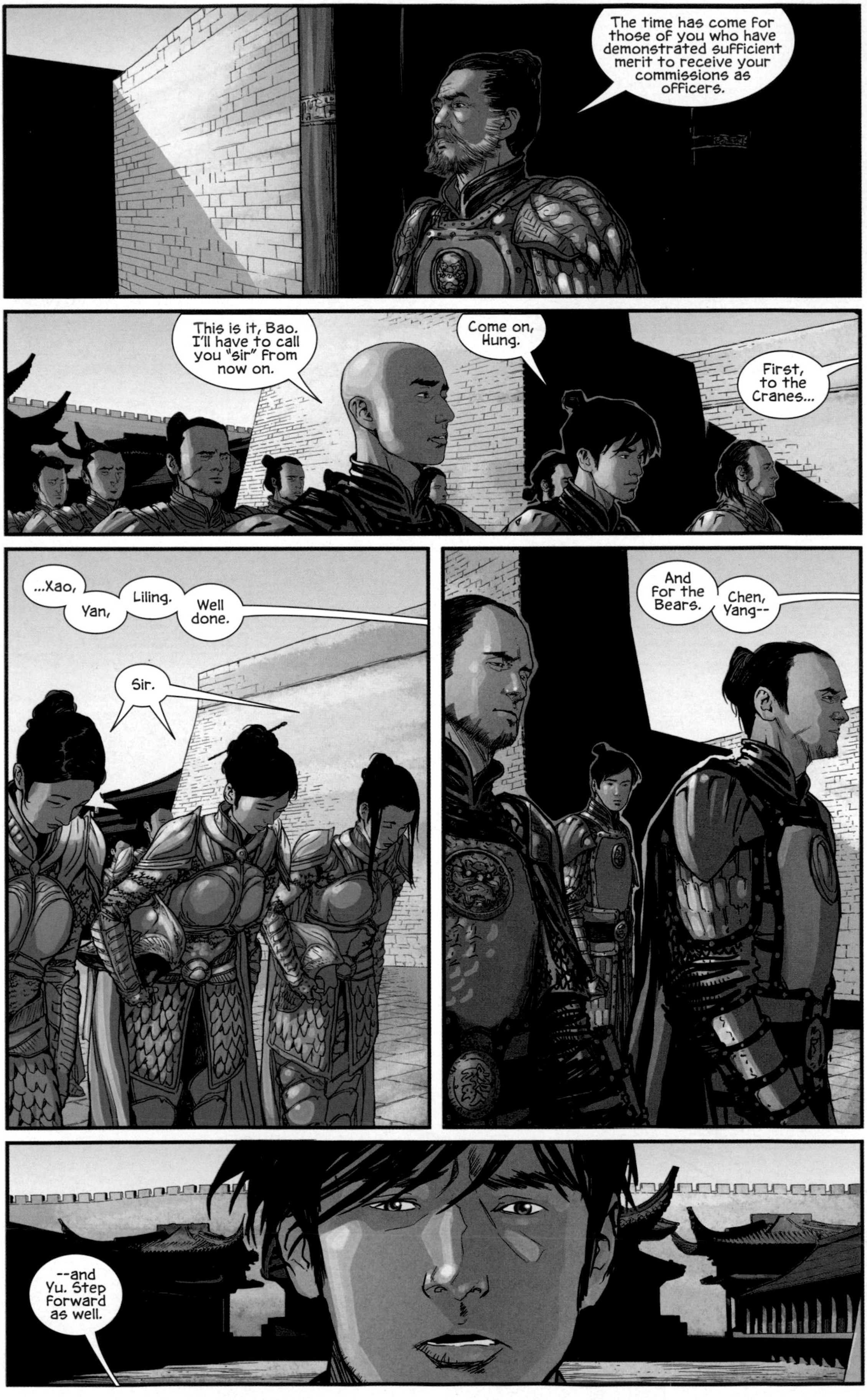
The time has come for those of you who have demonstrated sufficient merit to receive your commissions as officers.
This is it, Bao. I'll have to call you "sir" from now on.
Come on, Hung.
First, to the Cranes...
...Xao,
Yan,
Liling.
Well done.
Sir.
And for the Bears.
Chen, Yang--
--and Yu. Step forward as well.

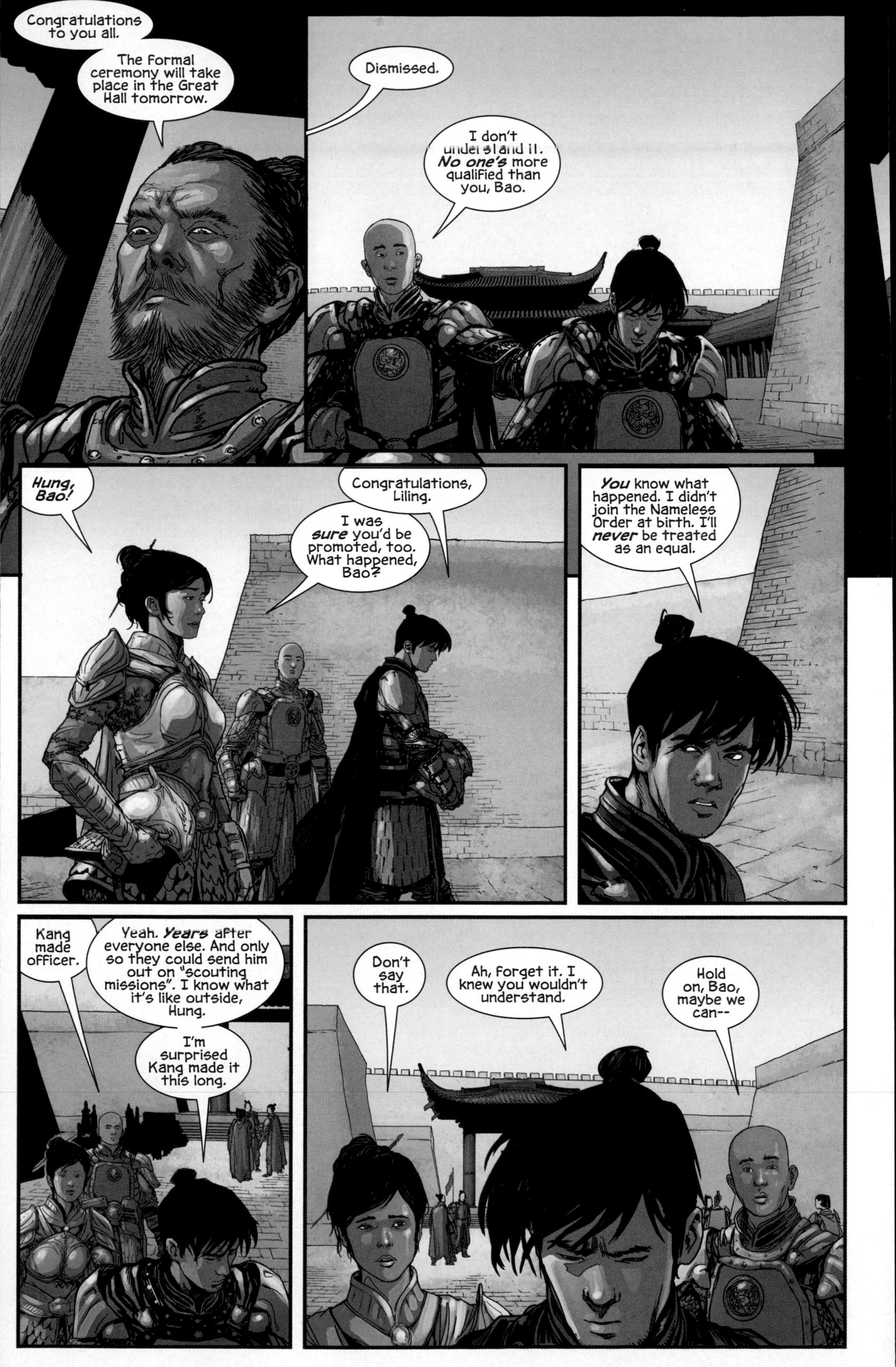
Congratulations to you all.
The formal ceremony will take place in the Great Hall tomorrow.
Dismissed.
I don't understand it. No one's more qualified than you, Bao.
Hung, Bao!
Congratulations, Liling.
I was sure you'd be promoted, too. What happened, Bao?
You know what happened. I didn't join the Nameless Order at birth. I'll never be treated as an equal.
Kang made officer.
Yeah. Years after everyone else. And only so they could send him out on "scouting missions". I know what it's like outside, Hung.
I'm surprised Kang made it this long.
Don't say that.
Ah, forget it. I knew you wouldn't understand.
Hold on, Bao, maybe we can--

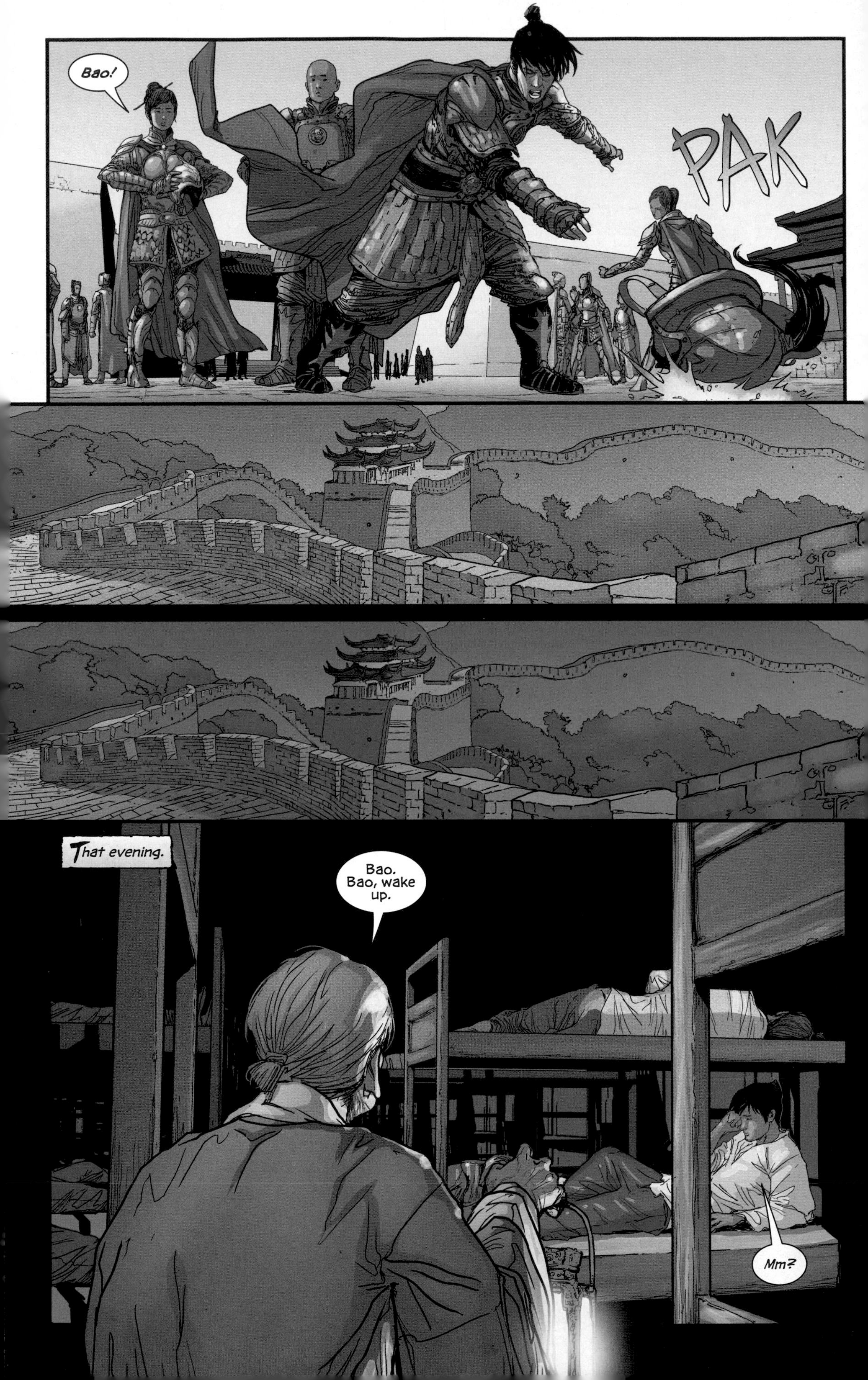
Bao!
PAK
That evening.
Bao.
Bao, wake up.
Mm?

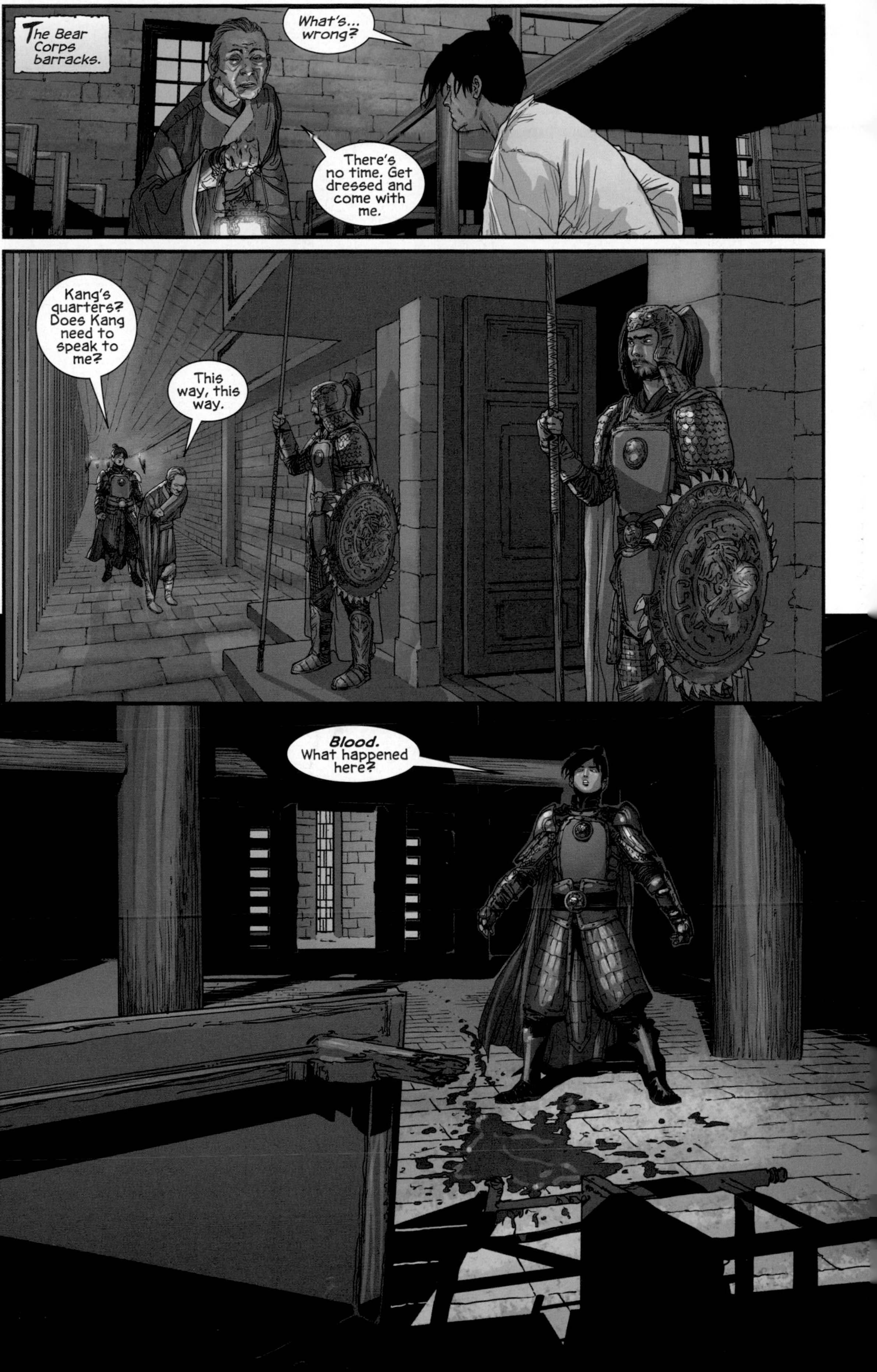
The Bear Corps barracks.
What's... wrong?
There's no time. Get dressed and come with me.
Kang's quarters? Does Kang need to speak to me?
This way, this way.
Blood. What happened here?

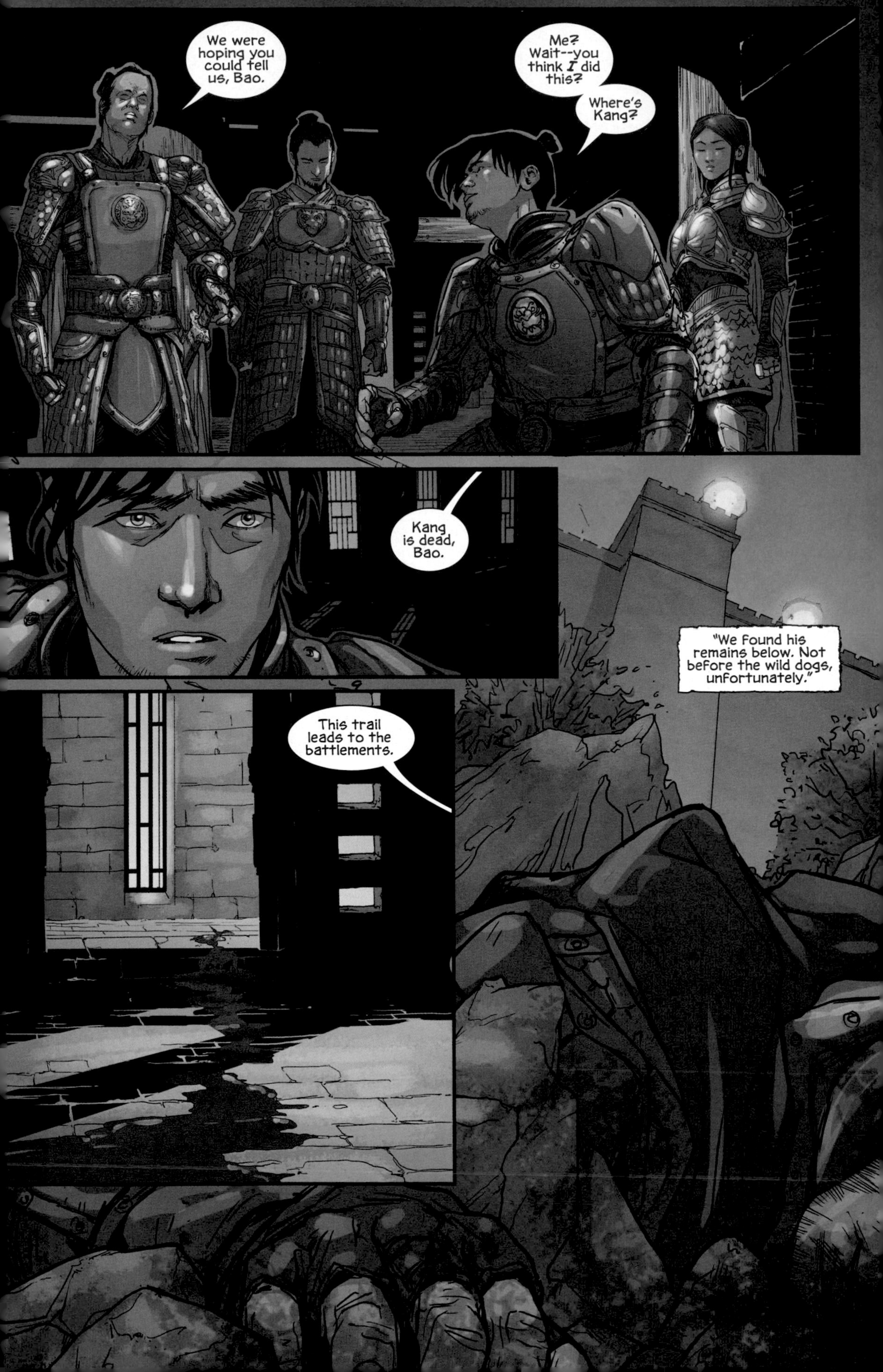
We were hoping you could tell us, Bao.
Me? Wait--you think I did this?
Where's Kang?
Kang is dead, Bao.
"We found his remains below. Not before the wild dogs, unfortunately."
This trail leads to the battlements.

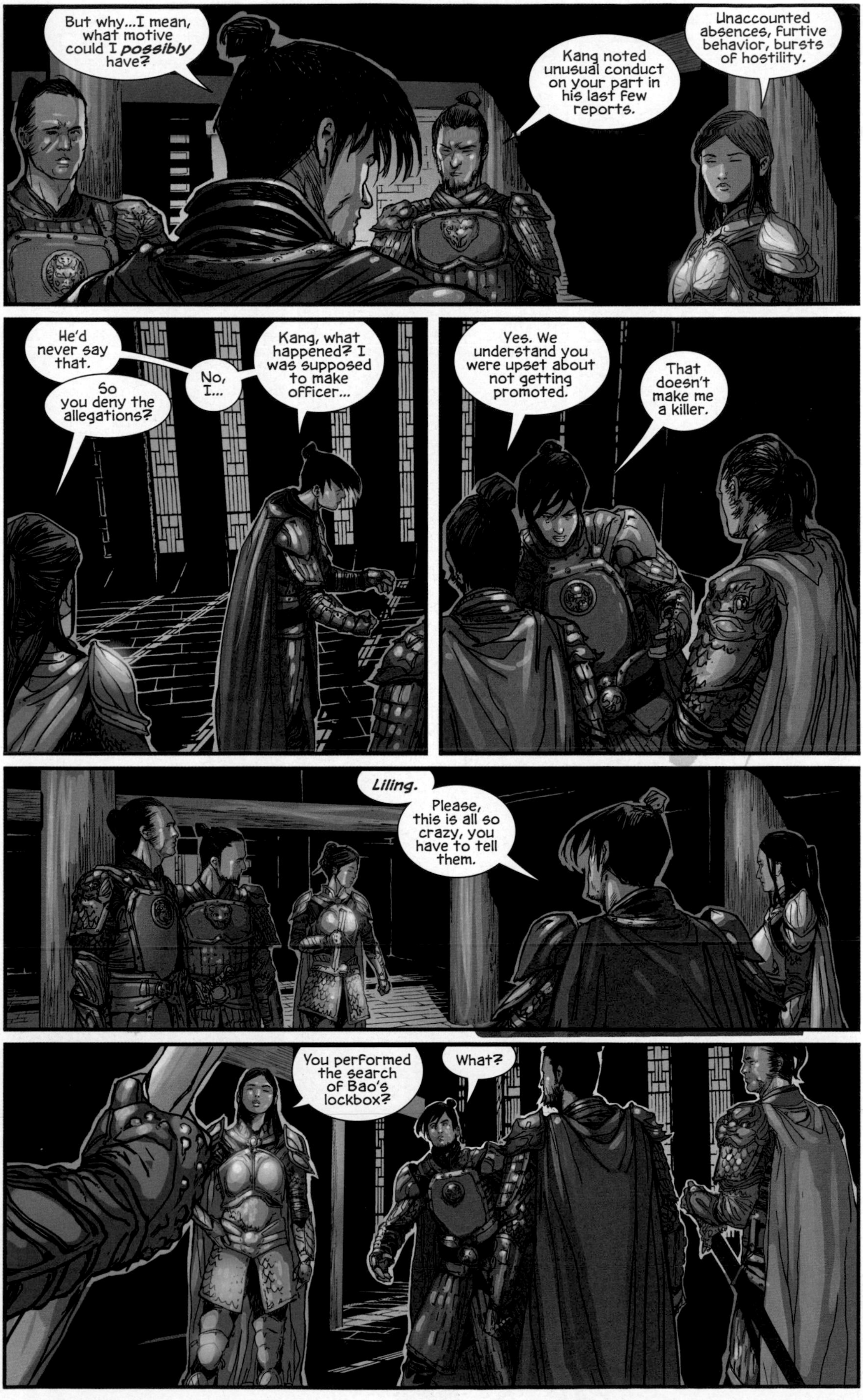
But why...I mean, what motive could I *possibly* have?
Kang noted unusual conduct on your part in his last few reports.
Unaccounted absences, furtive behavior, bursts of hostility.
He'd never say that.
So you deny the allegations?
No, I...
Kang, what happened? I was supposed to make officer...
Yes. We understand you were upset about not getting promoted.
That doesn't make me a killer.
Liling.
Please, this is all so crazy, you have to tell them.
You performed the search of Bao's lockbox?
What?

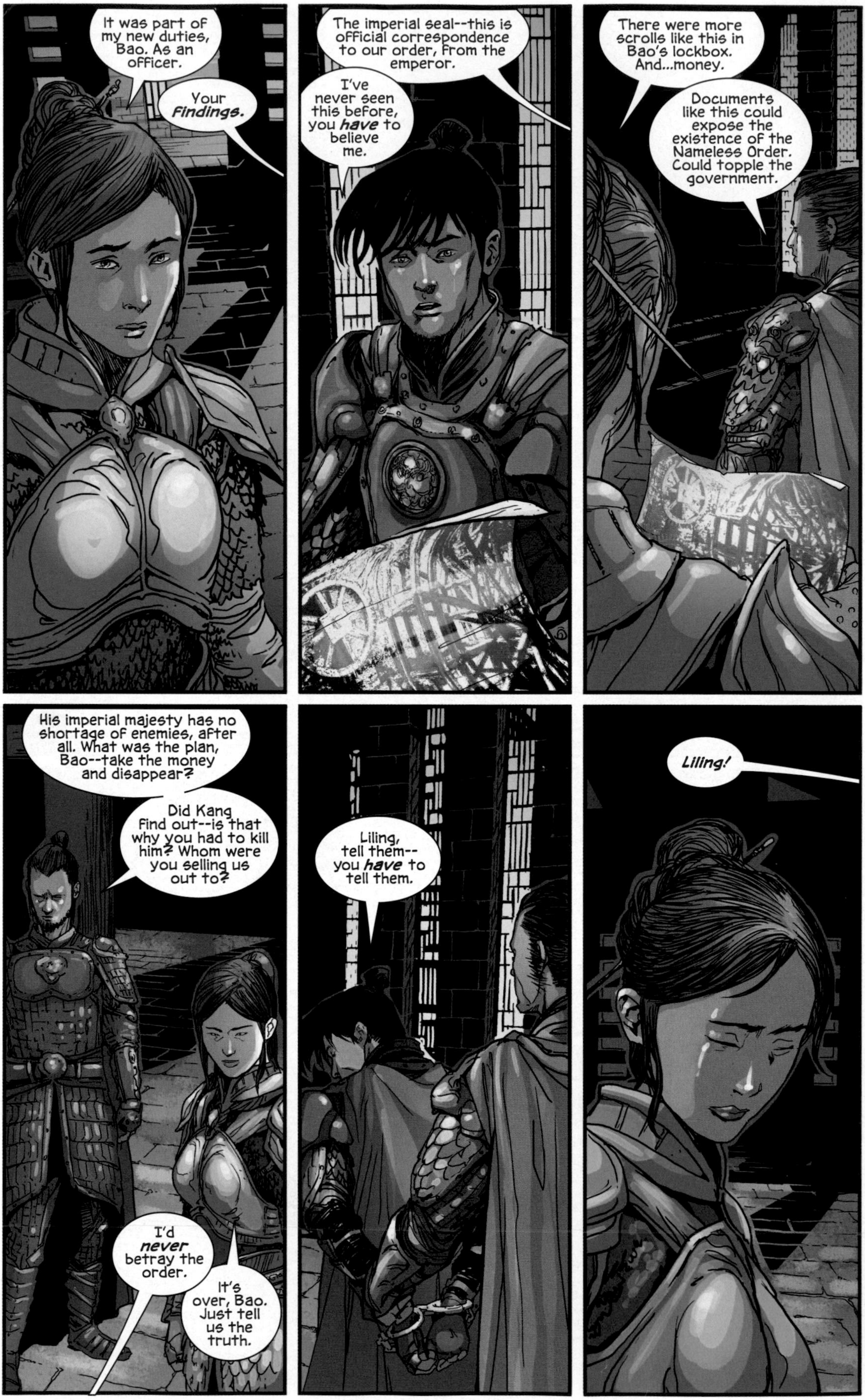
It was part of my new duties, Bao. As an officer.
Your findings.
The imperial seal--this is official correspondence to our order, from the emperor.
I've never seen this before, you have to believe me.
There were more scrolls like this in Bao's lockbox. And...money.
Documents like this could expose the existence of the Nameless Order. Could topple the government.
His imperial majesty has no shortage of enemies, after all. What was the plan, Bao--take the money and disappear?
Did Kang find out--is that why you had to kill him? Whom were you selling us out to?
I'd never betray the order.
It's over, Bao. Just tell us the truth.
Liling, tell them--you have to tell them.
Liling!

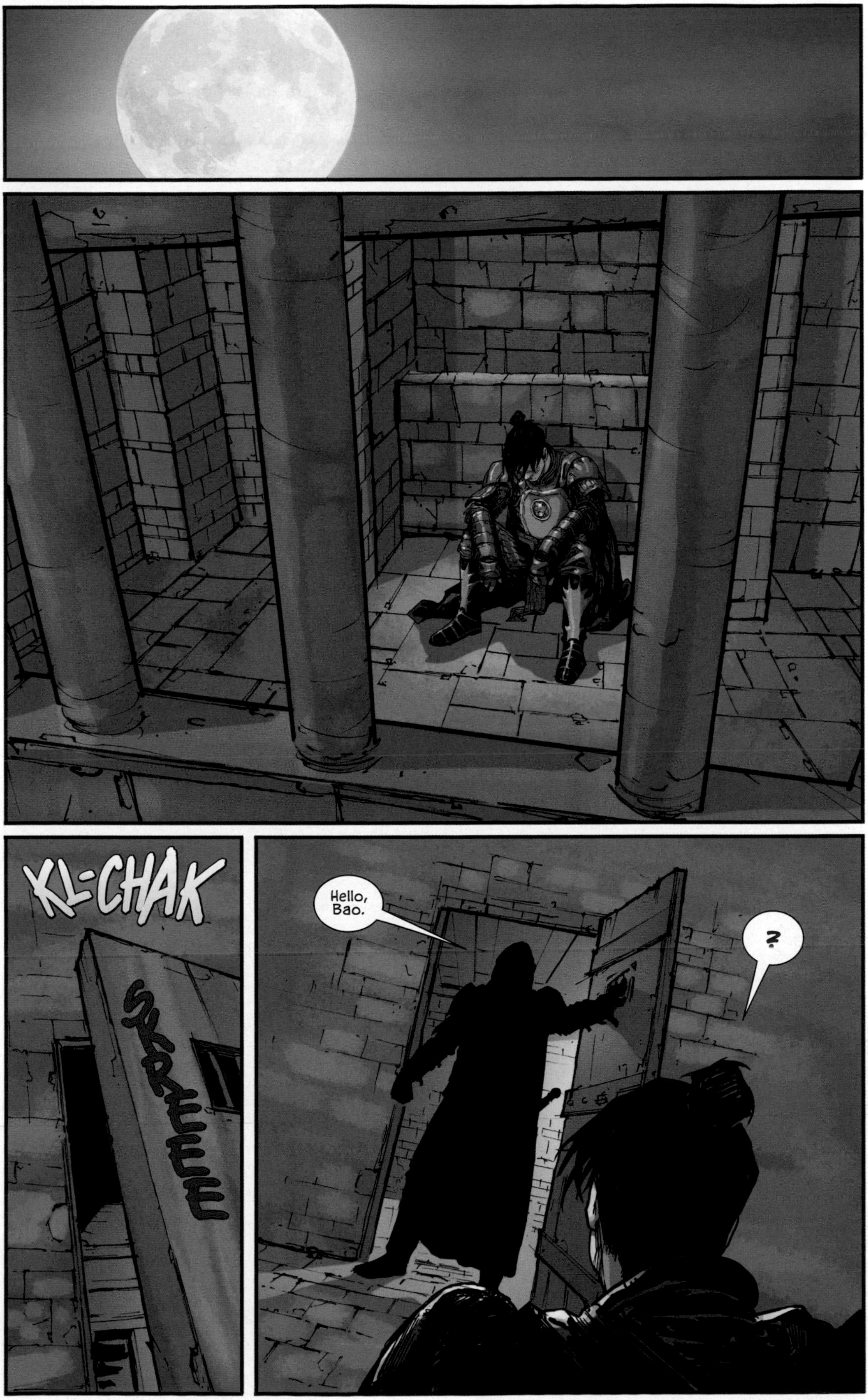
KL-CHAK
SKREEE
Hello, Bao.
?

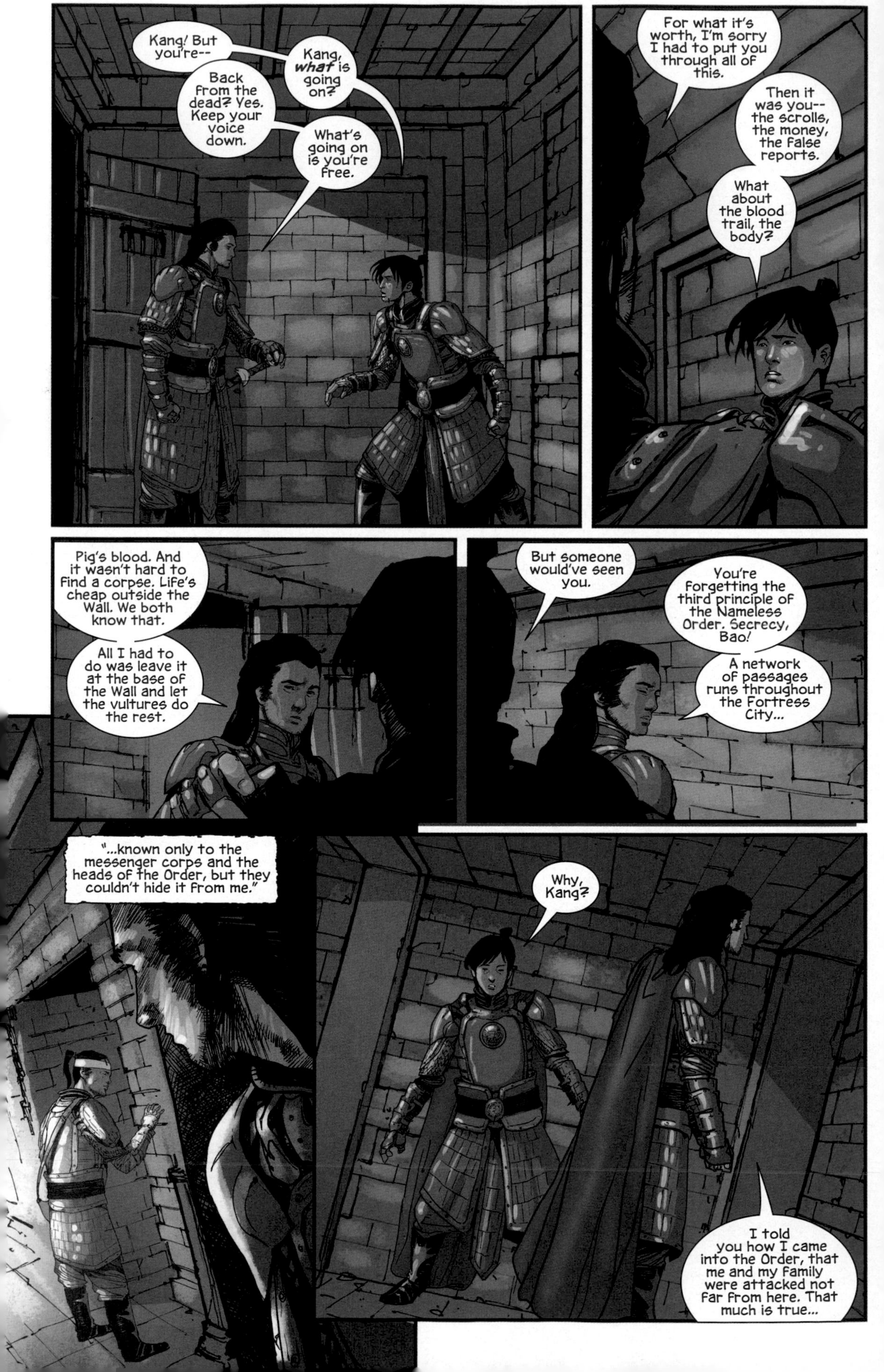

Kang! But you're--
Kang, *what* is going on?
Back from the dead? Yes. Keep your voice down.
What's going on is you're free.
For what it's worth, I'm sorry I had to put you through all of this.
Then it was you--the scrolls, the money, the false reports.
What about the blood trail, the body?
Pig's blood. And it wasn't hard to find a corpse. Life's cheap outside the Wall. We both know that.
All I had to do was leave it at the base of the Wall and let the vultures do the rest.
But someone would've seen you.
You're forgetting the third principle of the Nameless Order. Secrecy, Bao!
A network of passages runs throughout the Fortress City...
"...known only to the messenger corps and the heads of the Order, but they couldn't hide it from me."
Why, Kang?
I told you how I came into the Order, that me and my family were attacked not far from here. That much is true...

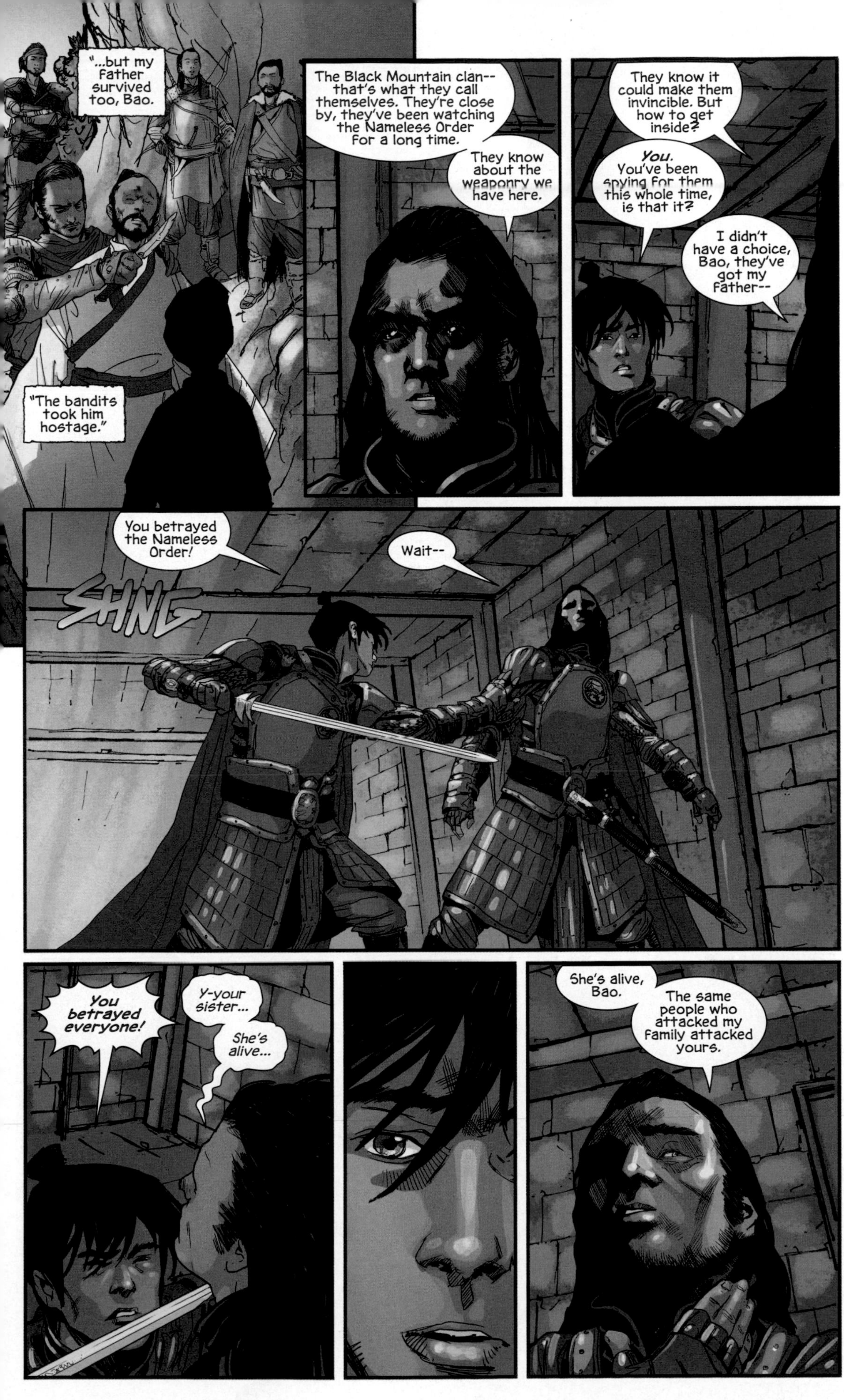
"...but my father survived too, Bao.
"The bandits took him hostage."
The Black Mountain clan--that's what they call themselves. They're close by, they've been watching the Nameless Order for a long time.
They know about the weaponry we have here.
They know it could make them invincible. But how to get inside?
You. You've been spying for them this whole time, is that it?
I didn't have a choice, Bao, they've got my father--
You betrayed the Nameless Order!
Wait--
SHNG
You betrayed everyone!
Y-your sister...
She's alive...
She's alive, Bao.
The same people who attacked my family attacked yours.

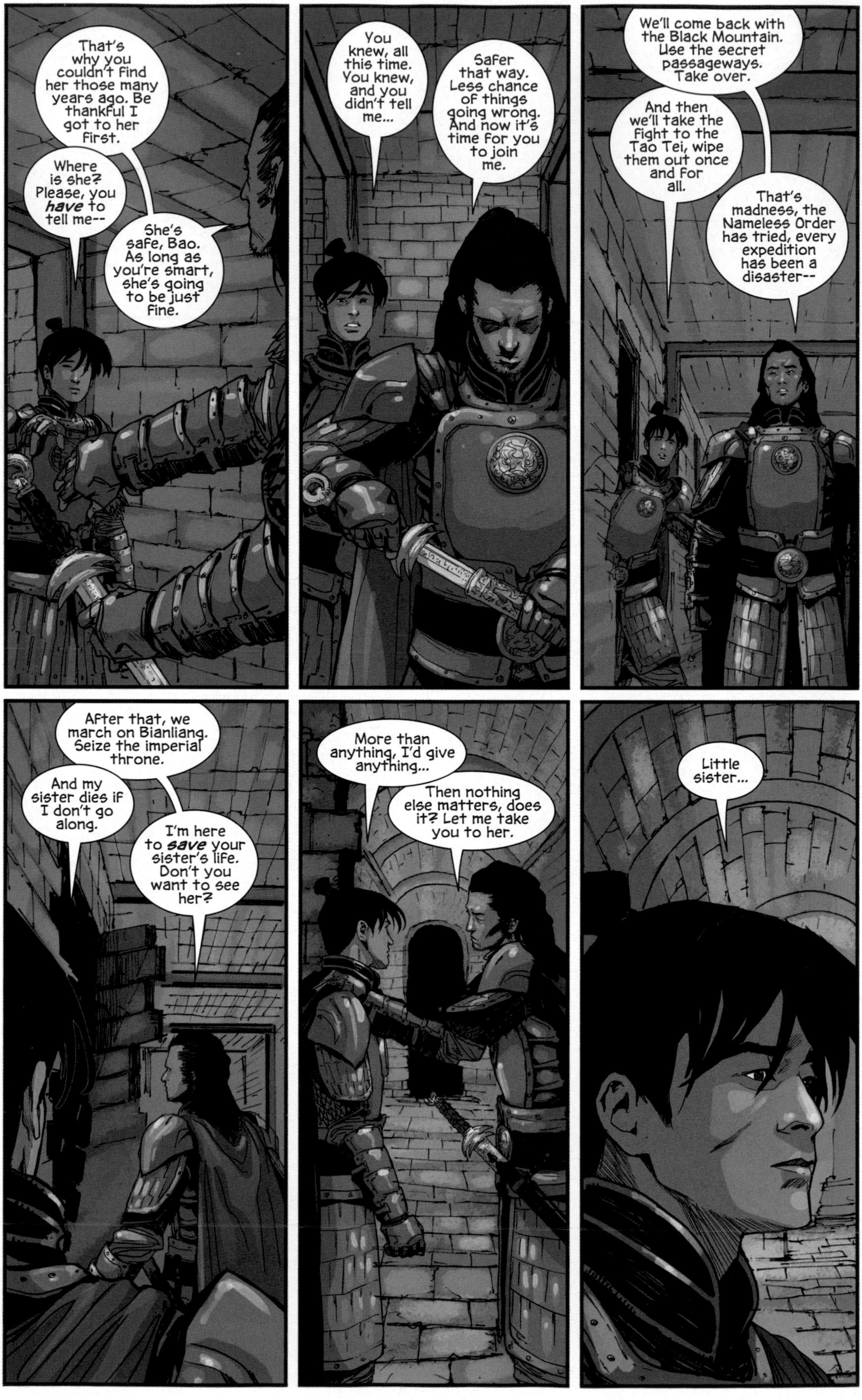
That's why you couldn't find her those many years ago. Be thankful I got to her first.
Where is she? Please, you *have* to tell me--
She's safe, Bao. As long as you're smart, she's going to be just fine.
You knew, all this time. You knew, and you didn't tell me...
Safer that way. Less chance of things going wrong. And now it's time for you to join me.
We'll come back with the Black Mountain. Use the secret passageways. Take over.
And then we'll take the fight to the Tao Tei, wipe them out once and for all.
That's madness, the Nameless Order has tried, every expedition has been a disaster--
After that, we march on Bianliang. Seize the imperial throne.
And my sister dies if I don't go along.
I'm here to *save* your sister's life. Don't you want to see her?
More than anything, I'd give anything...
Then nothing else matters, does it? Let me take you to her.
Little sister...

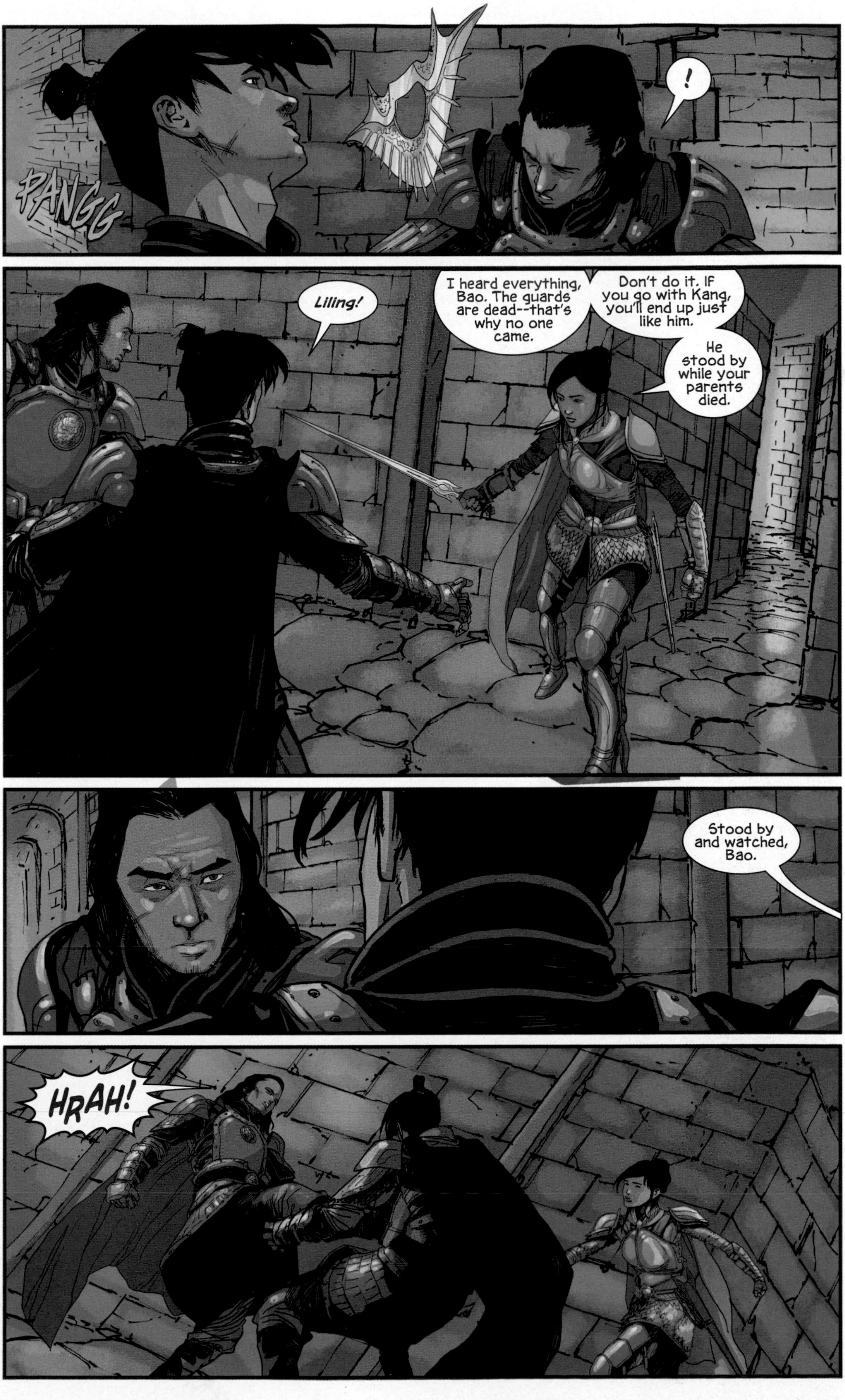
PANGG
!
Liling!
I heard everything, Bao. The guards are dead--that's why no one came.
Don't do it. If you go with Kang, you'll end up just like him.
He stood by while your parents died.
Stood by and watched, Bao.
HRAH!

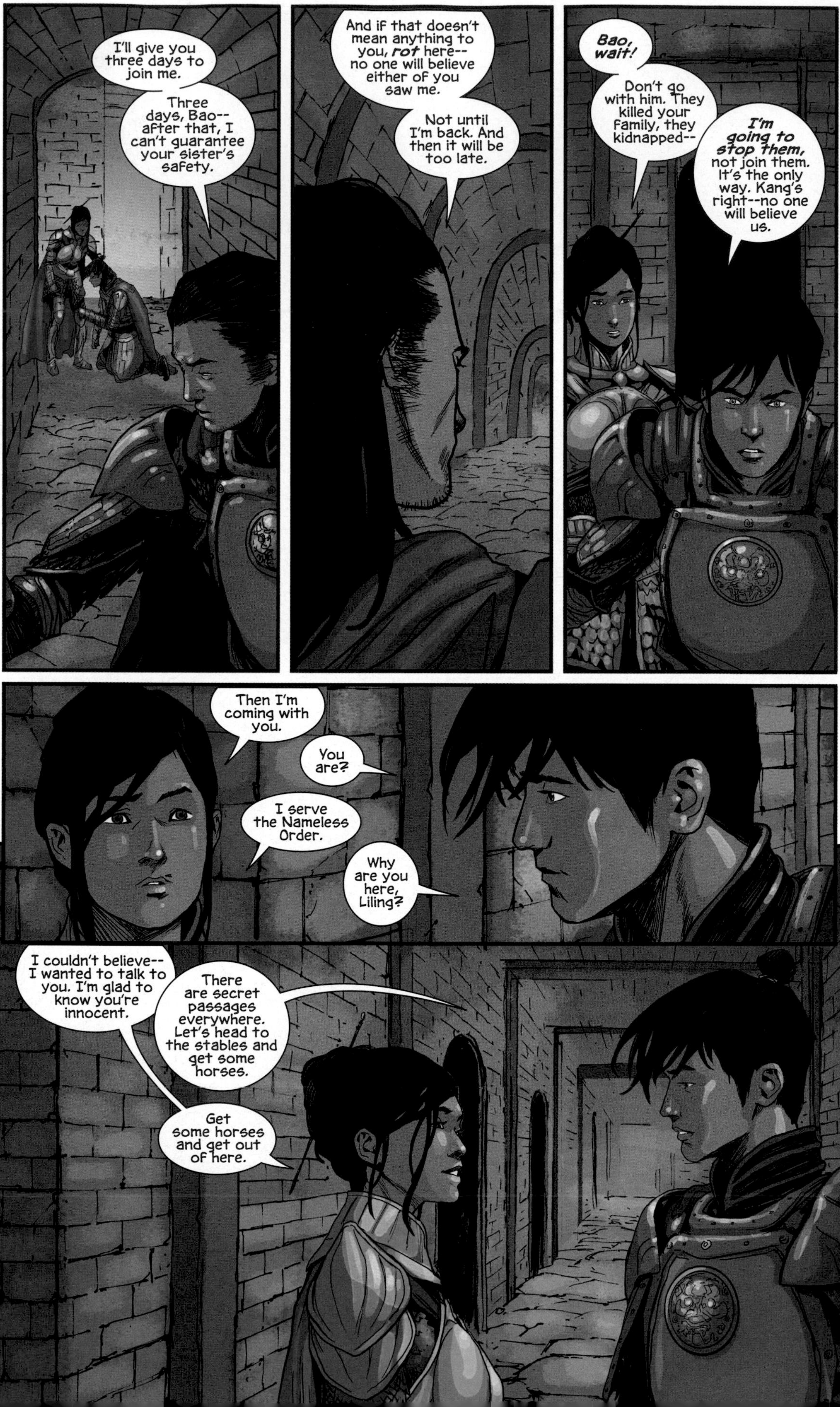

I'll give you three days to join me.
Three days, Bao--after that, I can't guarantee your sister's safety.
And if that doesn't mean anything to you, *rot* here--no one will believe either of you saw me.
Not until I'm back. And then it will be too late.
Bao, wait!
Don't go with him. They killed your family, they kidnapped--
I'm going to stop them, not join them. It's the only way. Kang's right--no one will believe us.
Then I'm coming with you.
You are?
I serve the Nameless Order.
Why are you here, Liling?
I couldn't believe--I wanted to talk to you. I'm glad to know you're innocent.
There are secret passages everywhere. Let's head to the stables and get some horses.
Get some horses and get out of here.

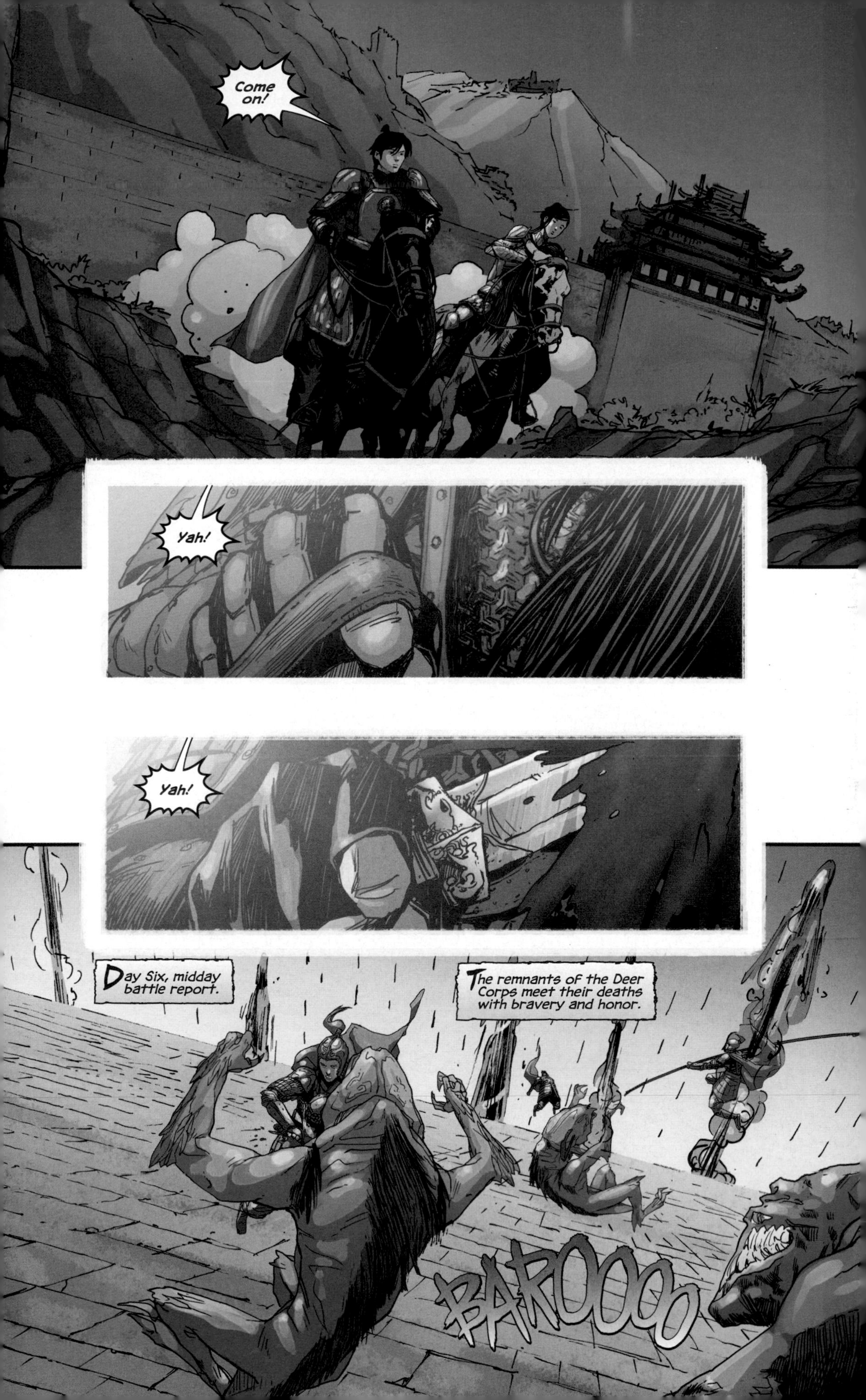
Come on!
Yah!
Yah!
Day Six, midday battle report.
The remnants of the Deer Corps meet their deaths with bravery and honor.
BAROOOO

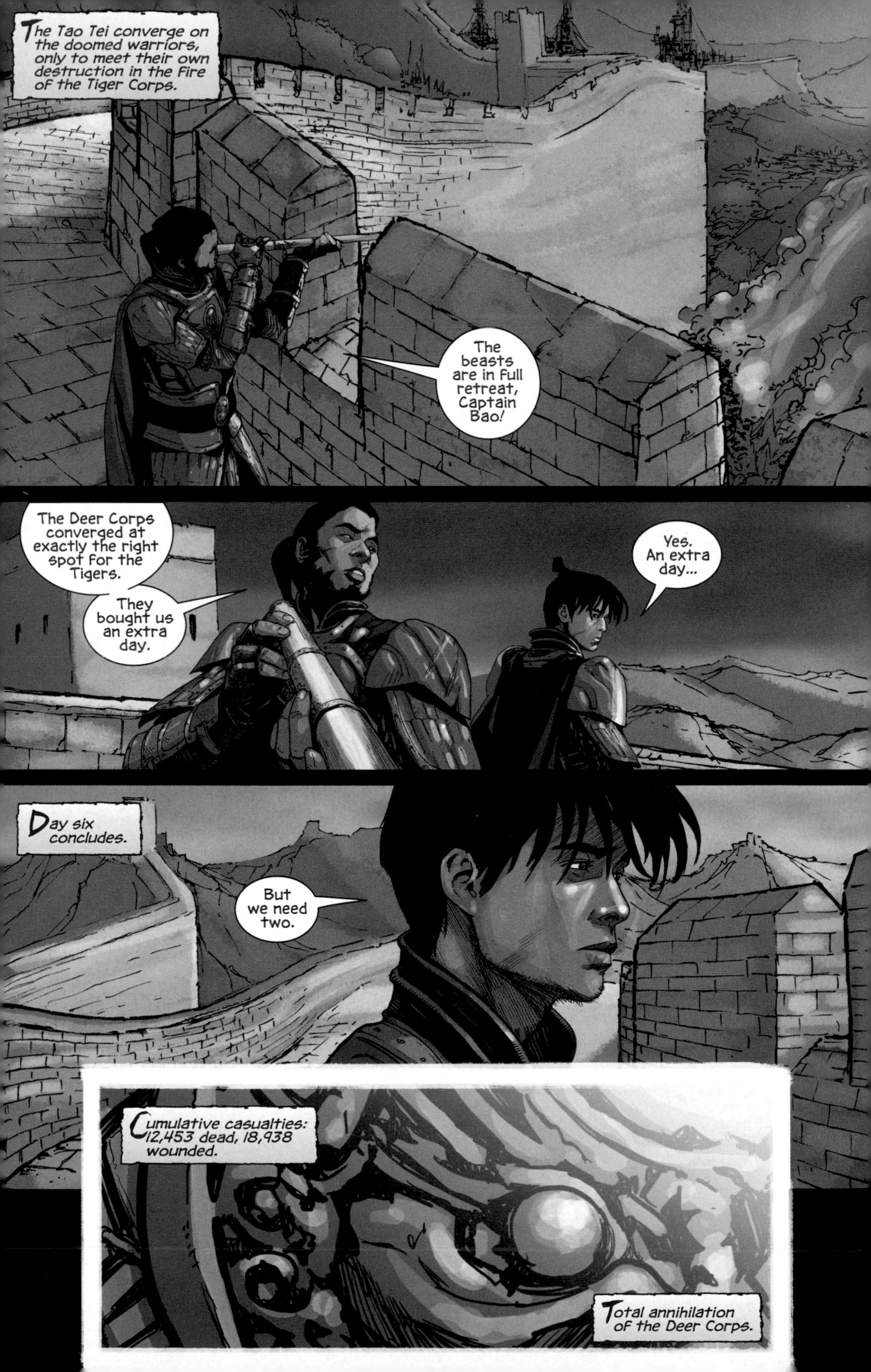
The Tao Tei converge on the doomed warriors, only to meet their own destruction in the fire of the Tiger Corps.
The beasts are in full retreat, Captain Bao!
The Deer Corps converged at exactly the right spot for the Tigers.
They bought us an extra day.
Yes. An extra day...
Day six concludes.
But we need two.
Cumulative casualties: 12,453 dead, 18,938 wounded.
Total annihilation of the Deer Corps.

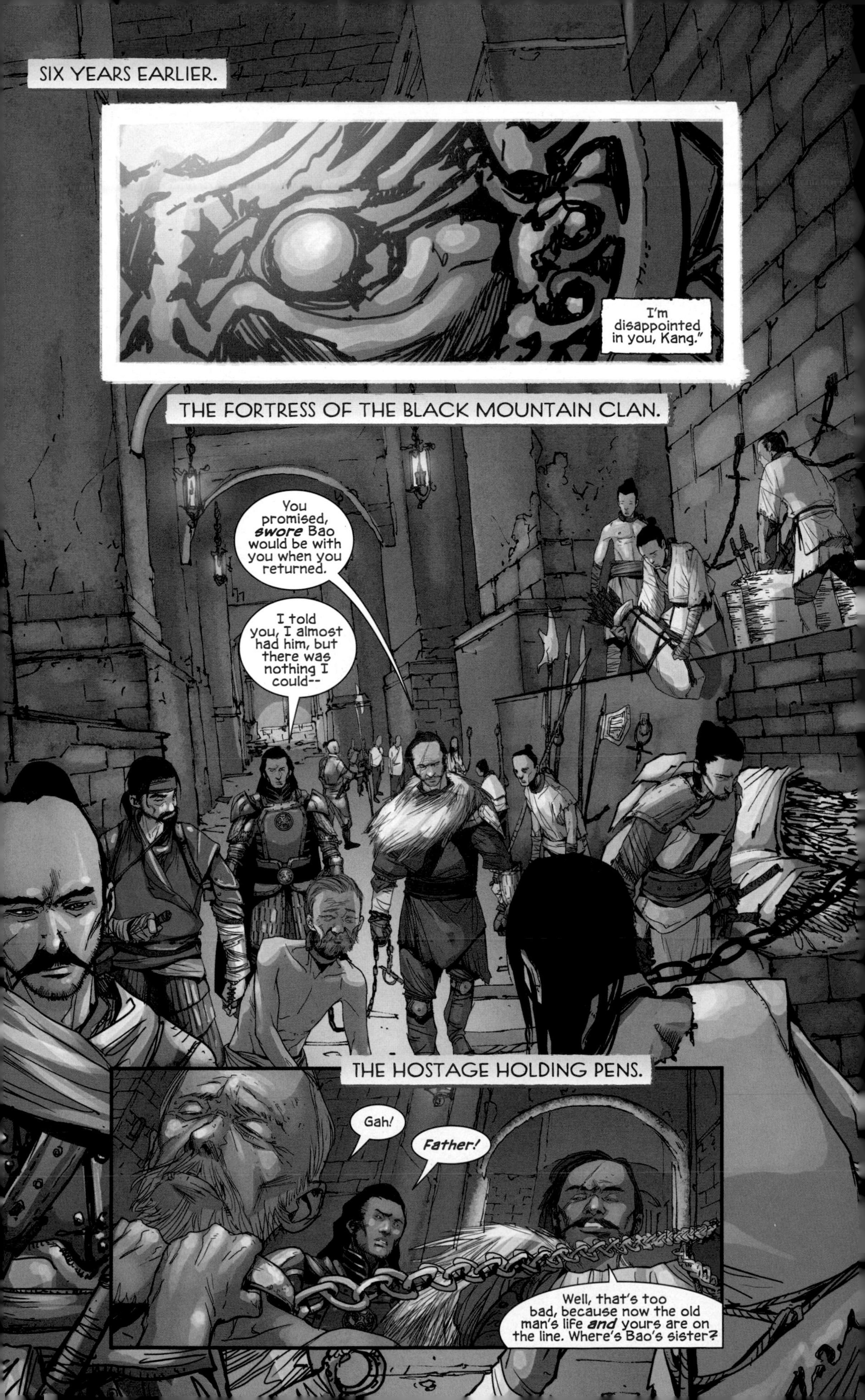
SIX YEARS EARLIER.
I'm disappointed in you, Kang."
THE FORTRESS OF THE BLACK MOUNTAIN CLAN.
You promised, *swore* Bao would be with you when you returned.
I told you, I almost had him, but there was nothing I could--
THE HOSTAGE HOLDING PENS.
Gah!
Father!
Well, that's too bad, because now the old man's life *and* yours are on the line. Where's Bao's sister?

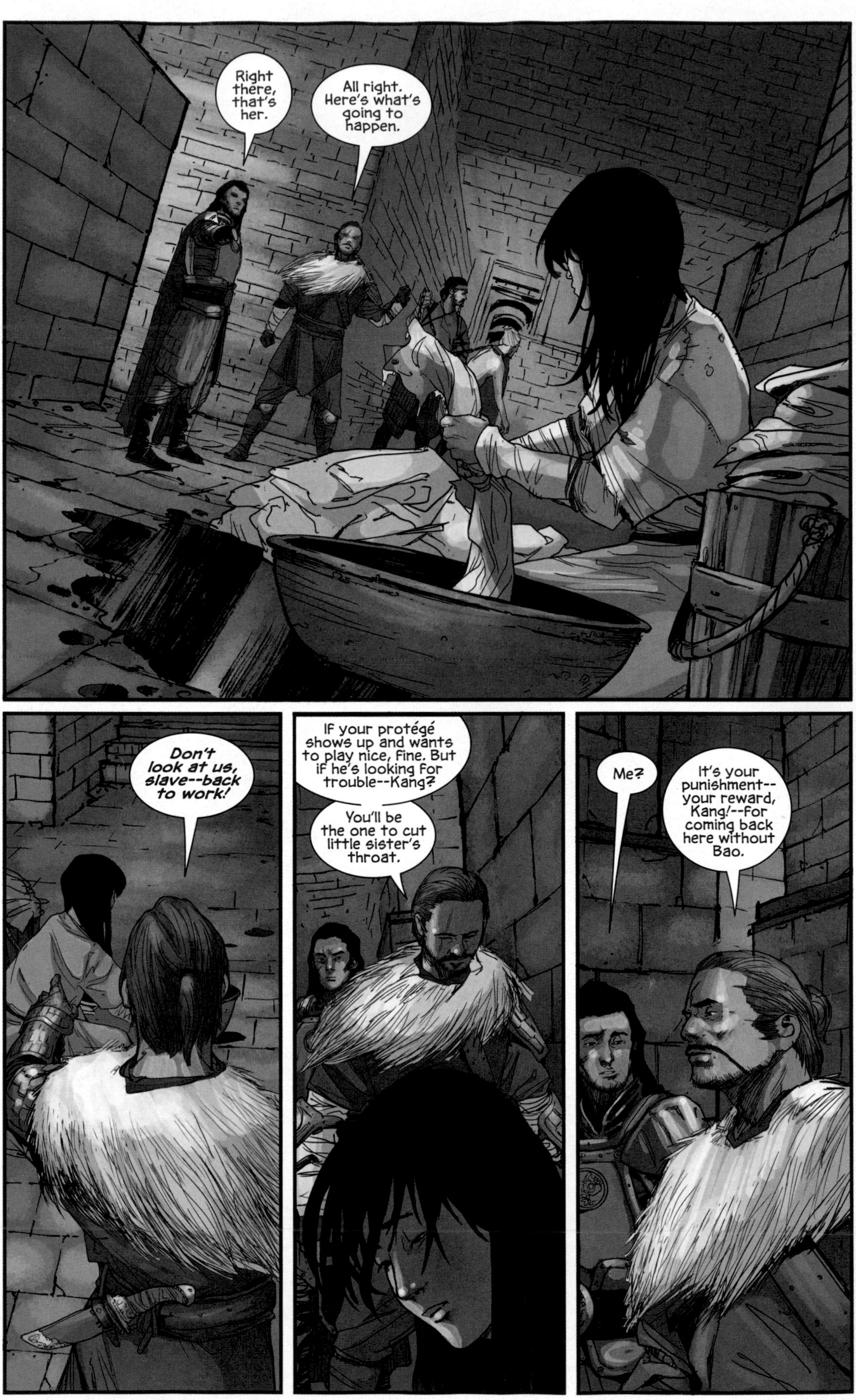

Right there, that's her.
All right. Here's what's going to happen.
Don't look at us, slave--back to work!
If your protégé shows up and wants to play nice, fine. But if he's looking for trouble--Kang?
You'll be the one to cut little sister's throat.
Me?
It's your punishment--your reward, Kang!--for coming back here without Bao.

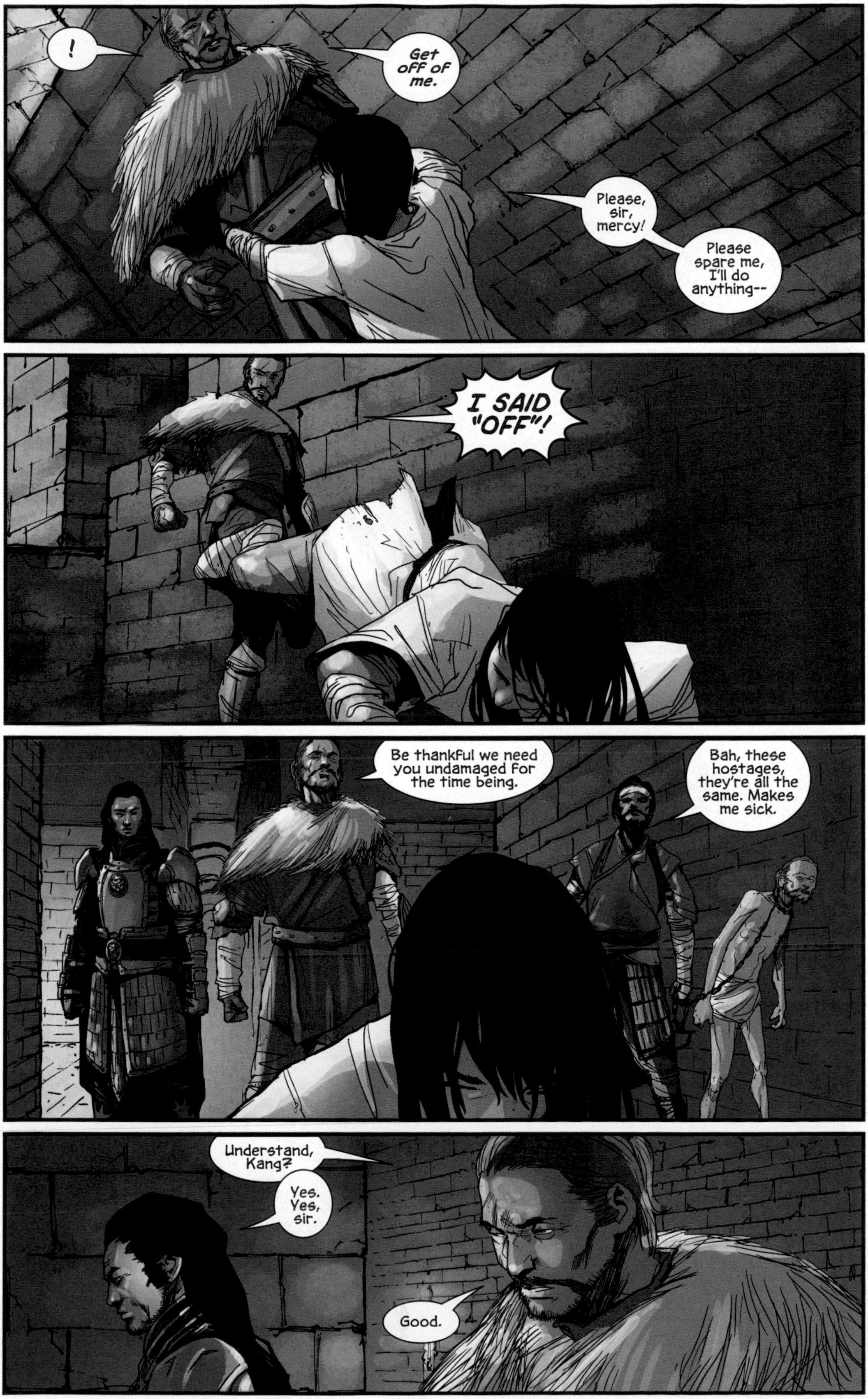

!
Get off of me.
Please, sir, mercy!
Please spare me, I'll do anything--
I SAID "OFF"!
Be thankful we need you undamaged for the time being.
Bah, these hostages, they're all the same. Makes me sick.
Understand, Kang?
Yes. Yes, sir.
Good.

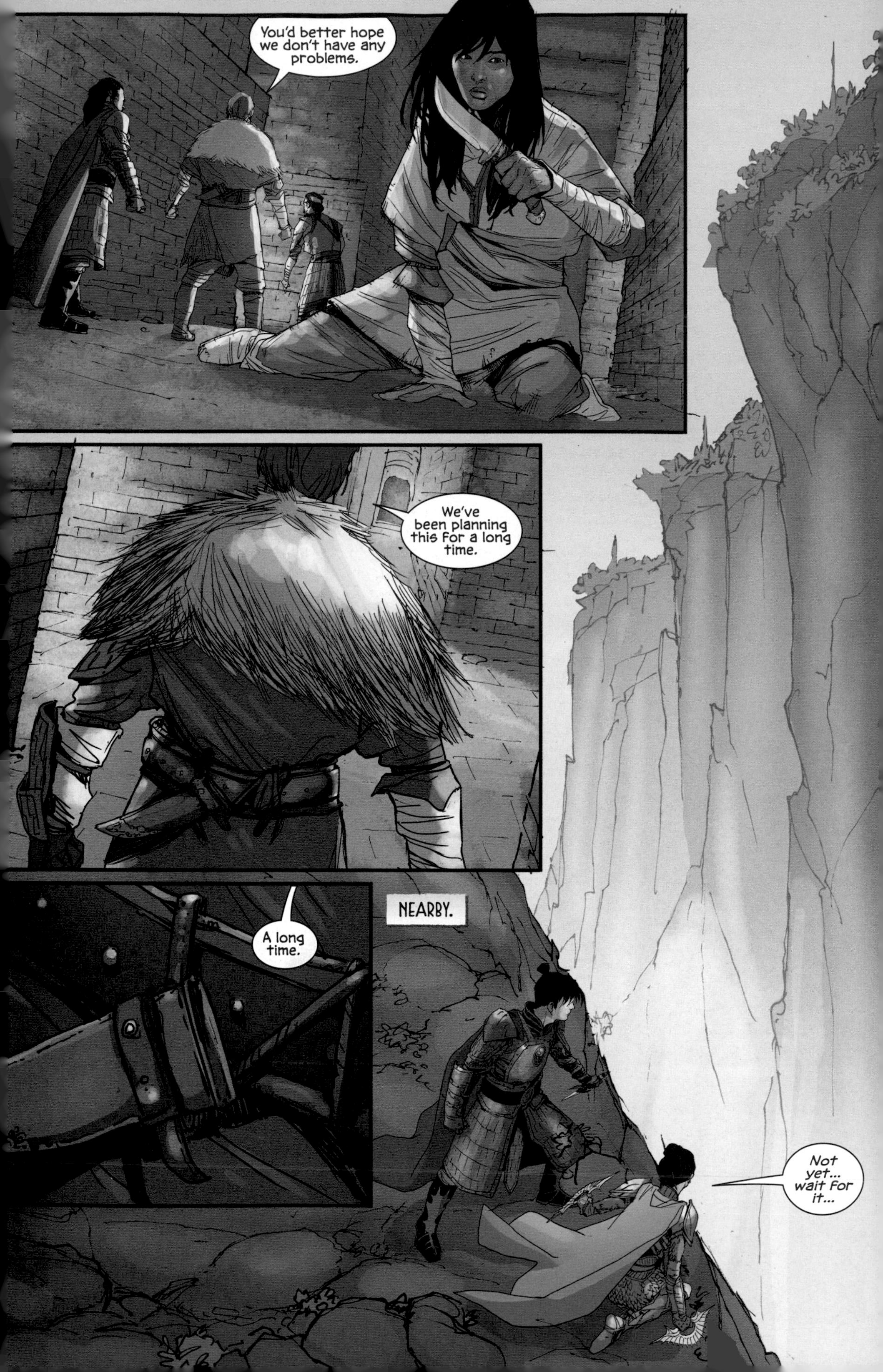
You'd better hope we don't have any problems.
We've been planning this for a long time.
A long time.
NEARBY.
Not yet... wait for it...

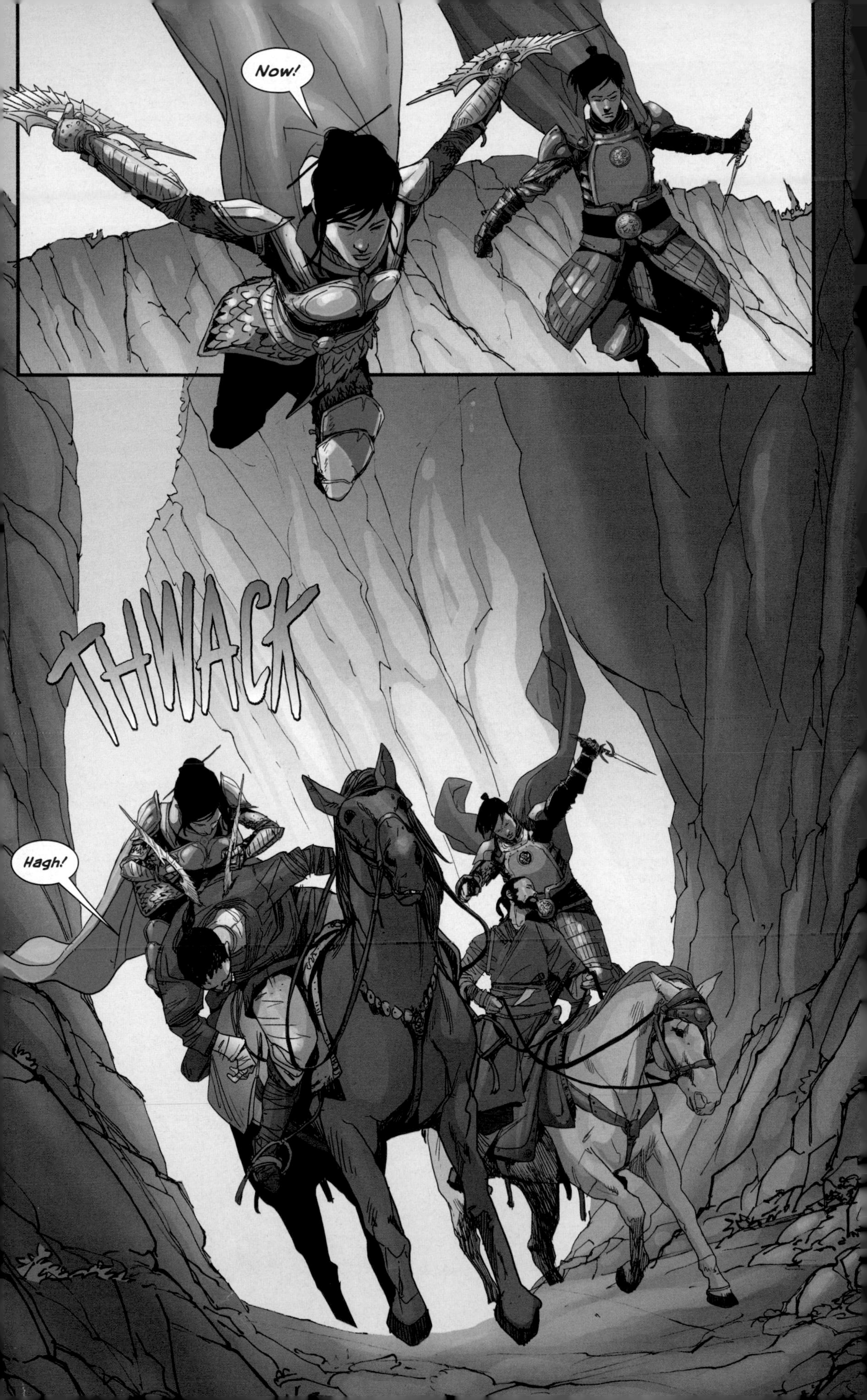
Now!
THWACK
Hagh!

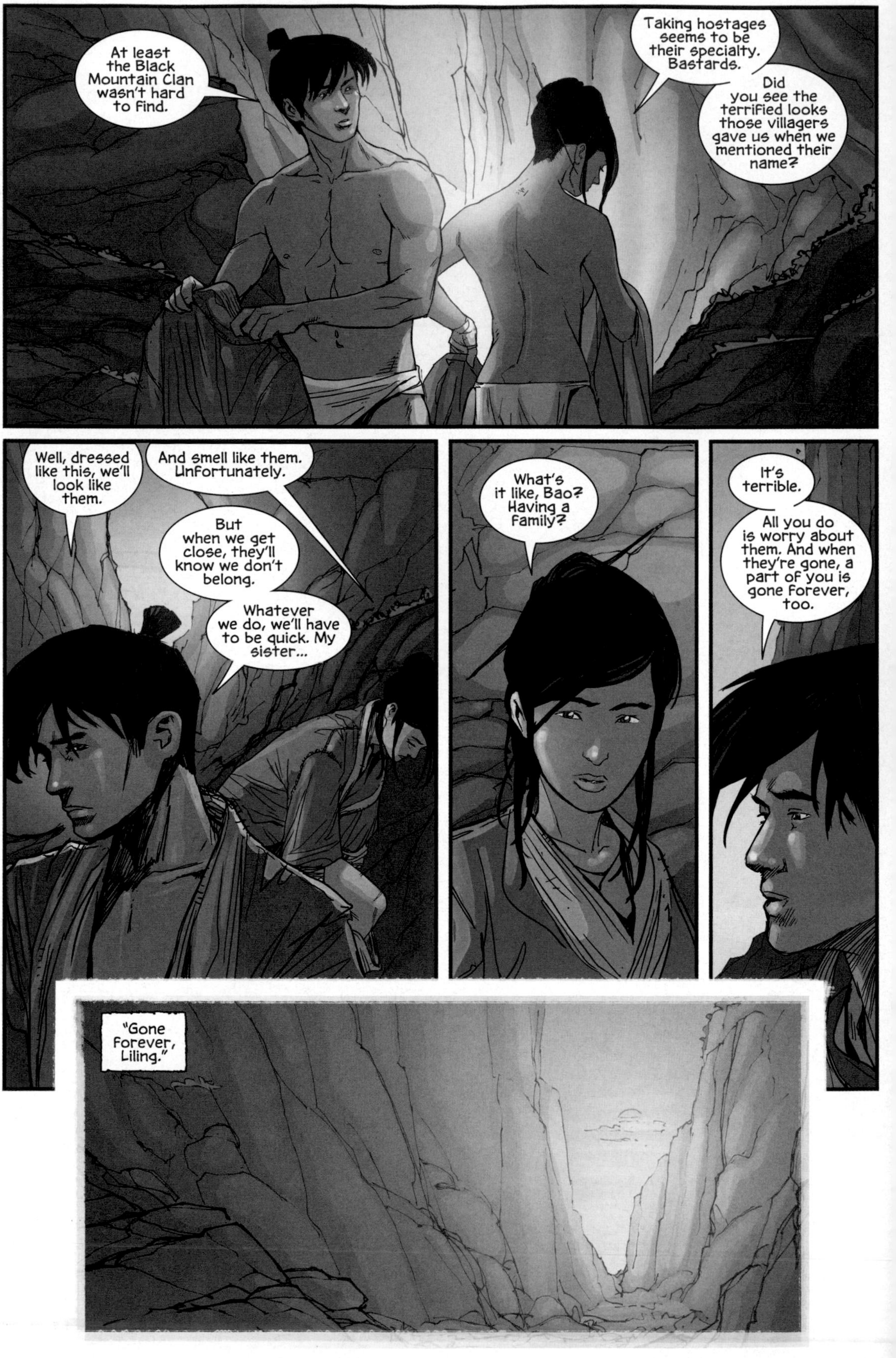
At least the Black Mountain Clan wasn't hard to find.
Taking hostages seems to be their specialty. Bastards.
Did you see the terrified looks those villagers gave us when we mentioned their name?
Well, dressed like this, we'll look like them.
And smell like them. Unfortunately.
But when we get close, they'll know we don't belong.
Whatever we do, we'll have to be quick. My sister...
What's it like, Bao? Having a family?
It's terrible.
All you do is worry about them. And when they're gone, a part of you is gone forever, too.
"Gone Forever, Liling."

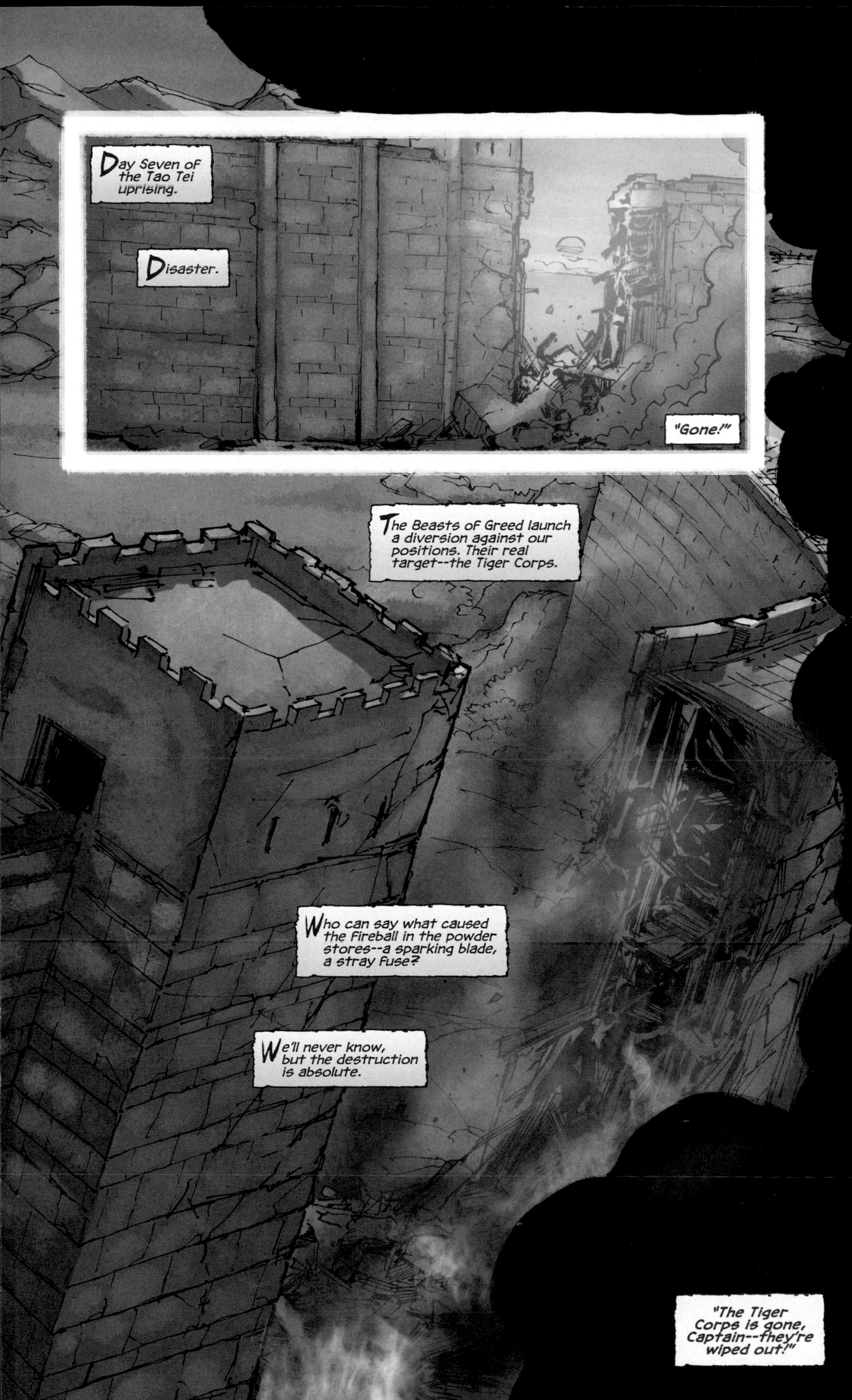
Day Seven of the Tao Tei uprising.
Disaster.
"Gone!"
The Beasts of Greed launch a diversion against our positions. Their real target--the Tiger Corps.
Who can say what caused the fireball in the powder stores--a sparking blade, a stray fuse?
We'll never know, but the destruction is absolute.
"The Tiger Corps is gone, Captain--they're wiped out!"

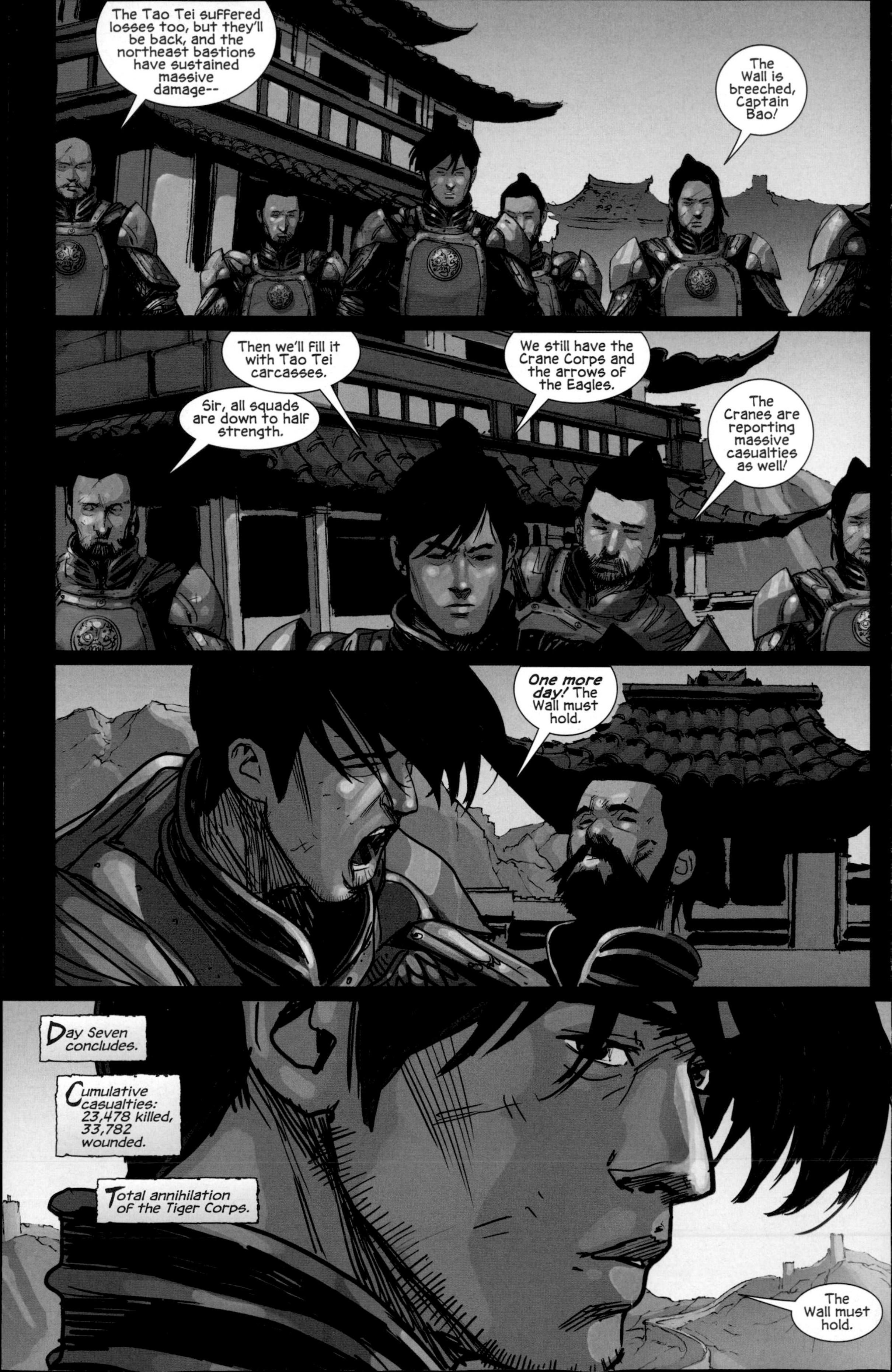
The Tao Tei suffered losses too, but they'll be back, and the northeast bastions have sustained massive damage--
The Wall is breeched, Captain Bao!
Sir, all squads are down to half strength.
Then we'll fill it with Tao Tei carcasses.
We still have the Crane Corps and the arrows of the Eagles.
The Cranes are reporting massive casualties as well!
One more day! The Wall must hold.
Day Seven concludes.
Cumulative casualties: 23,478 killed, 33,782 wounded.
Total annihilation of the Tiger Corps.
The Wall must hold.

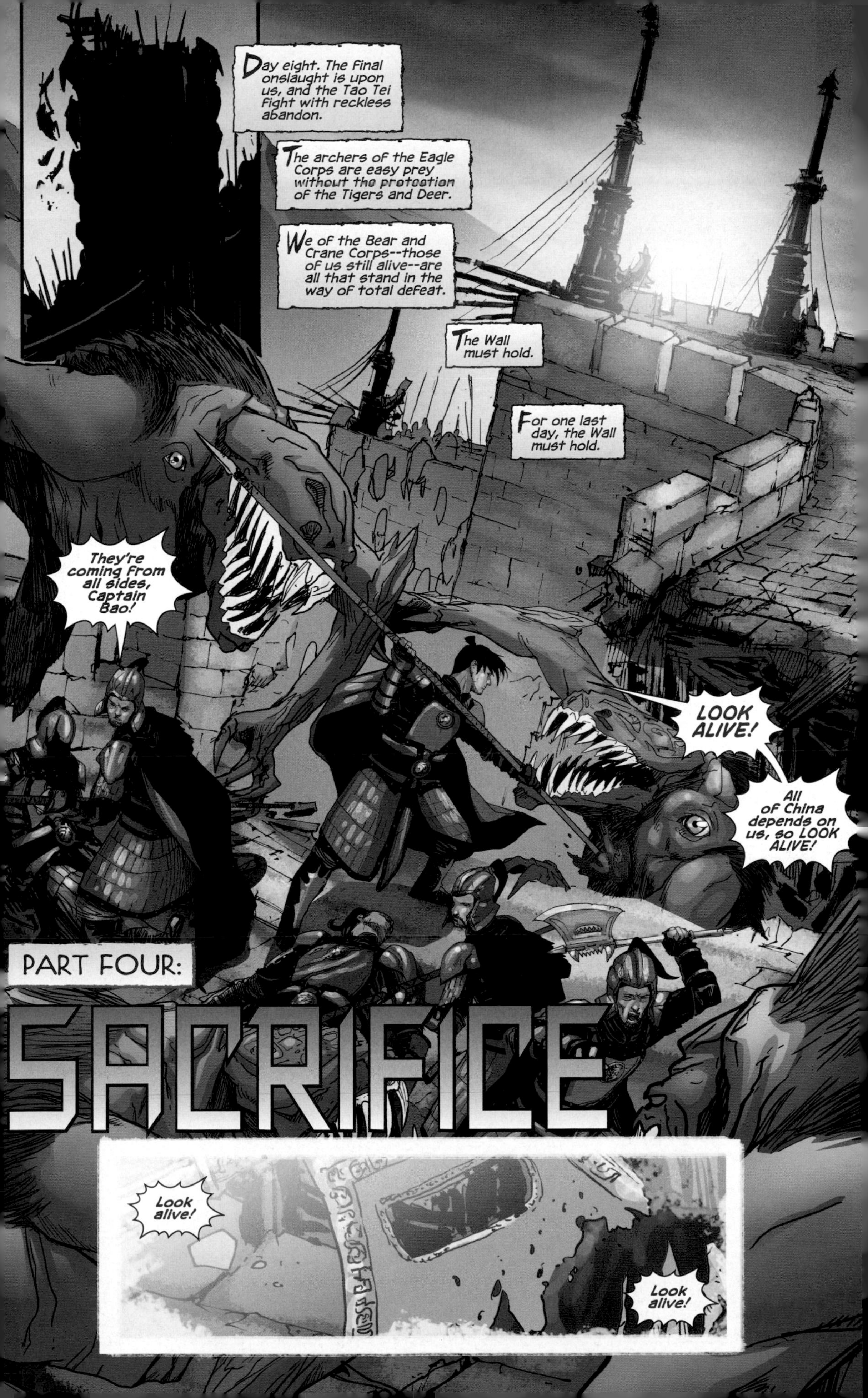
Day eight. The final onslaught is upon us, and the Tao Tei fight with reckless abandon.
The archers of the Eagle Corps are easy prey without the protection of the Tigers and Deer.
We of the Bear and Crane Corps--those of us still alive--are all that stand in the way of total defeat.
The Wall must hold.
For one last day, the Wall must hold.
They're coming from all sides, Captain Bao!
LOOK ALIVE!
All of China depends on us, so LOOK ALIVE!
PART FOUR:
SACRIFICE
Look alive!
Look alive!

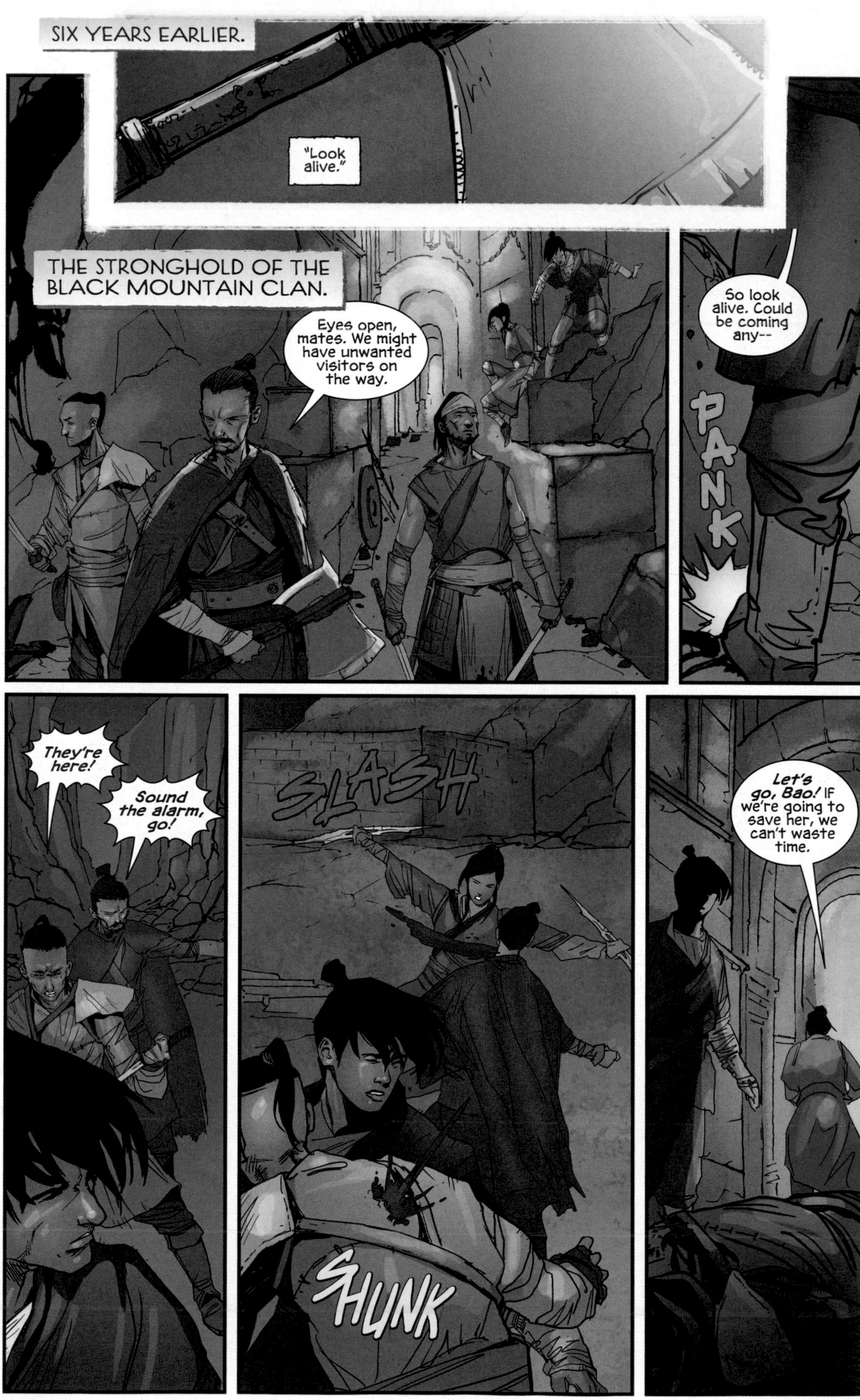
SIX YEARS EARLIER.
"Look alive."
THE STRONGHOLD OF THE BLACK MOUNTAIN CLAN.
Eyes open, mates. We might have unwanted visitors on the way.
So look alive. Could be coming any--
PANK
They're here!
Sound the alarm, go!
SLASH
SHUNK
Let's go, Bao! If we're going to save her, we can't waste time.

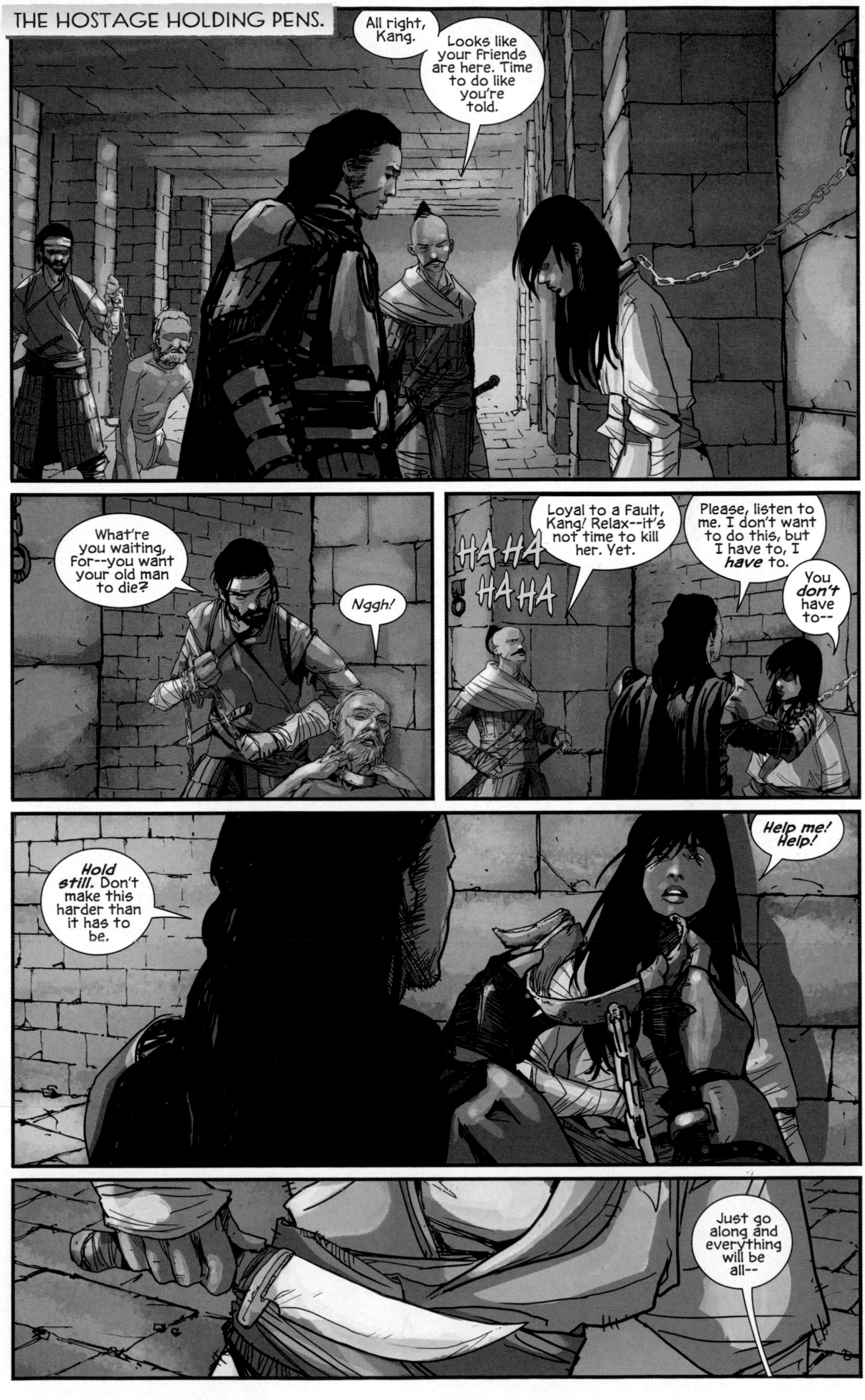
THE HOSTAGE HOLDING PENS.
All right, Kang.
Looks like your friends are here. Time to do like you're told.
What're you waiting, for--you want your old man to die?
Nggh!
HAHA HAHA
Loyal to a fault, Kang! Relax--it's not time to kill her. Yet.
Please, listen to me. I don't want to do this, but I have to, I *have* to.
You *don't* have to--
Hold still. Don't make this harder than it has to be.
Help me! Help!
Just go along and everything will be all--

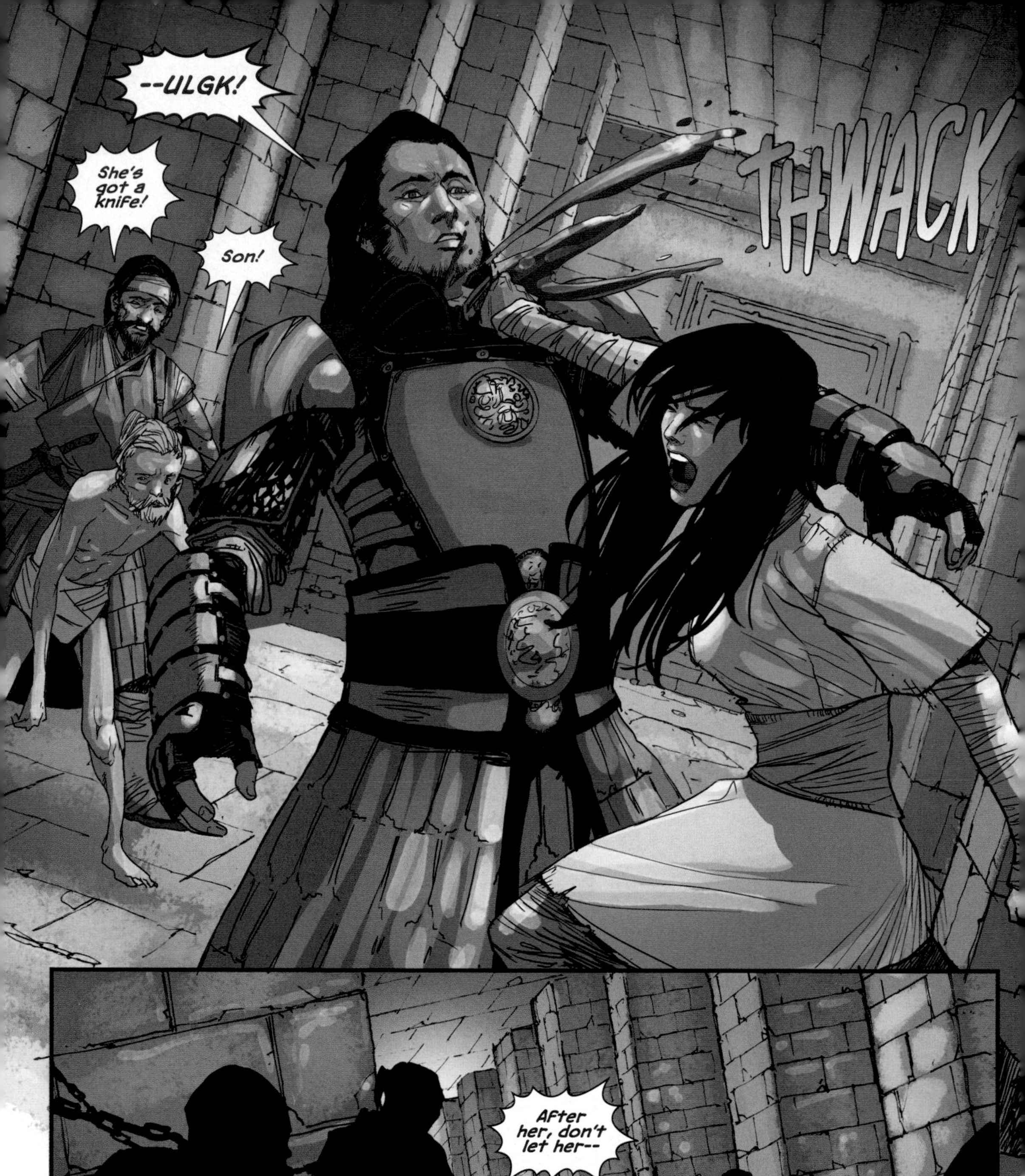
--ULGK!
She's got a knife!
Son!
THWACK
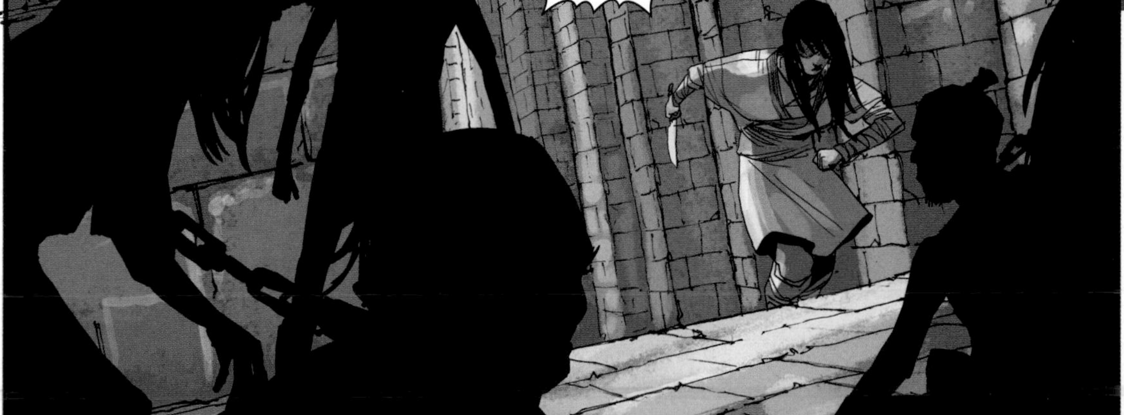
After her, don't let her--

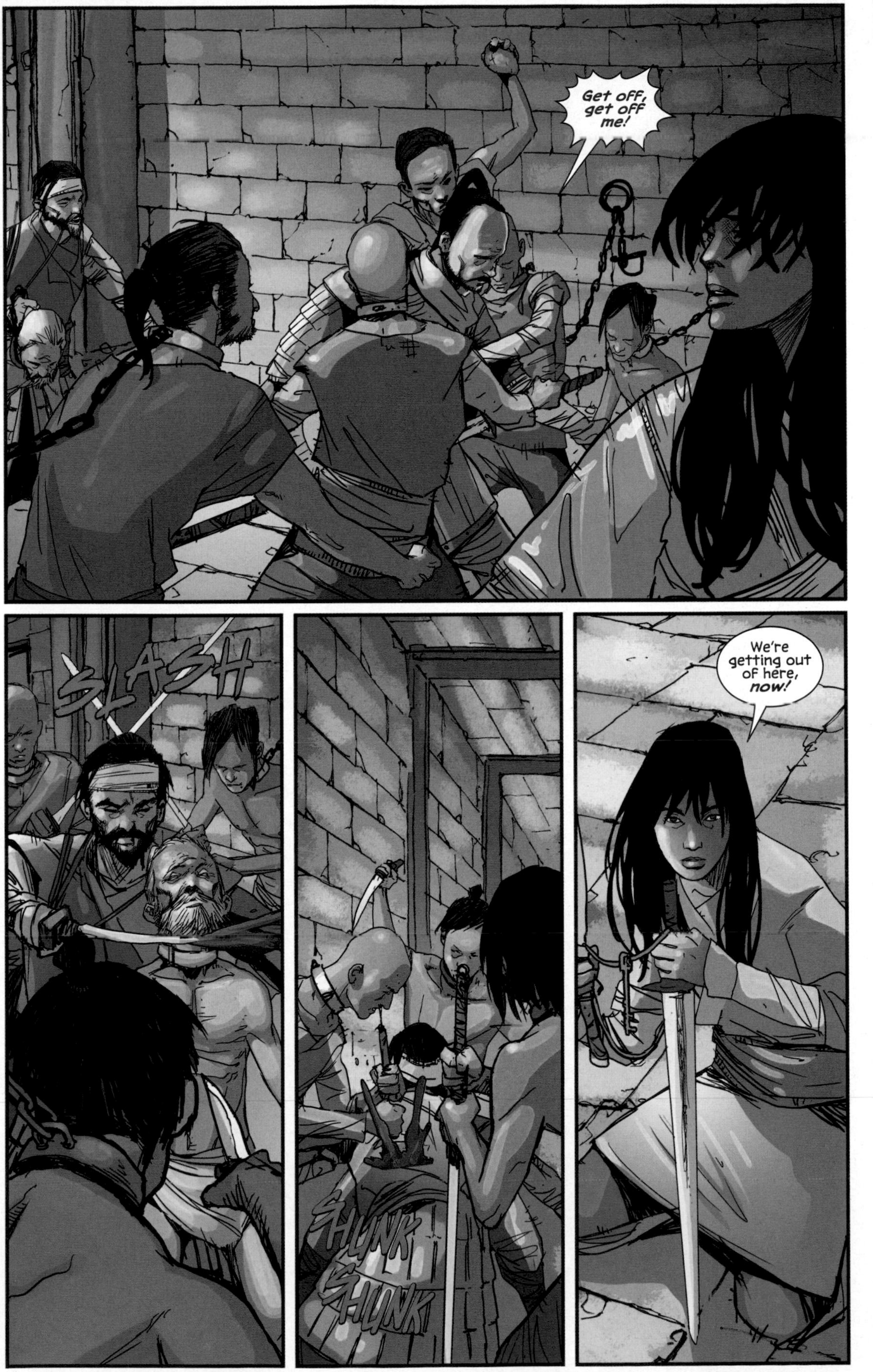
Get off, get off me!
SLASH
SHUNK SHUNK
We're getting out of here, *now!*

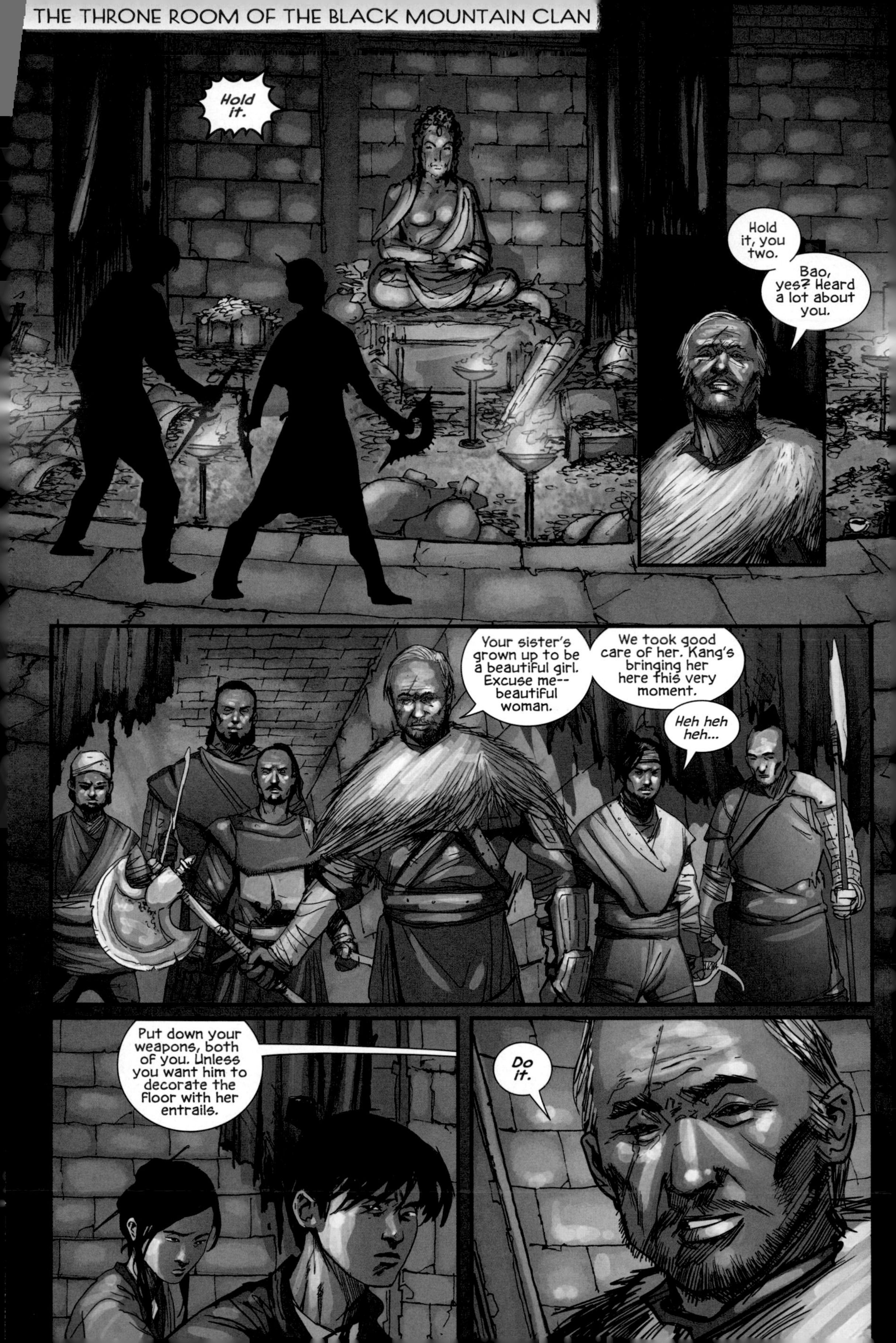
THE THRONE ROOM OF THE BLACK MOUNTAIN CLAN
Hold it.
Hold it, you two.
Bao, yes? Heard a lot about you.
Your sister's grown up to be a beautiful girl. Excuse me-- beautiful woman.
We took good care of her. Kang's bringing her here this very moment.
Heh heh heh...
Put down your weapons, both of you. Unless you want him to decorate the floor with her entrails.
Do it.

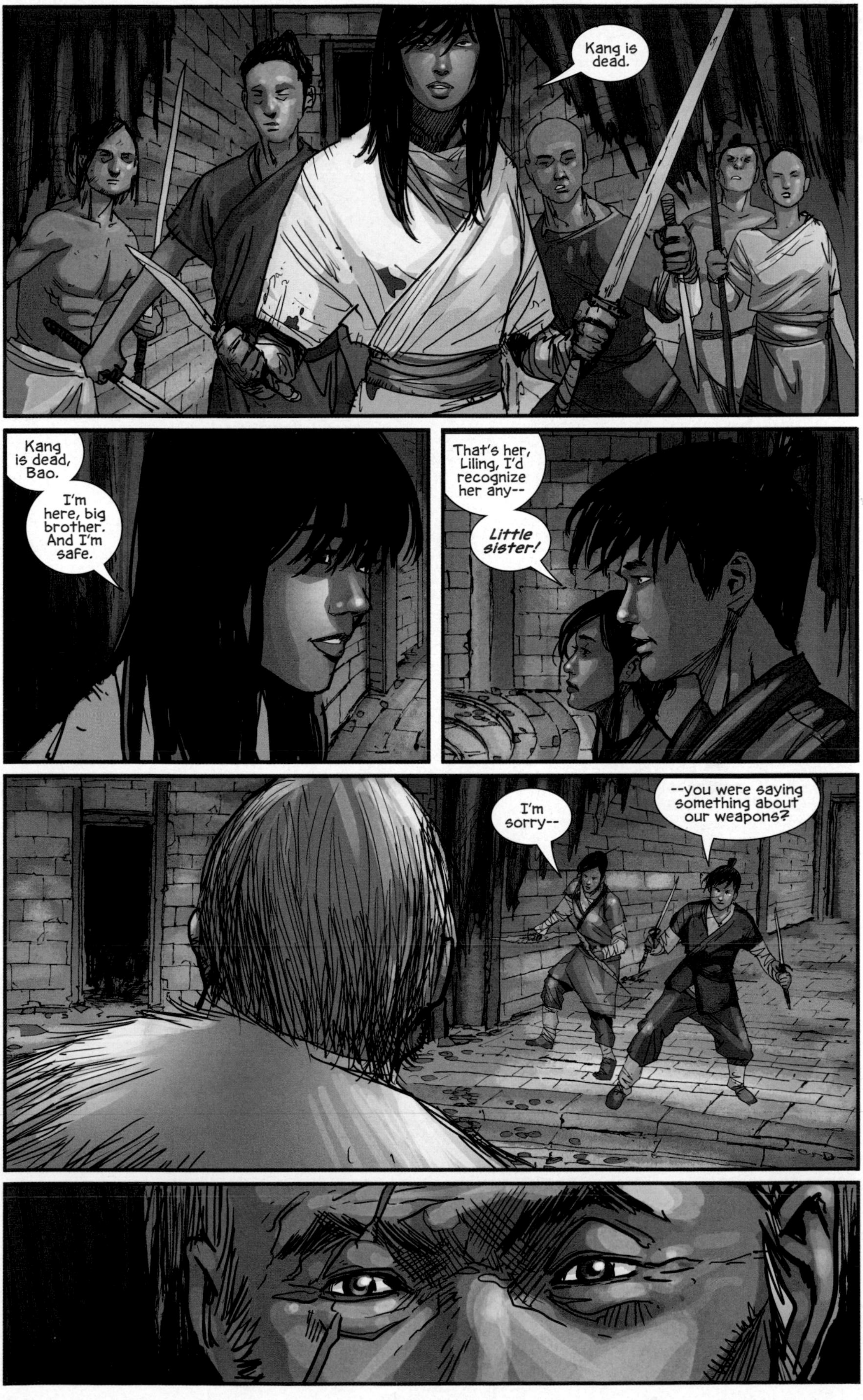
Kang is dead.
Kang is dead, Bao.
I'm here, big brother. And I'm safe.
That's her, Liling, I'd recognize her any--
Little sister!
I'm sorry--
--you were saying something about our weapons?

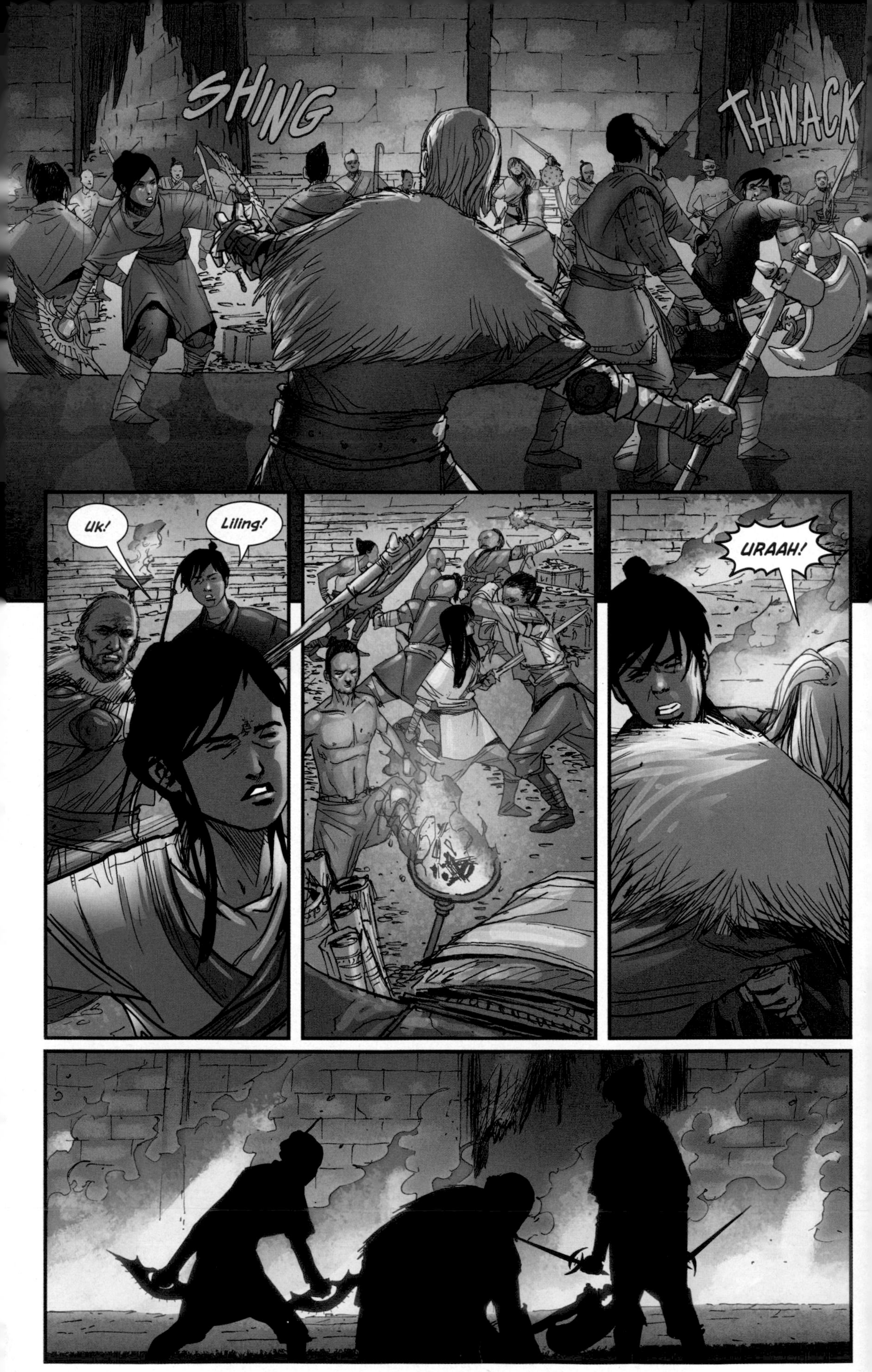
SHING
THWACK
UK!
Liling!
URAAH!

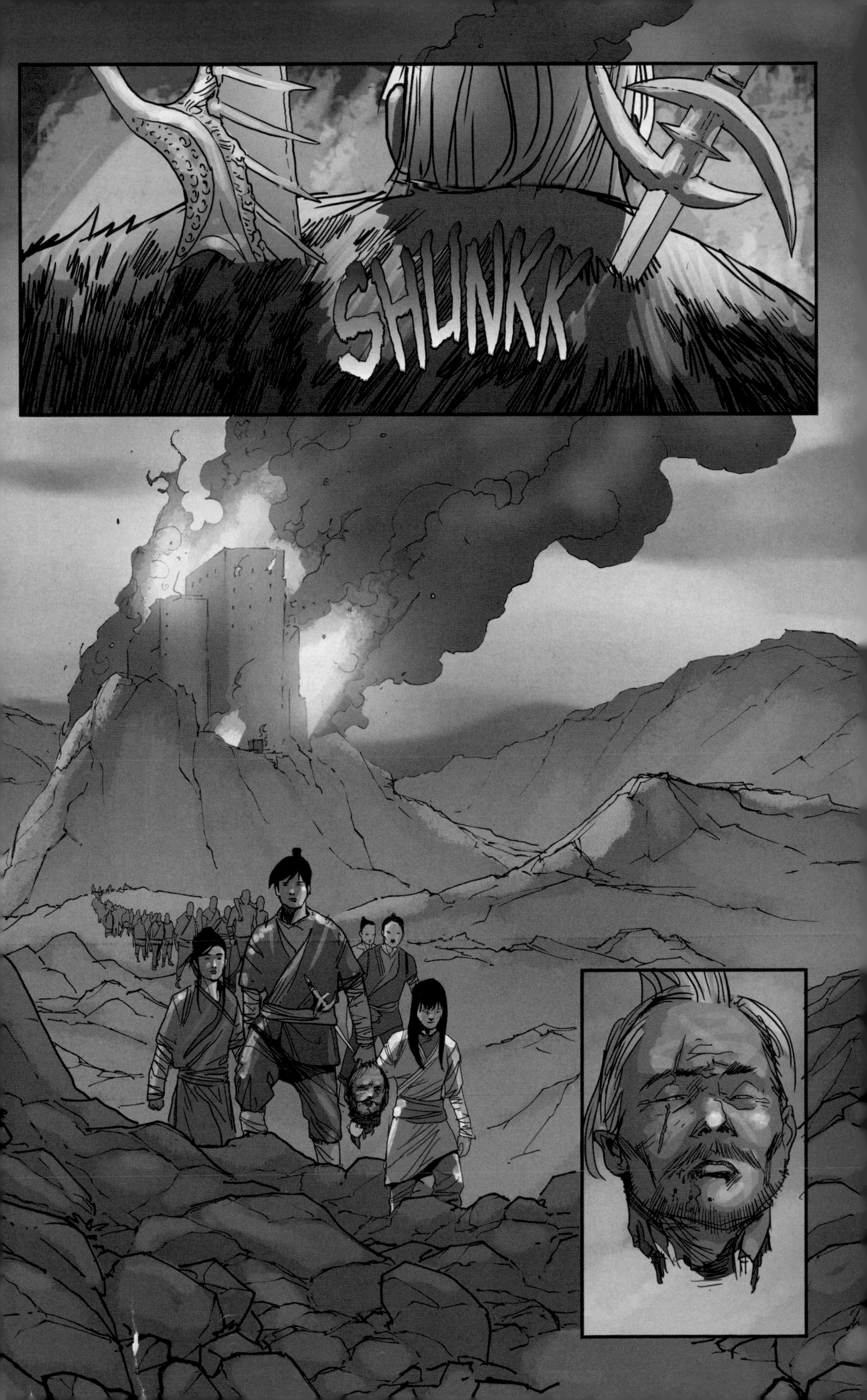
SHUNKK

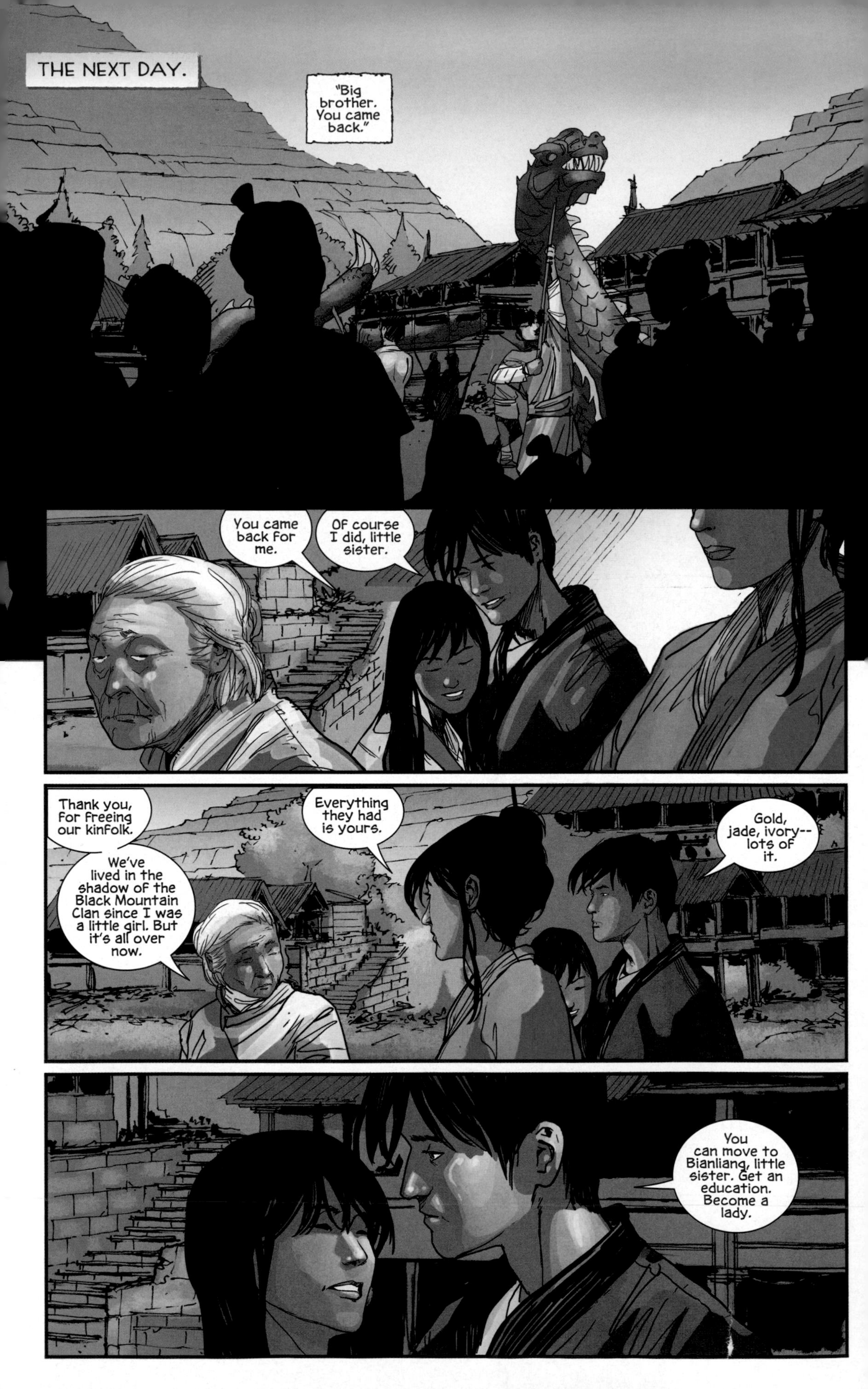
THE NEXT DAY.
"Big brother. You came back."
You came back for me.
Of course I did, little sister.
Thank you, for freeing our kinfolk.
We've lived in the shadow of the Black Mountain Clan since I was a little girl. But it's all over now.
Everything they had is yours.
Gold, jade, ivory-- lots of it.
You can move to Bianliang, little sister. Get an education. Become a lady.

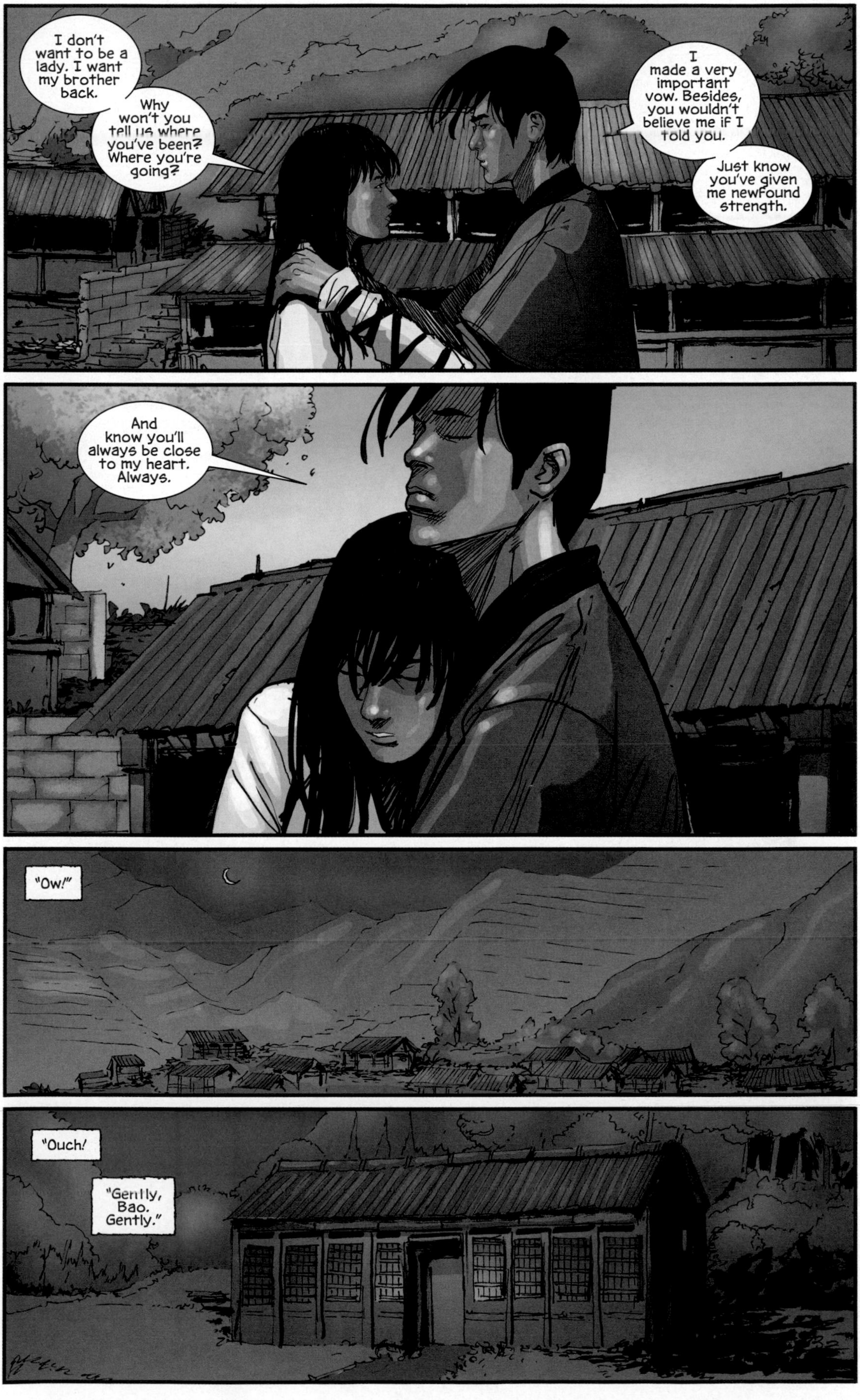
I don't want to be a lady. I want my brother back.
Why won't you tell us where you've been? Where you're going?
I made a very important vow. Besides, you wouldn't believe me if I told you.
Just know you've given me newfound strength.
And know you'll always be close to my heart. Always.
"Ow!"
"Ouch!
"Gently, Bao. Gently."

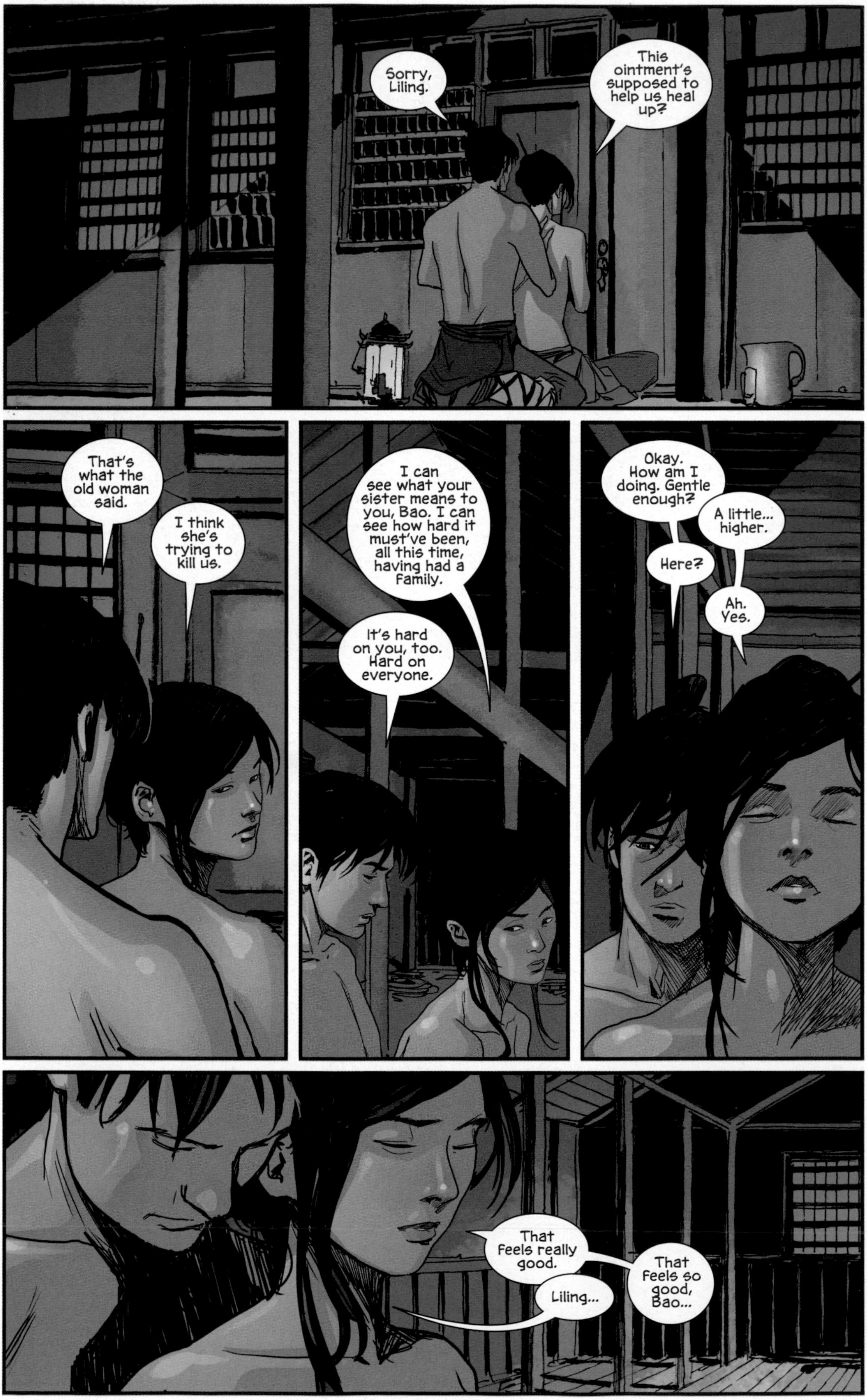
Sorry, Liling.
This ointment's supposed to help us heal up?
That's what the old woman said.
I think she's trying to kill us.
I can see what your sister means to you, Bao. I can see how hard it must've been, all this time, having had a family.
It's hard on you, too. Hard on everyone.
Okay. How am I doing. Gentle enough?
A little... higher.
Here?
Ah. Yes.
That feels really good.
Liling...
That feels so good, Bao...

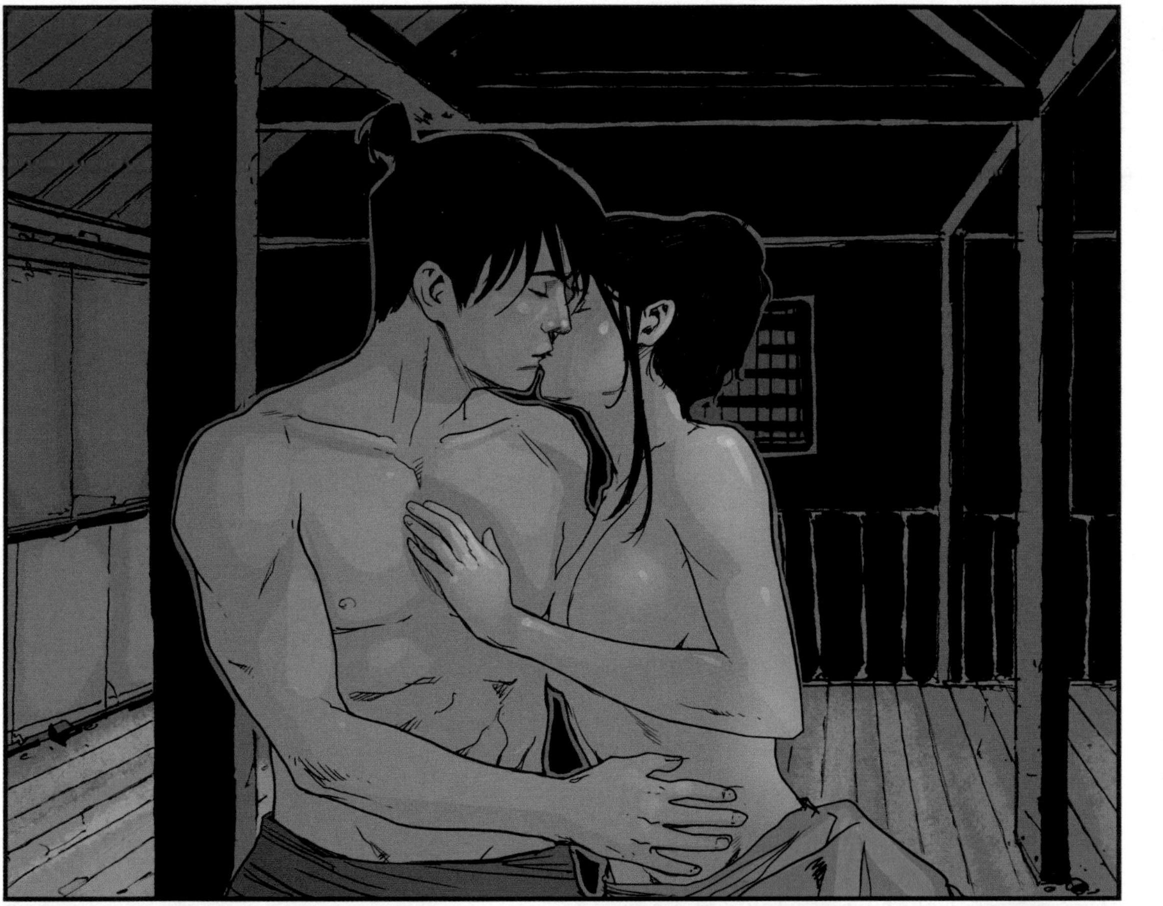
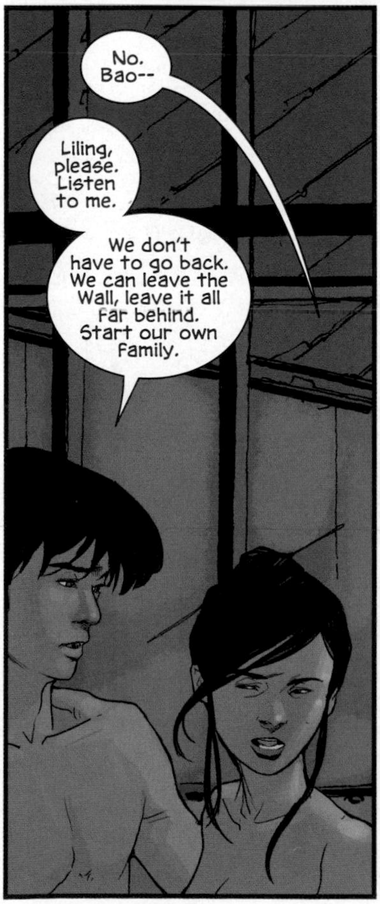
No. Bao--
Liling, please. Listen to me.
We don't have to go back. We can leave the Wall, leave it all far behind. Start our own family.
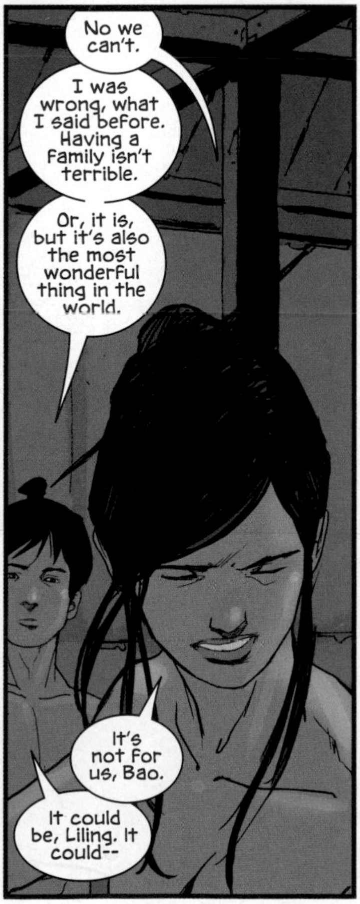
No we can't.
I was wrong, what I said before. Having a family isn't terrible.
Or, it is, but it's also the most wonderful thing in the world.
It's not for us, Bao.
It could be, Liling. It could--
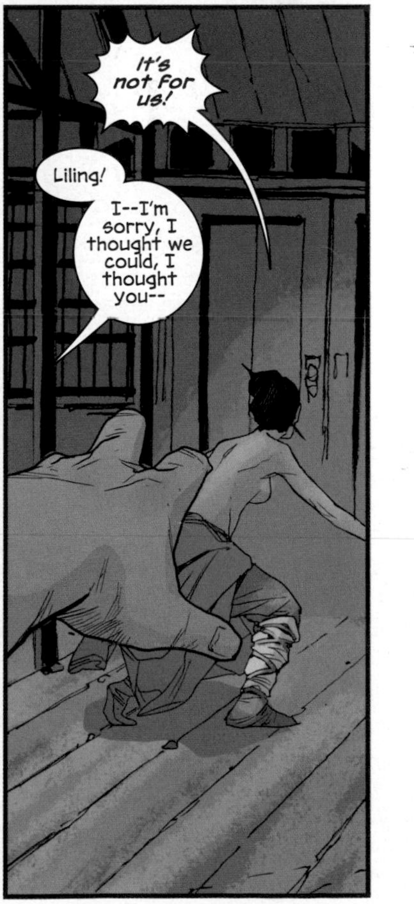
It's not for us!
Liling!
I--I'm sorry, I thought we could, I thought you--

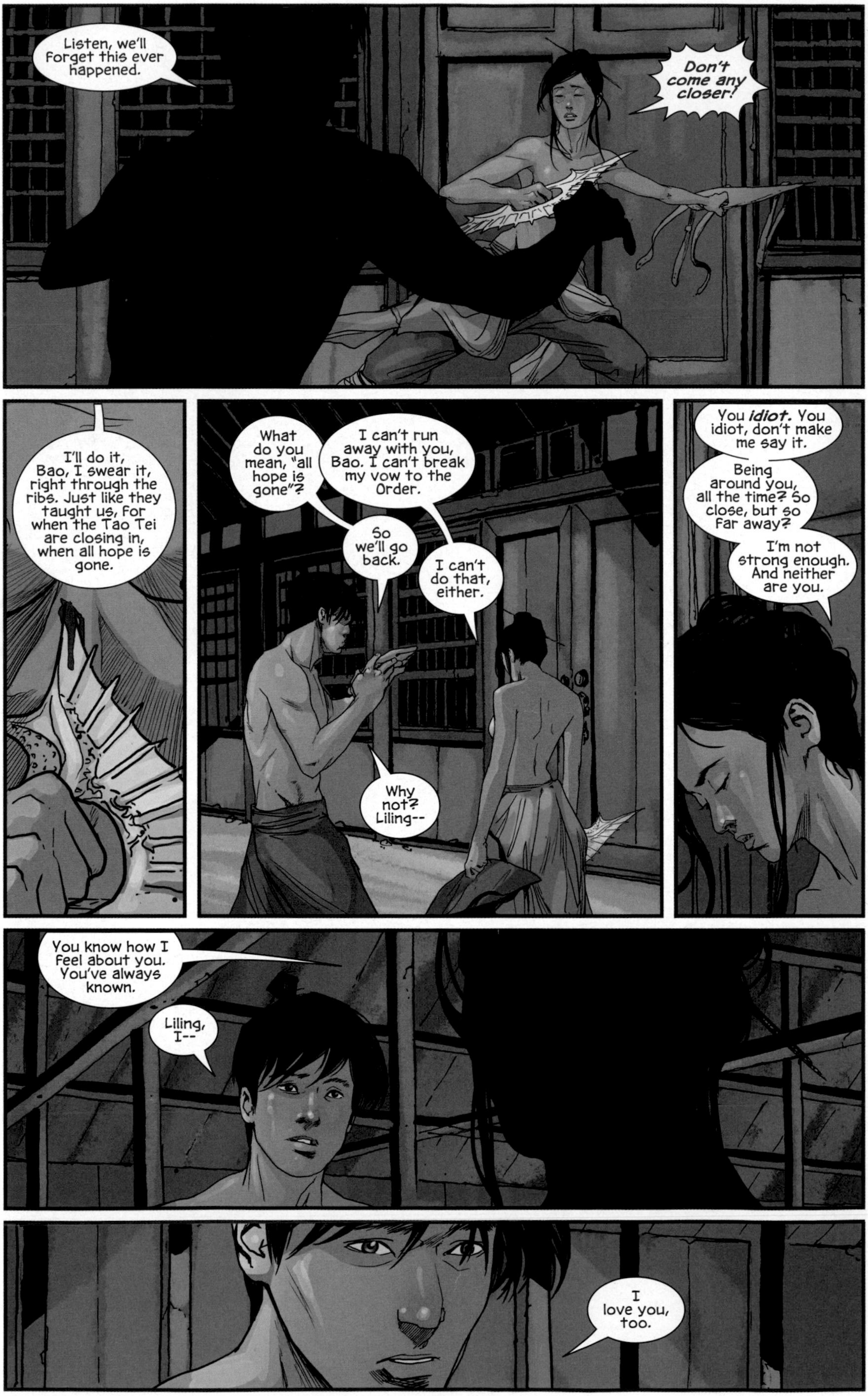
Listen, we'll forget this ever happened.
Don't come any closer!
I'll do it, Bao, I swear it, right through the ribs. Just like they taught us, for when the Tao Tei are closing in, when all hope is gone.
What do you mean, "all hope is gone"?
I can't run away with you, Bao. I can't break my vow to the Order.
So we'll go back.
I can't do that, either.
Why not? Liling--
You idiot. You idiot, don't make me say it.
Being around you, all the time? So close, but so far away?
I'm not strong enough. And neither are you.
You know how I feel about you. You've always known.
Liling, I--
I love you, too.

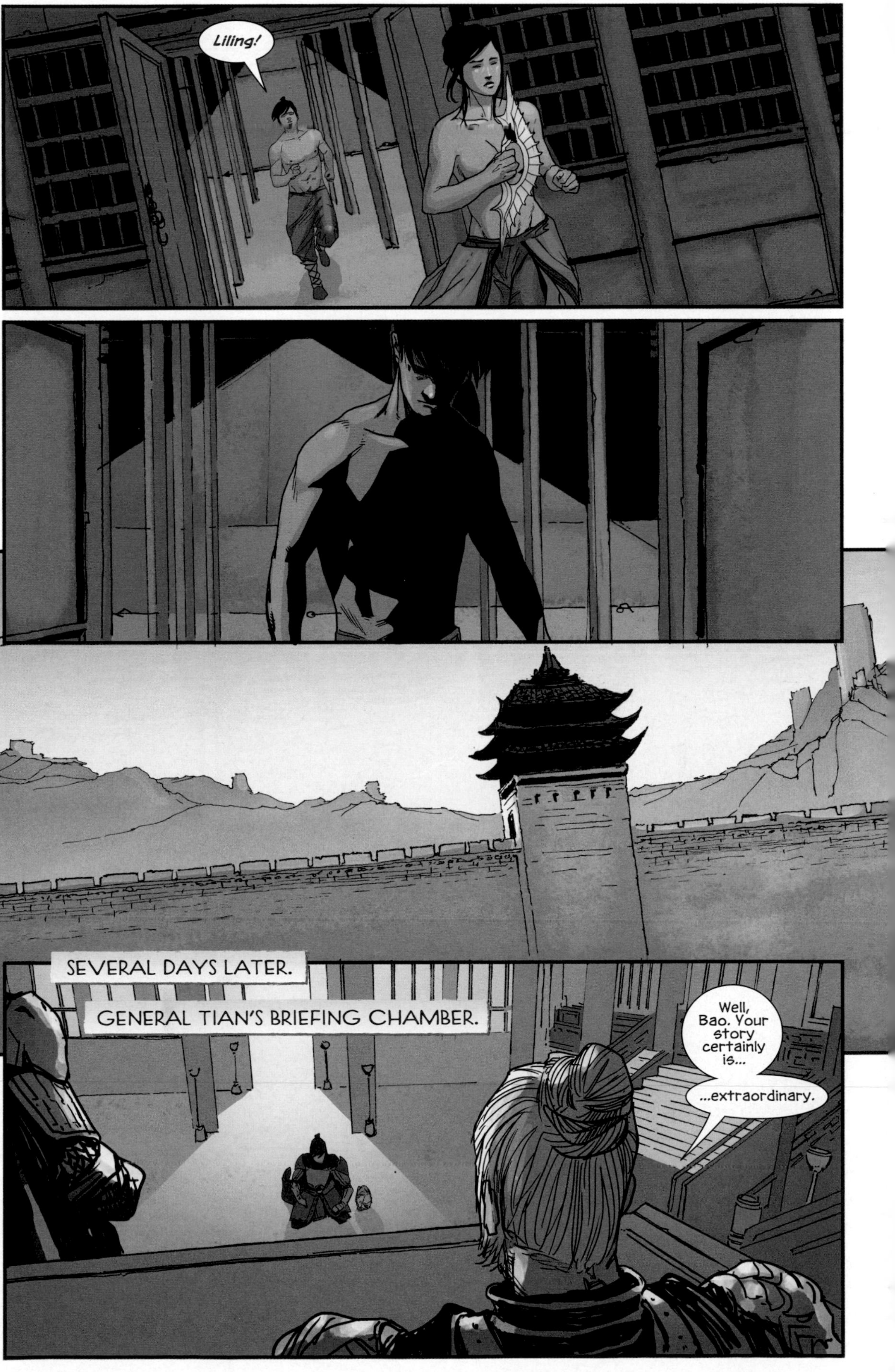
Liling!
SEVERAL DAYS LATER.
GENERAL TIAN'S BRIEFING CHAMBER.
Well, Bao. Your story certainly is...
...extraordinary.

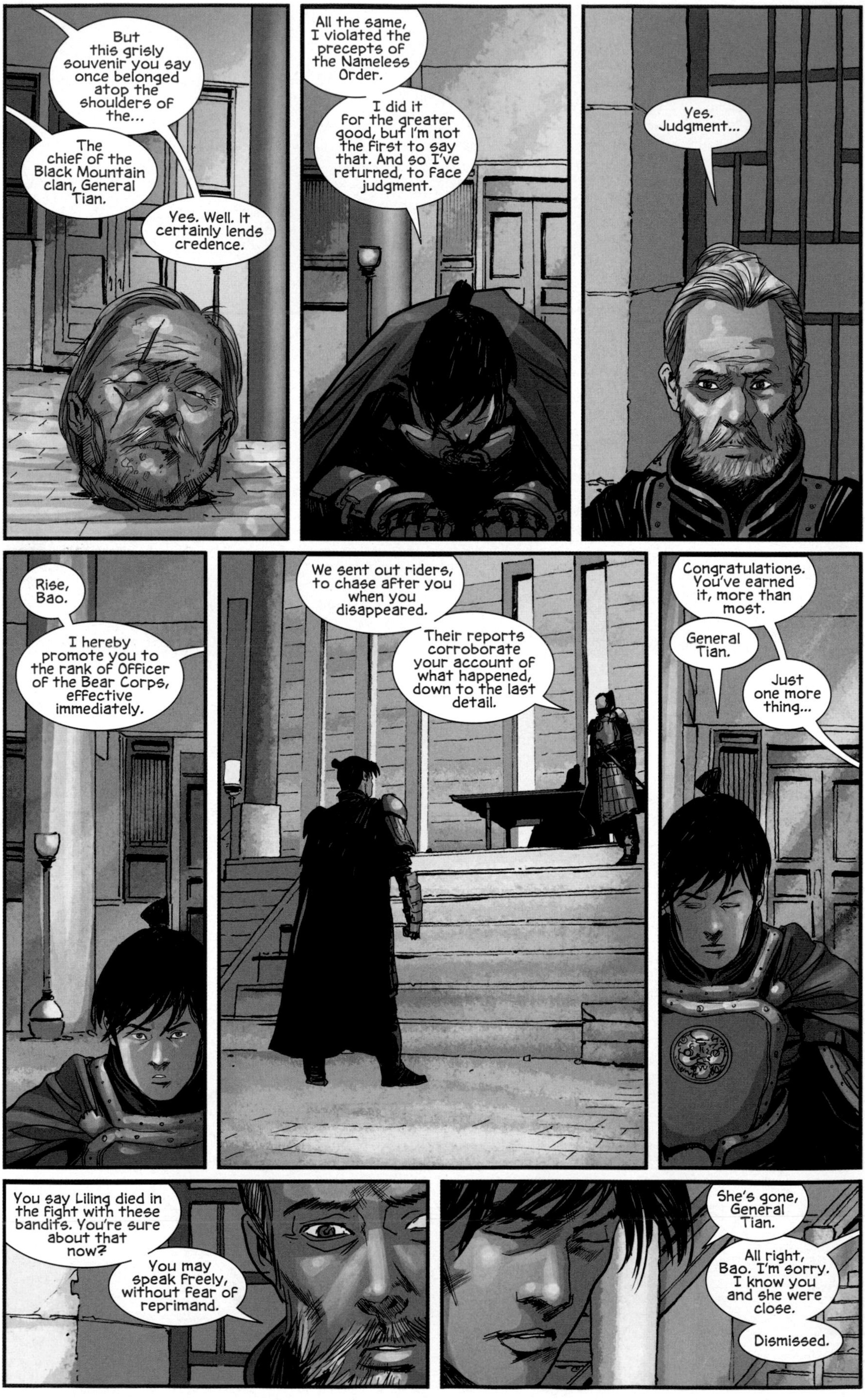
But this grisly souvenir you say once belonged atop the shoulders of the...
The chief of the Black Mountain clan, General Tian.
Yes. Well. It certainly lends credence.
All the same, I violated the precepts of the Nameless Order.
I did it for the greater good, but I'm not the first to say that. And so I've returned, to face judgment.
Yes. Judgment...
Rise, Bao.
I hereby promote you to the rank of Officer of the Bear Corps, effective immediately.
We sent out riders, to chase after you when you disappeared.
Their reports corroborate your account of what happened, down to the last detail.
Congratulations. You've earned it, more than most.
General Tian.
Just one more thing...
You say Liling died in the fight with these bandits. You're sure about that now?
You may speak freely, without fear of reprimand.
She's gone, General Tian.
All right, Bao. I'm sorry. I know you and she were close.
Dismissed.

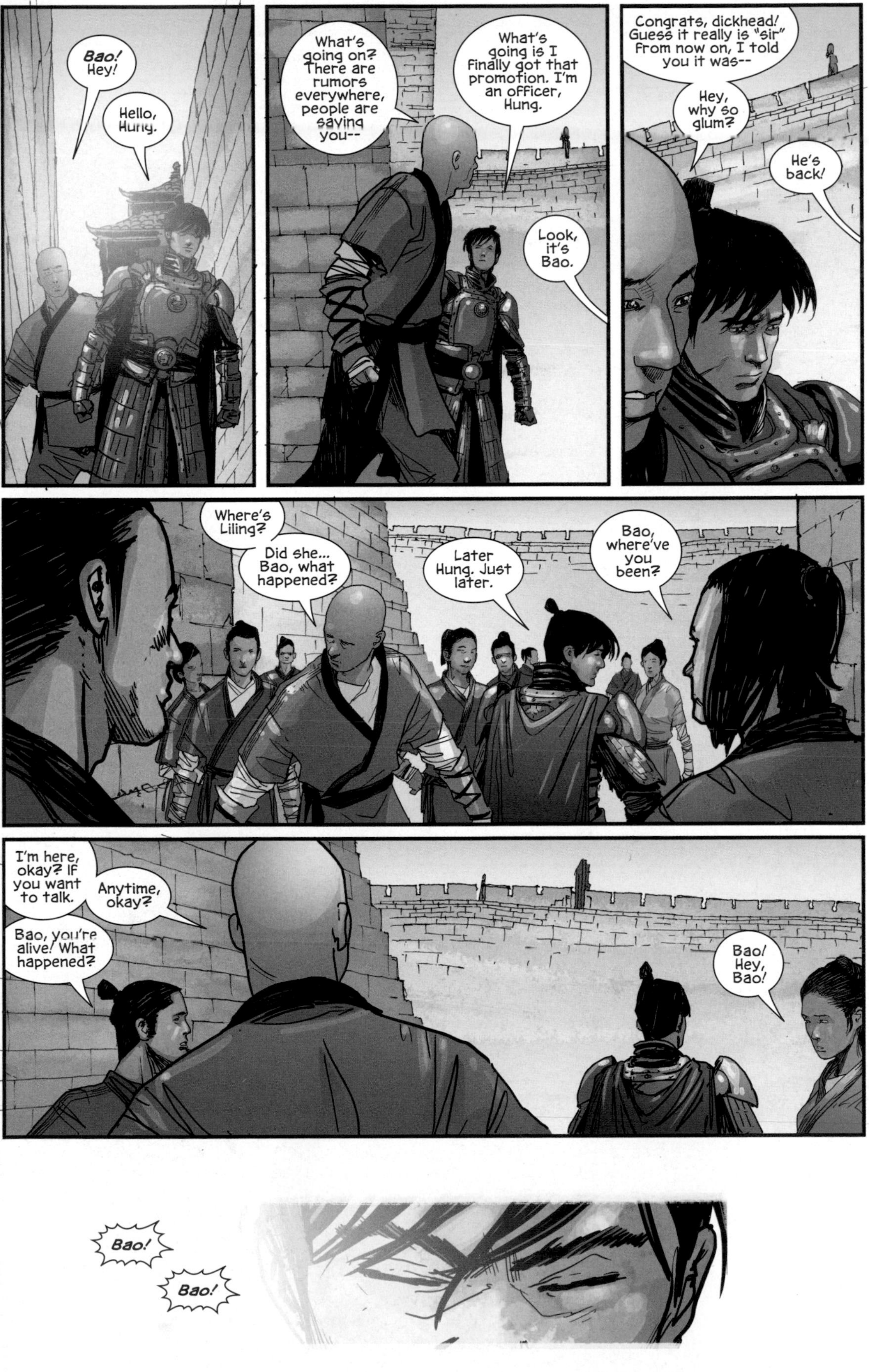

Bao! Hey!
Hello, Hung.
What's going on? There are rumors everywhere, people are saying you--
What's going is I finally got that promotion. I'm an officer, Hung.
Look, it's Bao.
Congrats, dickhead! Guess it really is "sir" from now on, I told you it was--
Hey, why so glum?
He's back!
Where's Liling?
Did she... Bao, what happened?
Later Hung. Just later.
Bao, where've you been?
I'm here, okay? If you want to talk.
Anytime, okay?
Bao, you're alive! What happened?
Bao! Hey, Bao!
Bao!
Bao!

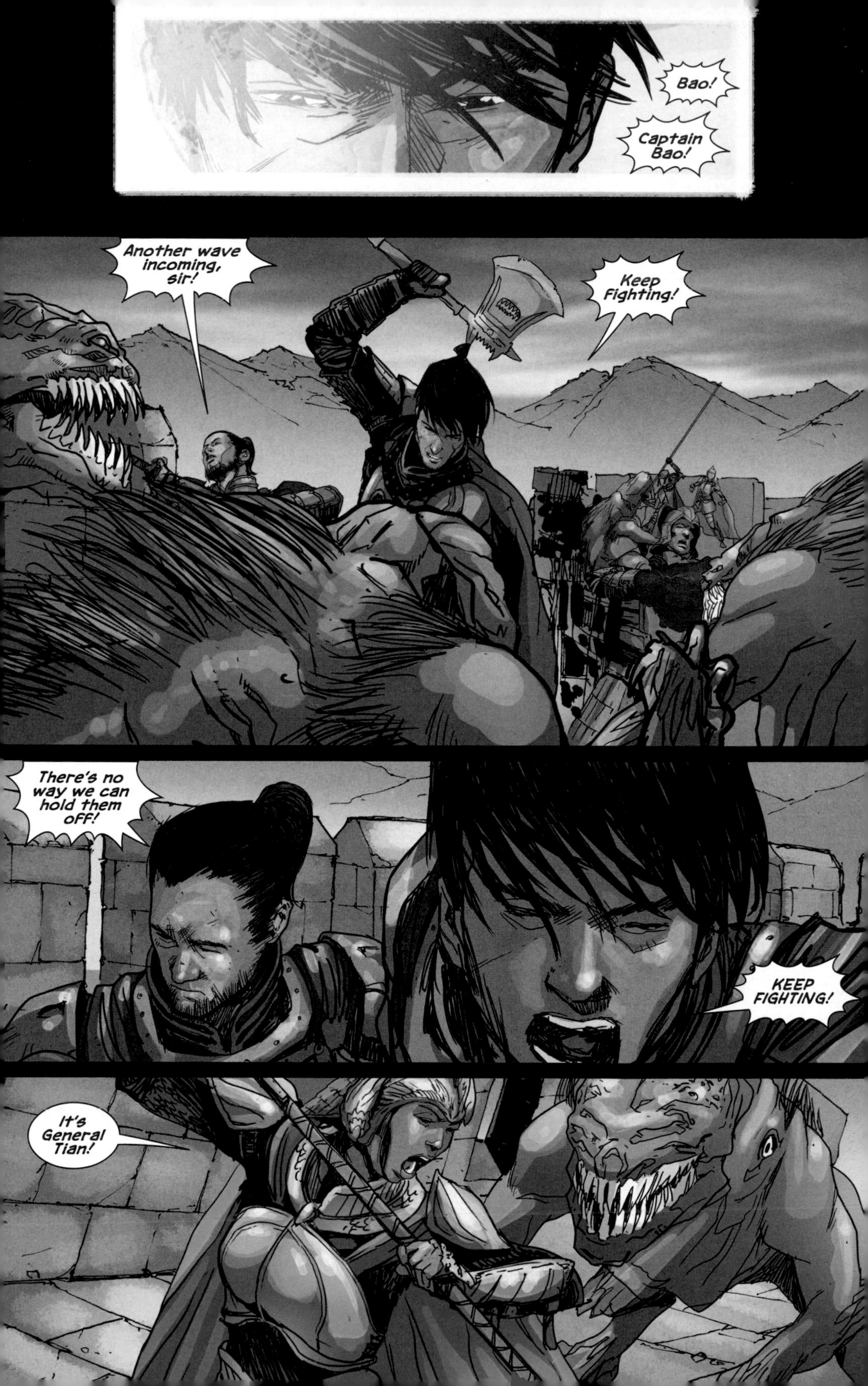
Bao!
Captain Bao!
Another wave incoming, sir!
Keep Fighting!
There's no way we can hold them off!
KEEP FIGHTING!
It's General Tian!

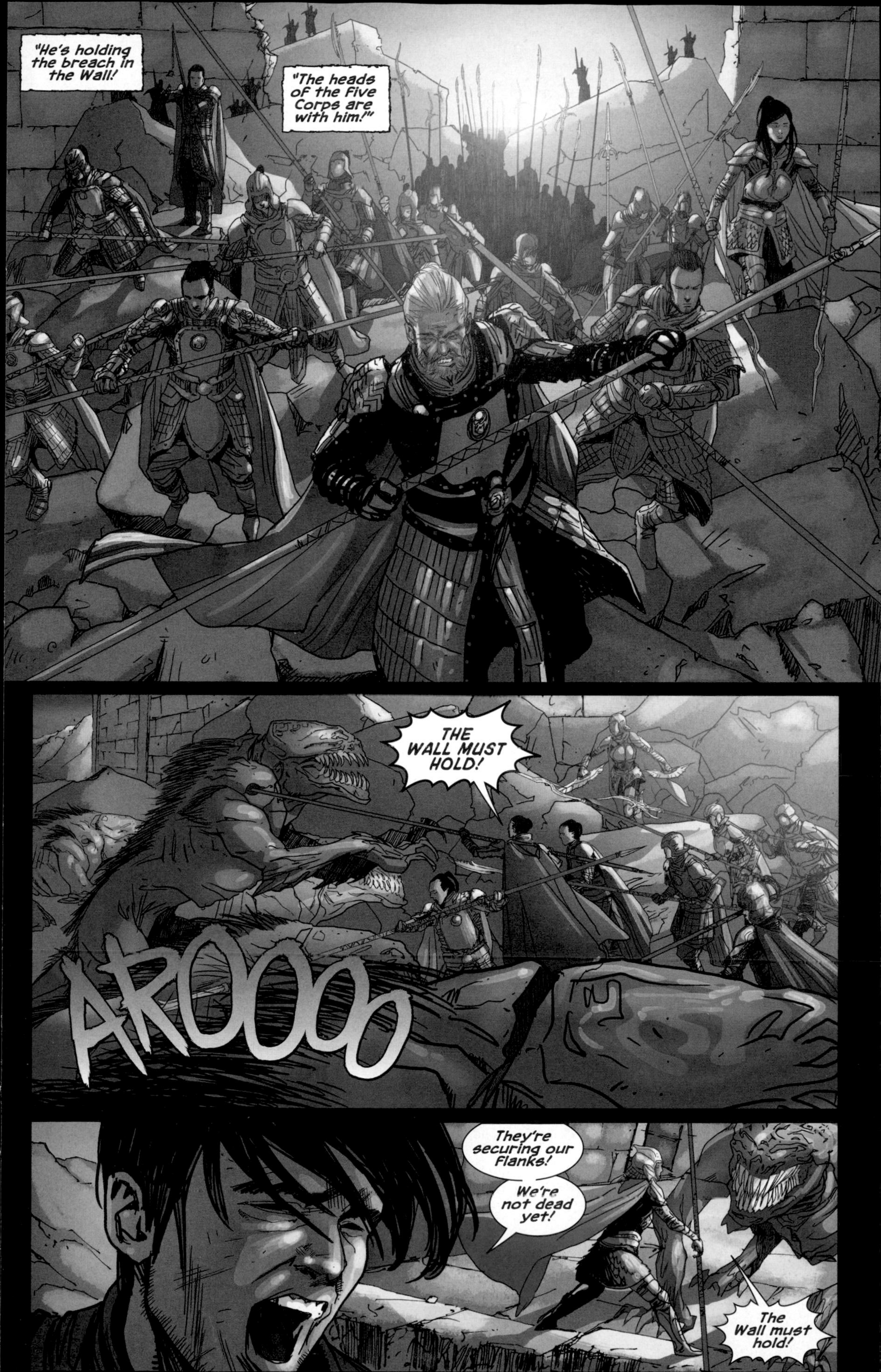
"He's holding the breach in the Wall!
"The heads of the Five Corps are with him!"
THE WALL MUST HOLD!
AROOOO
They're securing our Flanks!
We're not dead yet!
The Wall must hold!

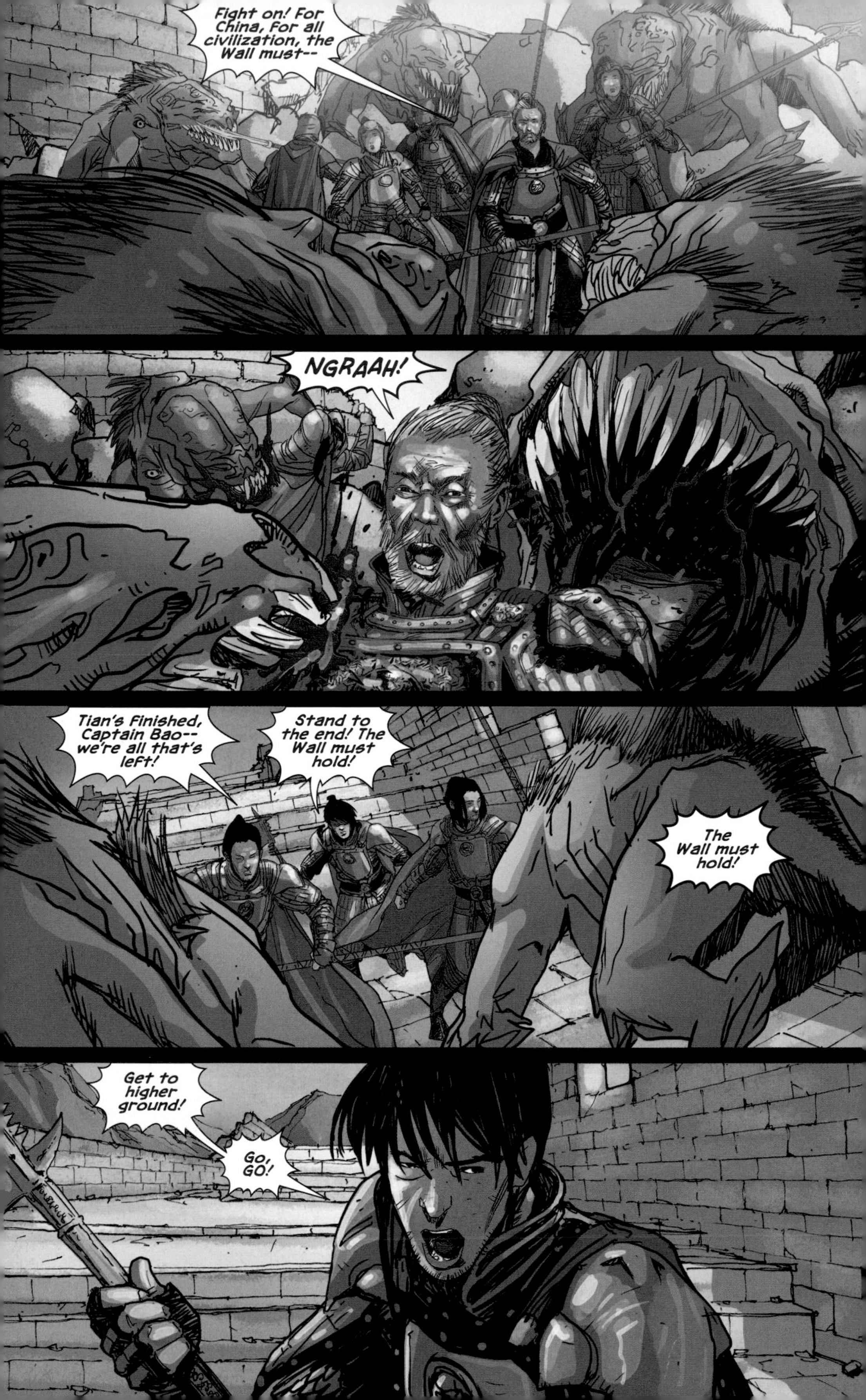
Fight on! For China, For all civilization, the Wall must--
NGRAAH!
Tian's Finished, Captain Bao-- we're all that's left!
Stand to the end! The Wall must hold!
The Wall must hold!
Get to higher ground!
Go, GO!

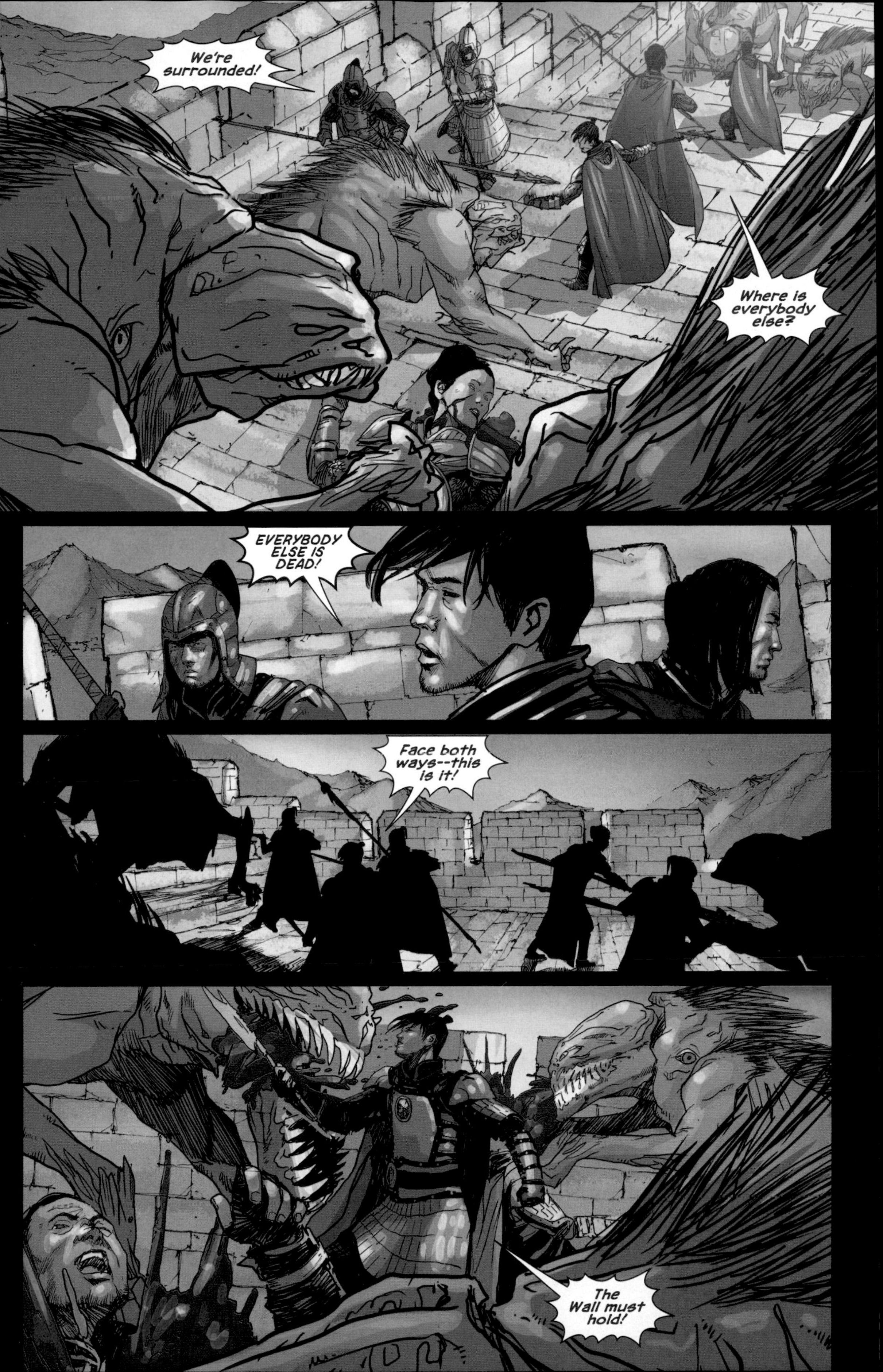
We're surrounded!
Where is everybody else?
EVERYBODY ELSE IS DEAD!
Face both ways--this is it!
The Wall must hold!

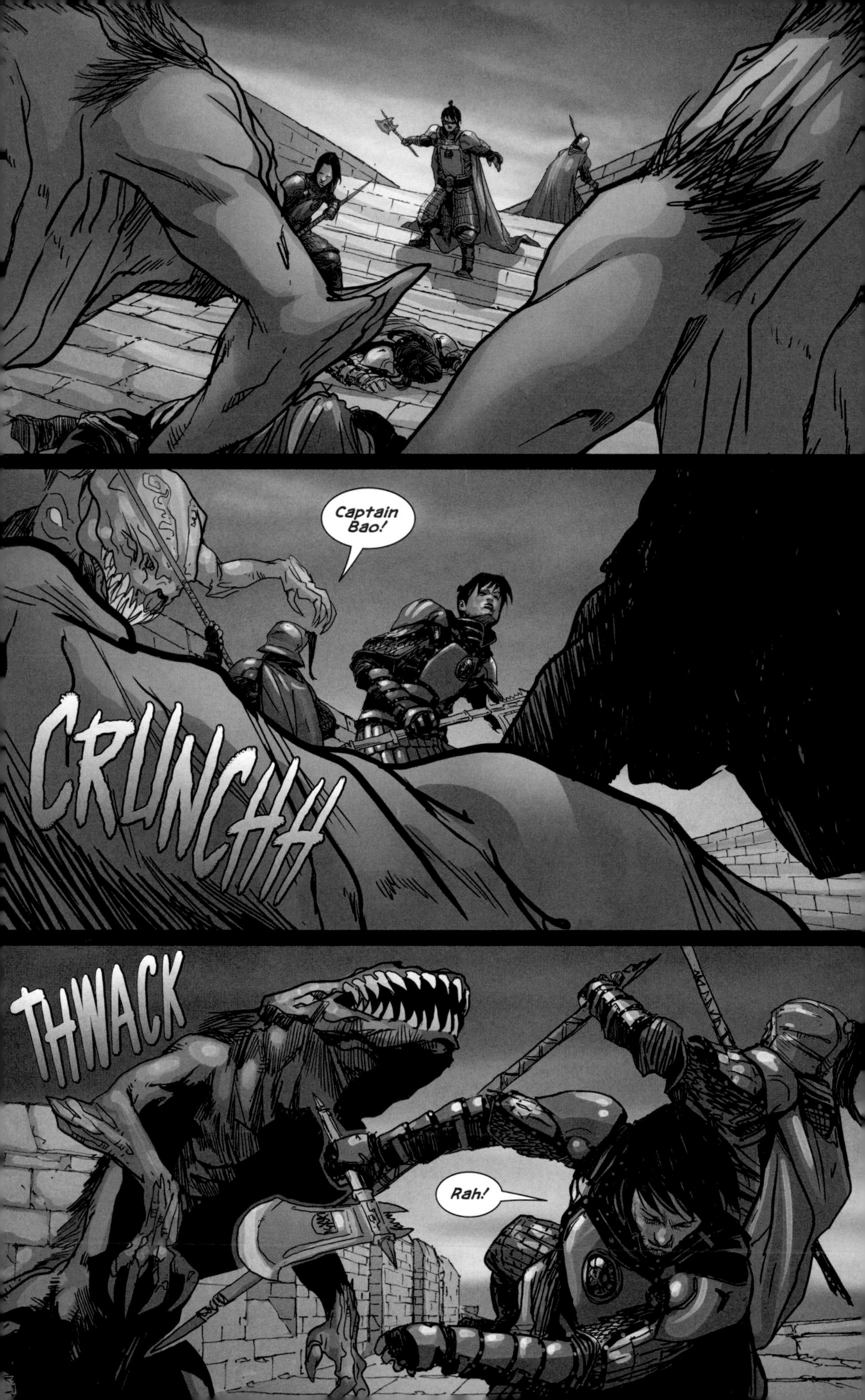
Captain Bao!
CRUNCHH
THWACK
Rah!

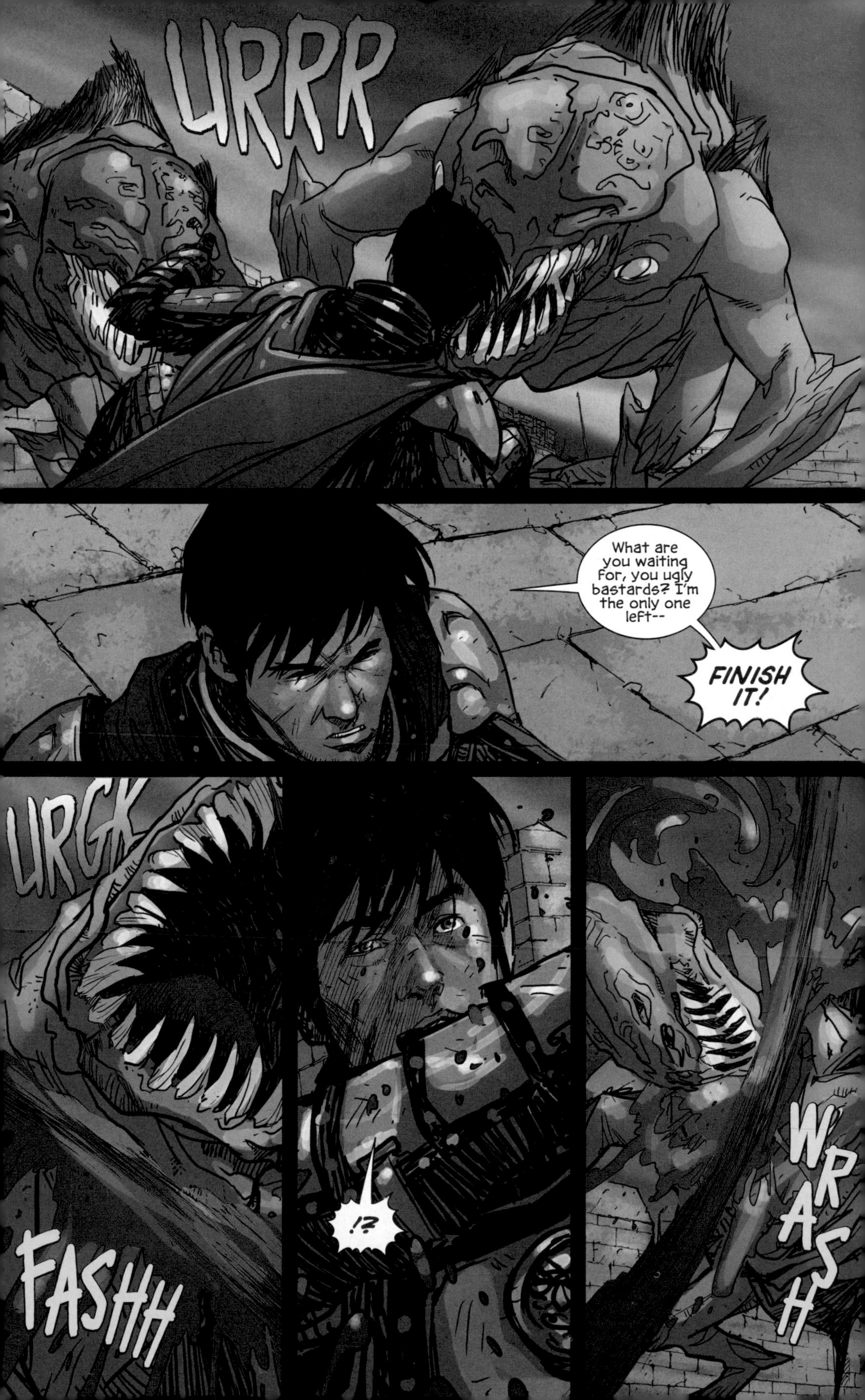
URRR
What are you waiting for, you ugly bastards? I'm the only one left--
FINISH IT!
URGK
FASHH
!?
WRASH

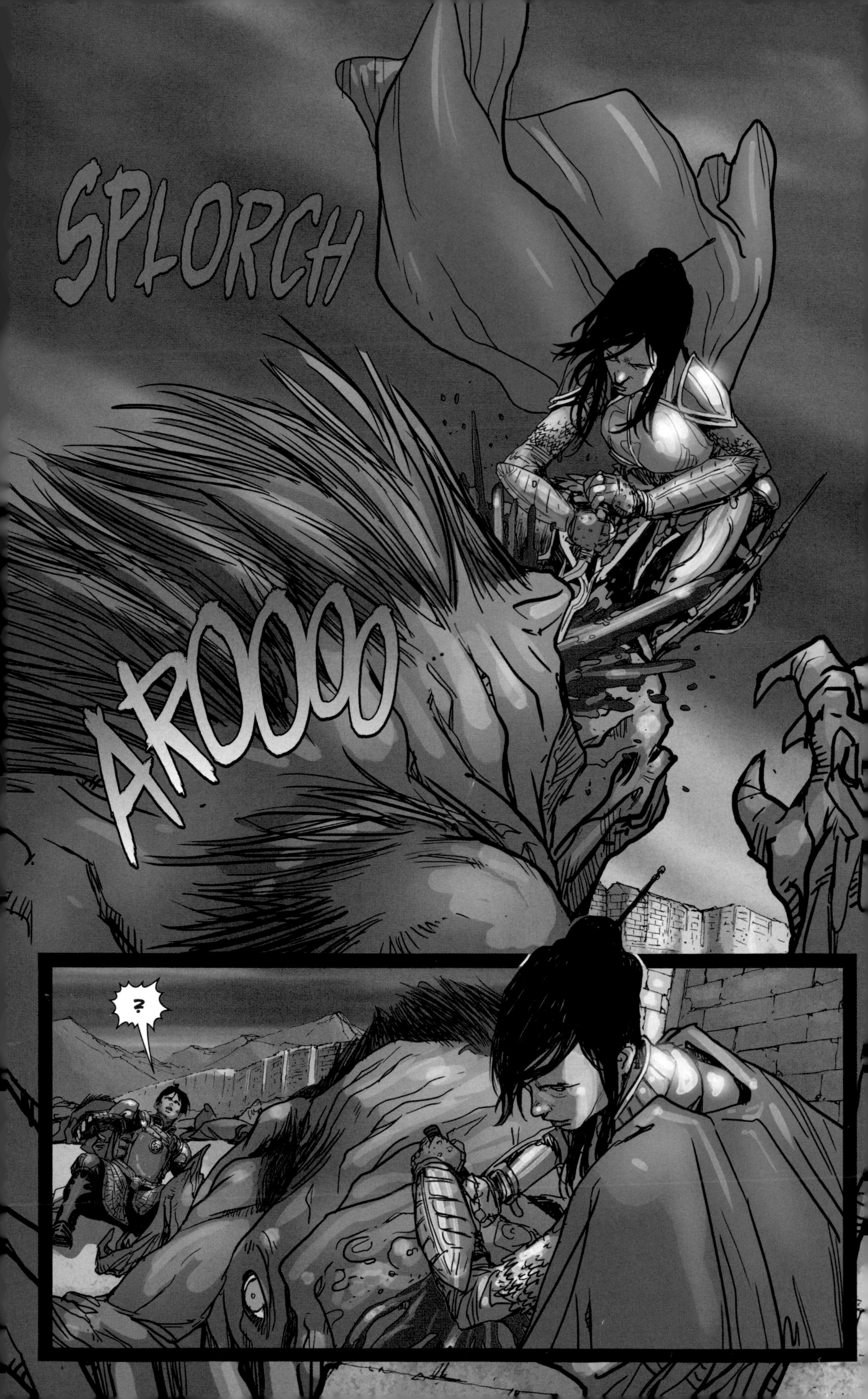
SPLORCH
AROOOO
?

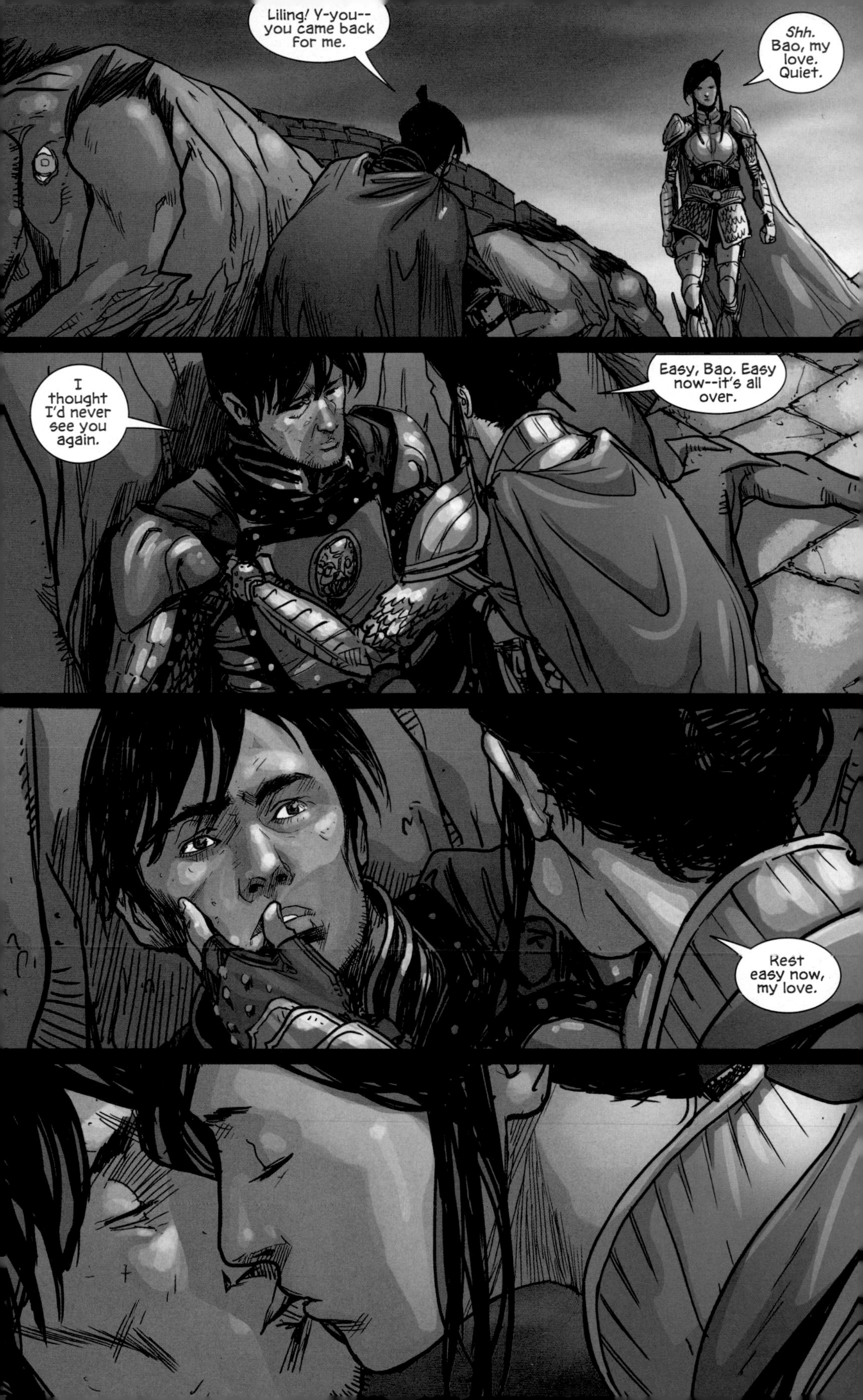
Liling! Y-you-- you came back for me.
Shh. Bao, my love. Quiet.
I thought I'd never see you again.
Easy, Bao. Easy now--it's all over.
Rest easy now, my love.

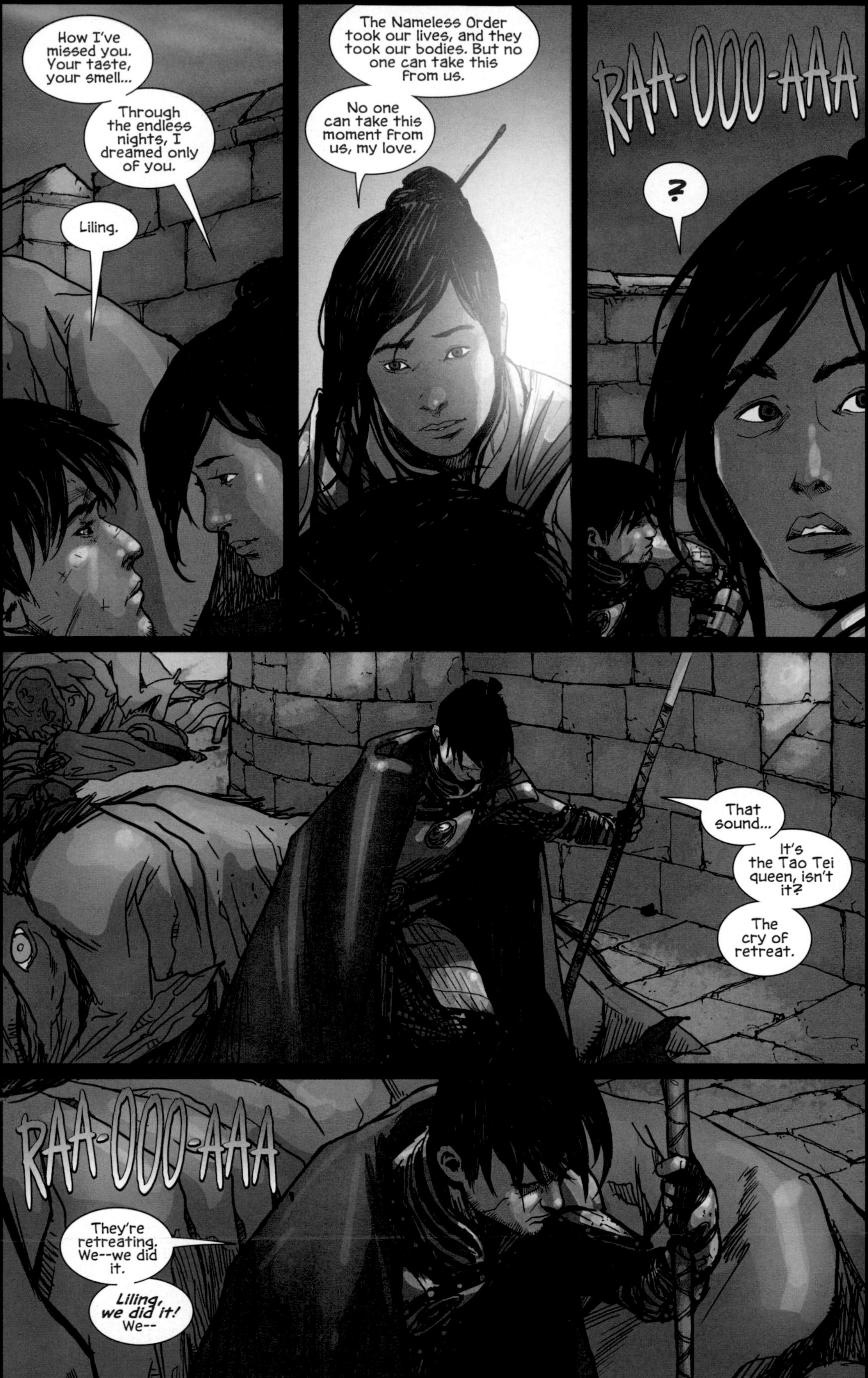
How I've missed you. Your taste, your smell...
Through the endless nights, I dreamed only of you.
Liling.
The Nameless Order took our lives, and they took our bodies. But no one can take this from us.
No one can take this moment from us, my love.
RAA-OOO-AAA
?
That sound...
It's the Tao Tei queen, isn't it?
The cry of retreat.
RAA-OOO-AAA
They're retreating. We--we did it.
Liling, we did it! We--

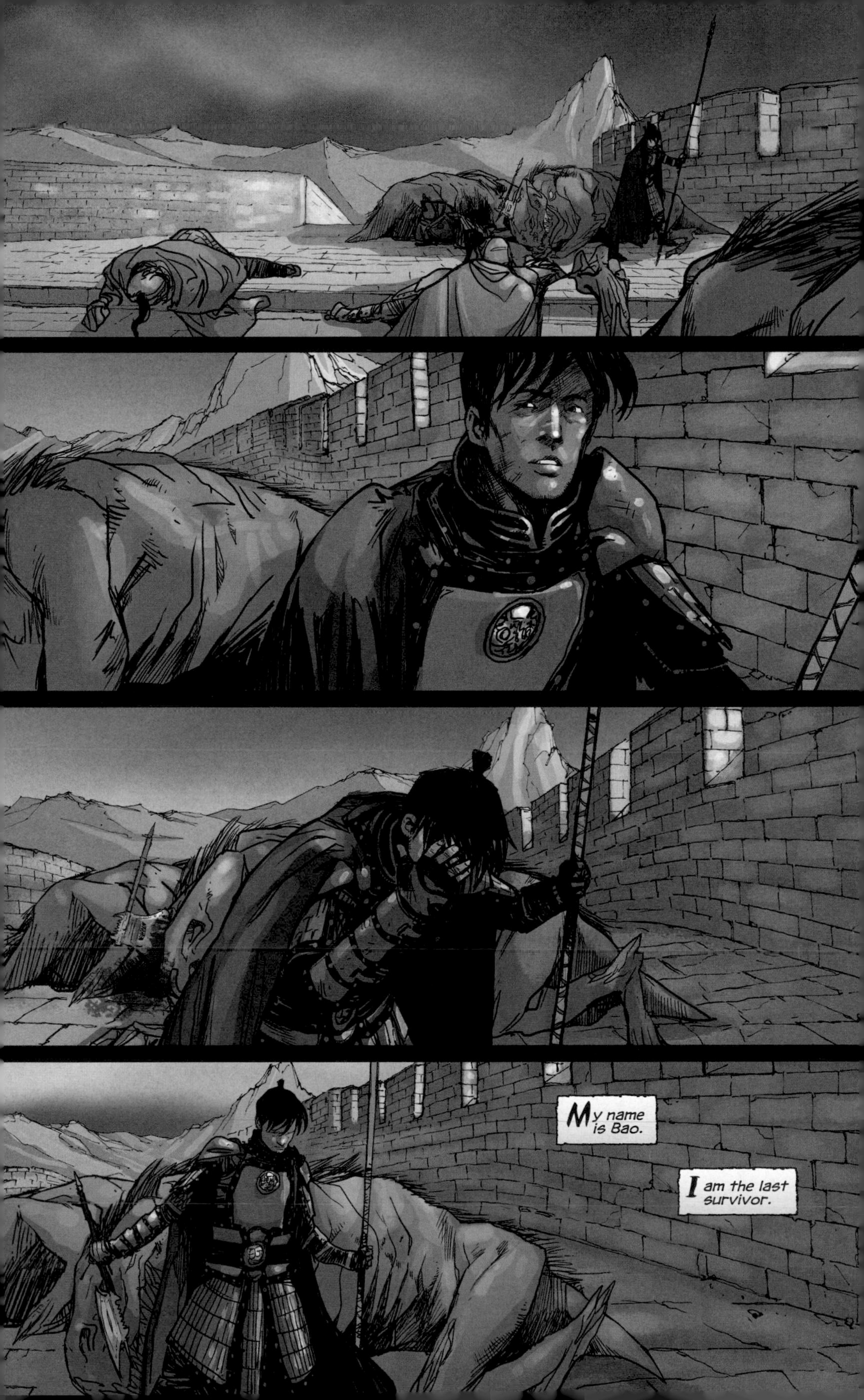
My name is Bao.
I am the last survivor.

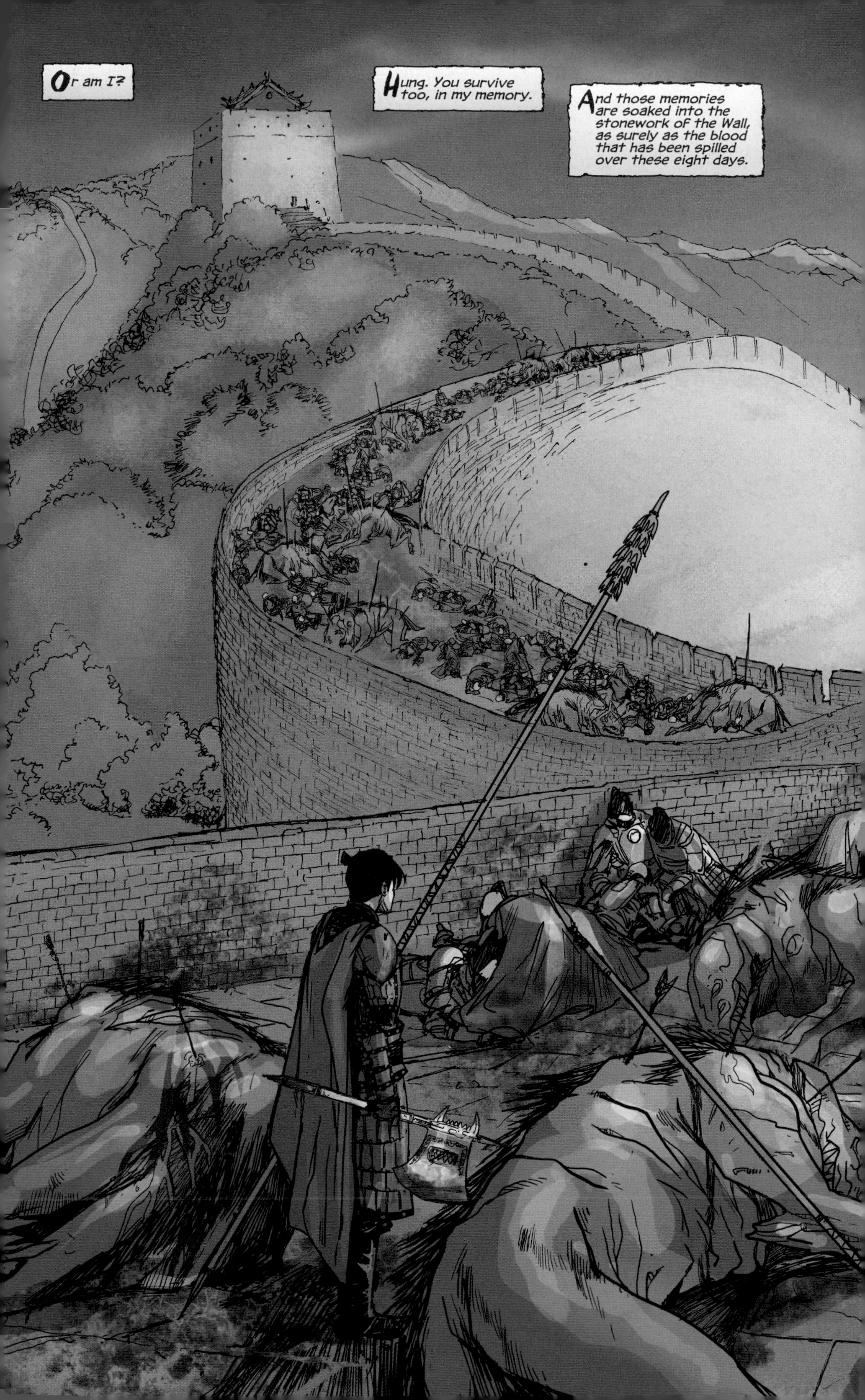
Or am I?
Hung. You survive too, in my memory.
And those memories are soaked into the stonework of the Wall, as surely as the blood that has been spilled over these eight days.

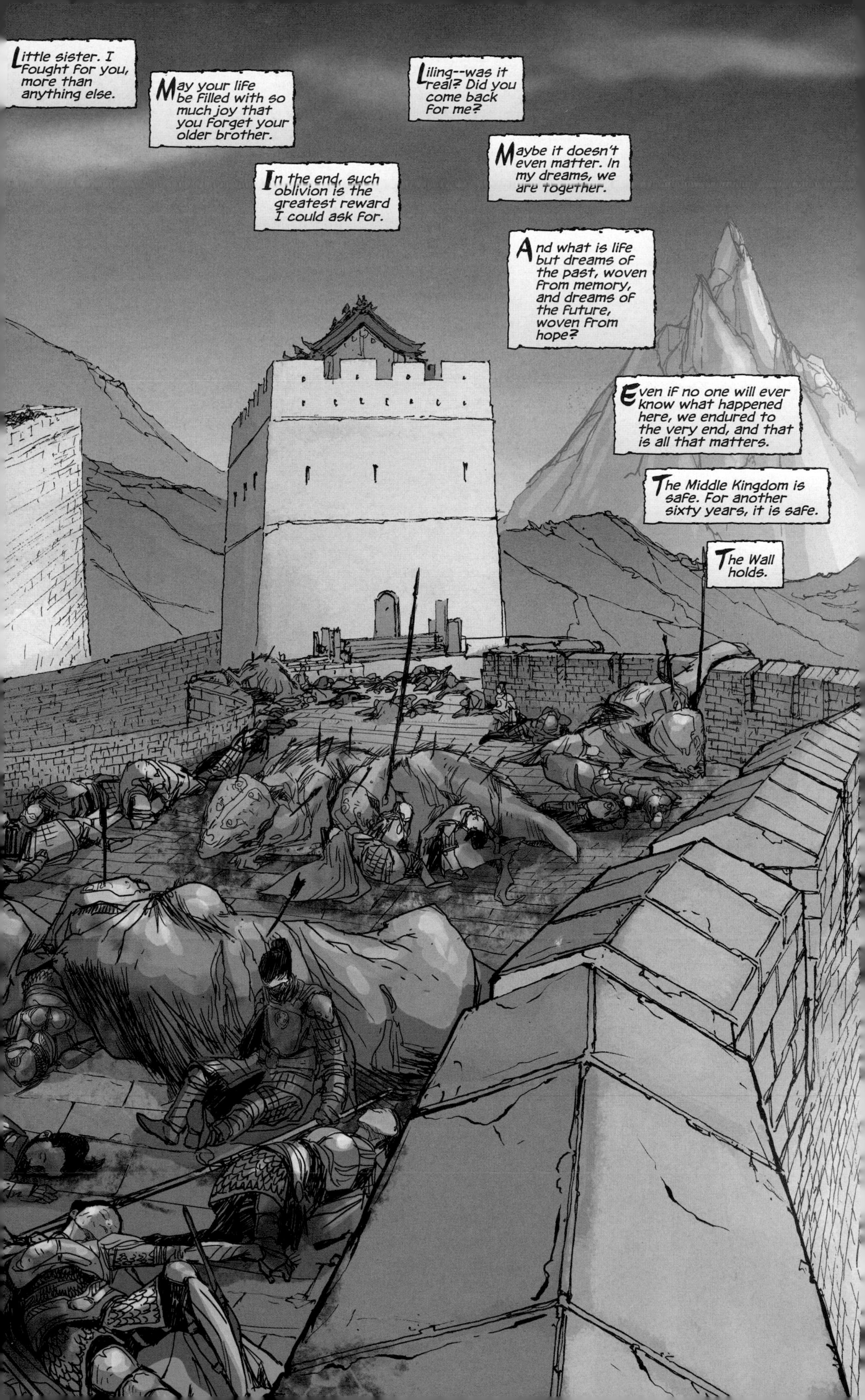
Little sister. I fought for you, more than anything else.
May your life be filled with so much joy that you forget your older brother.
In the end, such oblivion is the greatest reward I could ask for.
Liling--was it real? Did you come back for me?
Maybe it doesn't even matter. In my dreams, we are together.
And what is life but dreams of the past, woven from memory, and dreams of the future, woven from hope?
Even if no one will ever know what happened here, we endured to the very end, and that is all that matters.
The Middle Kingdom is safe. For another sixty years, it is safe.
The Wall holds.

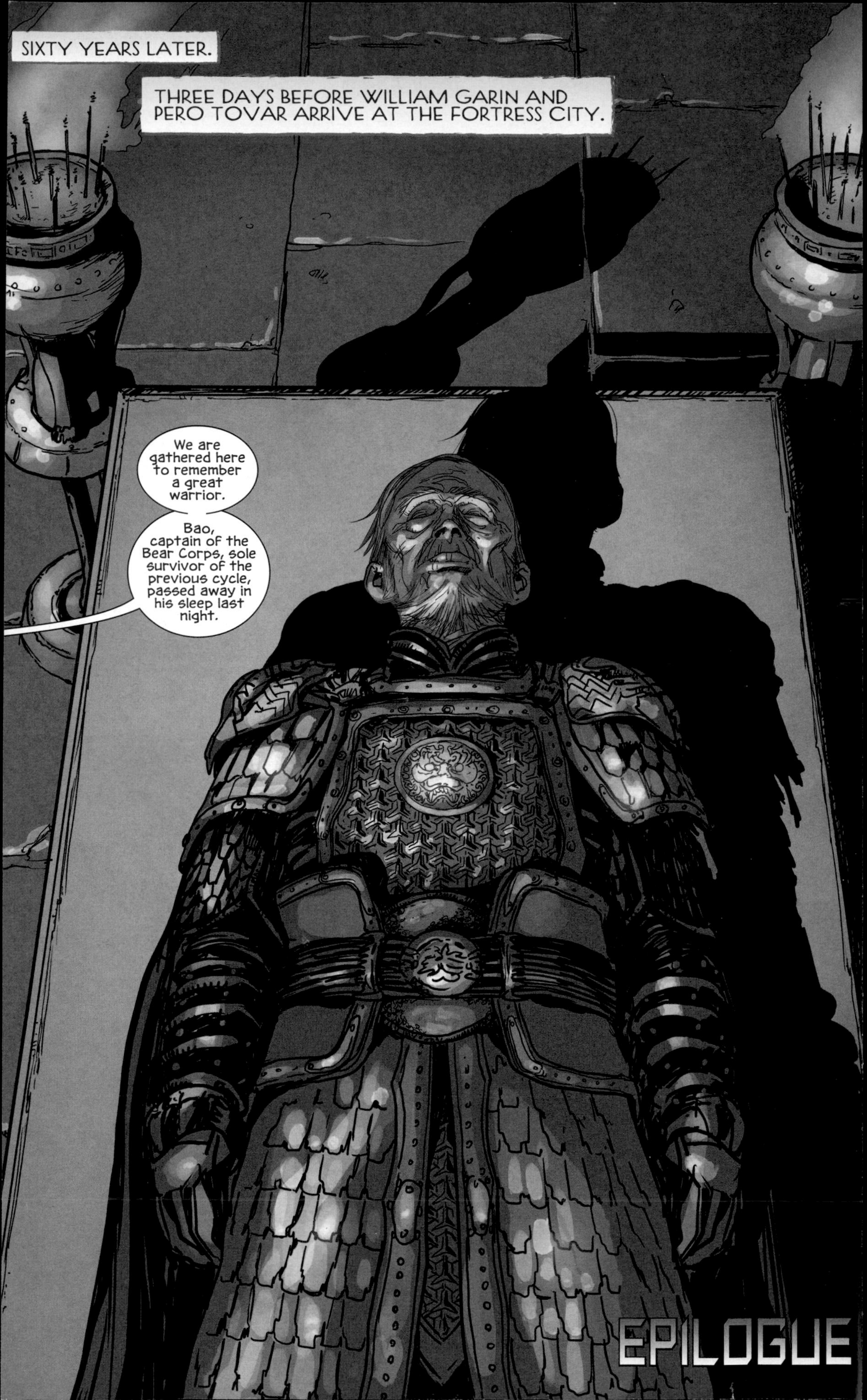
SIXTY YEARS LATER.
THREE DAYS BEFORE WILLIAM GARIN AND PERO TOVAR ARRIVE AT THE FORTRESS CITY.
We are gathered here to remember a great warrior.
Bao, captain of the Bear Corps, sole survivor of the previous cycle, passed away in his sleep last night.
EPILOGUE

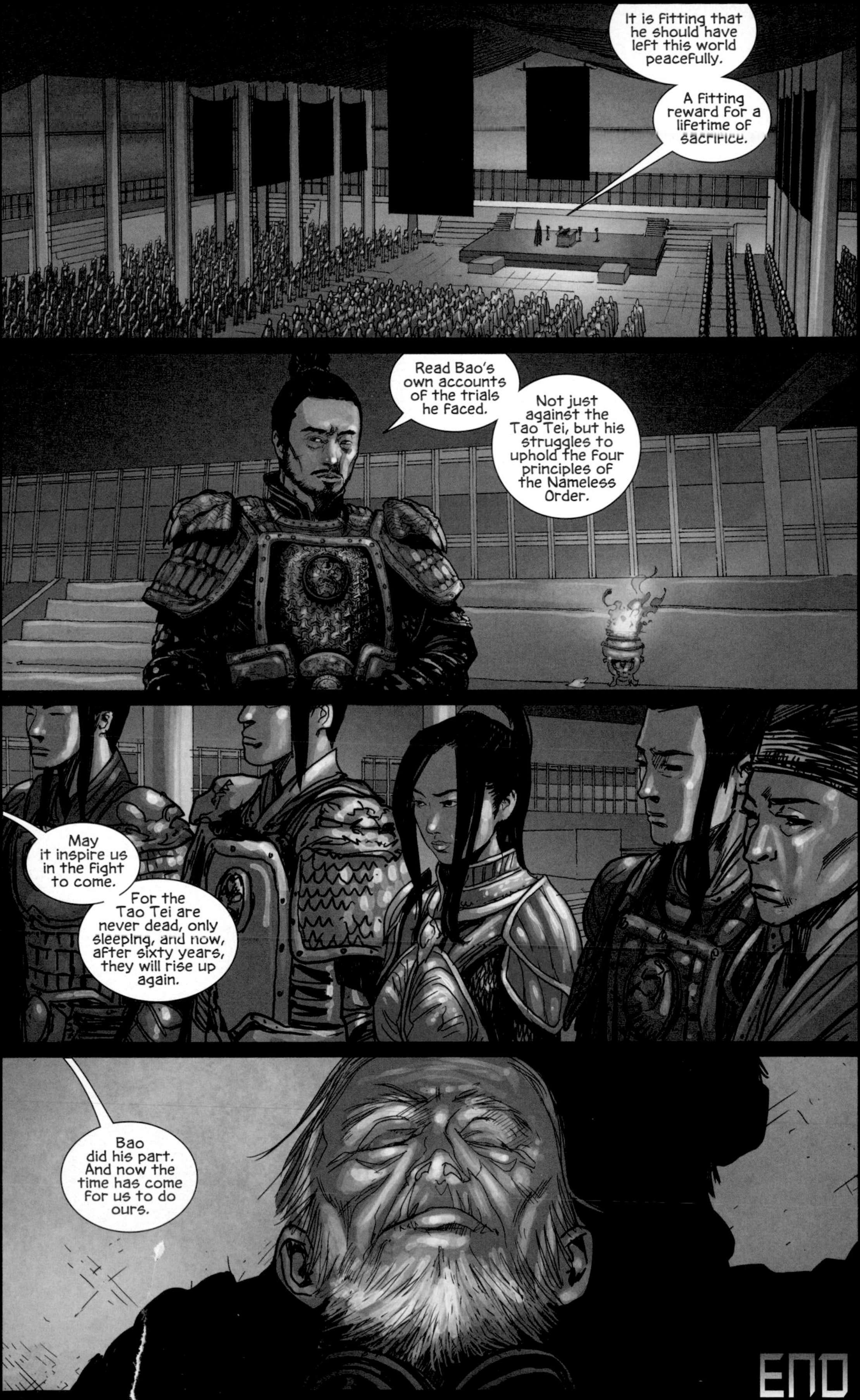
It is fitting that he should have left this world peacefully.
A fitting reward for a lifetime of sacrifice.
Read Bao's own accounts of the trials he faced.
Not just against the Tao Tei, but his struggles to uphold the four principles of the Nameless Order.
May it inspire us in the fight to come.
For the Tao Tei are never dead, only sleeping, and now, after sixty years, they will rise up again.
Bao did his part. And now the time has come for us to do ours.
END

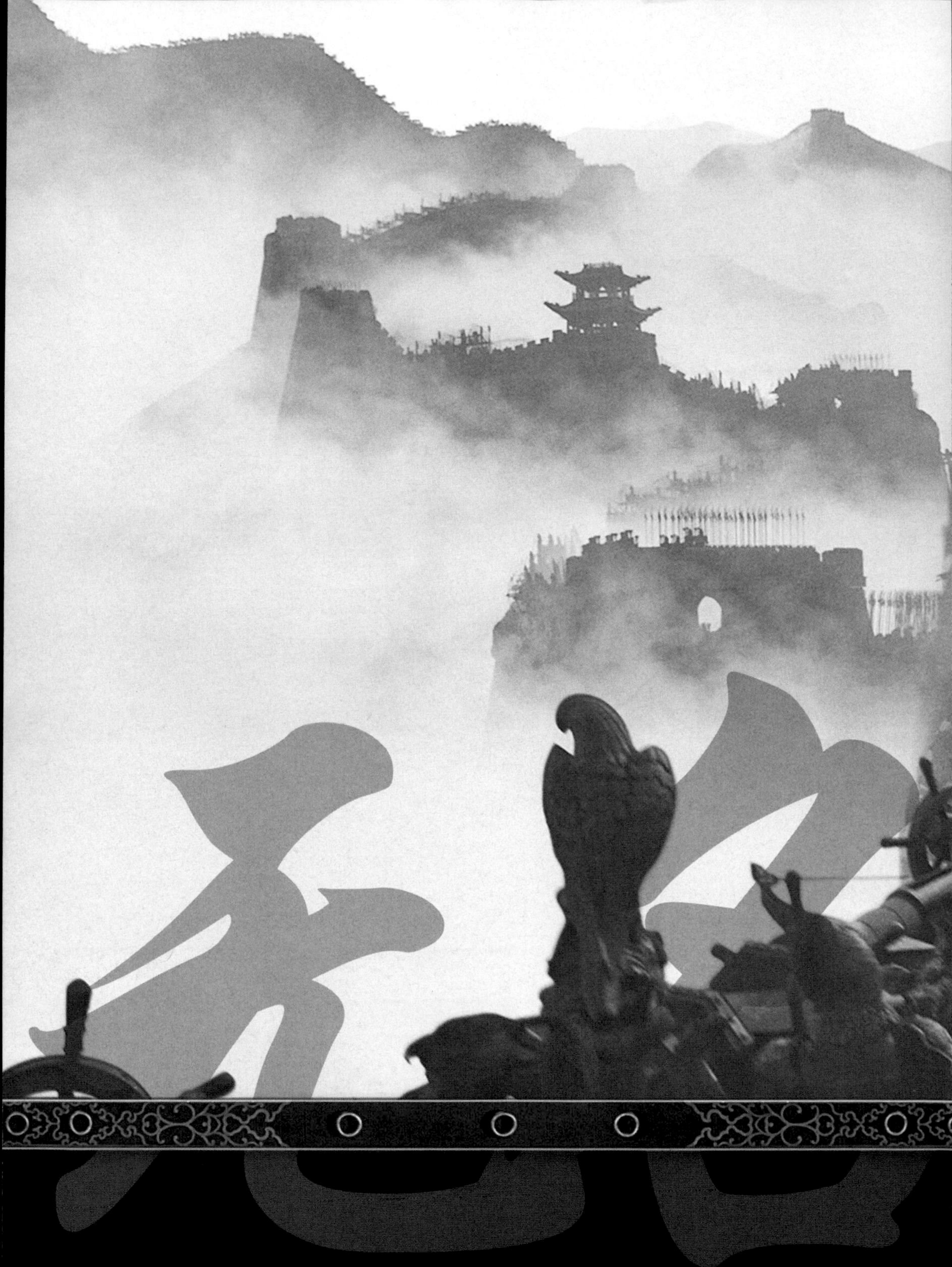

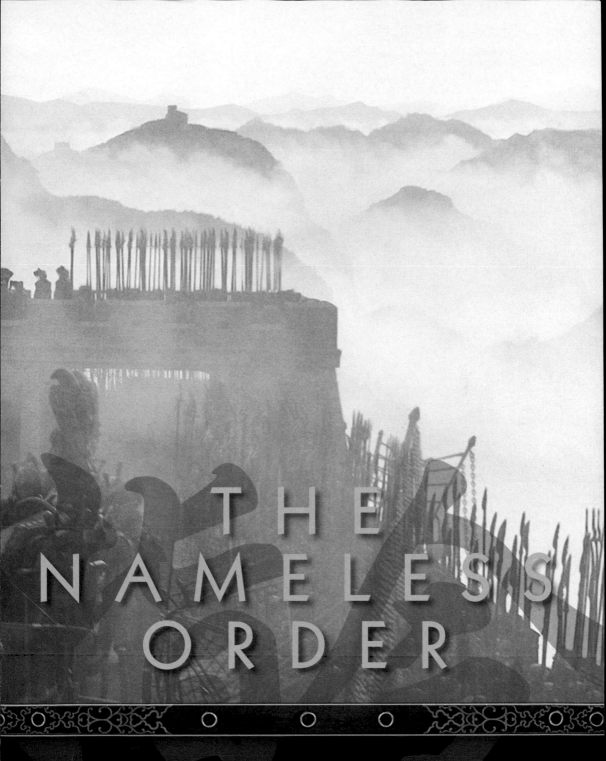

THE
NAMELESS
ORDER

AN ELITE FIGHTING FORCE HIDDEN FROM HISTORY,
SACRIFICING EVERYTHING TO KEEP HUMANITY SAFE.
10,000 WARRIORS STRONG. FIVE UNIQUE FACTIONS,
ALL CHANNELING POWERFUL FORCES OF NATURE.

BEAR HAND-TO-HAND

BRAVE FIGHTERS, STRONG AS THE BEAR, THAT HAVE SACRIFICED EVERYTHING TO JOIN THE GREATEST WARRIORS ON EARTH.

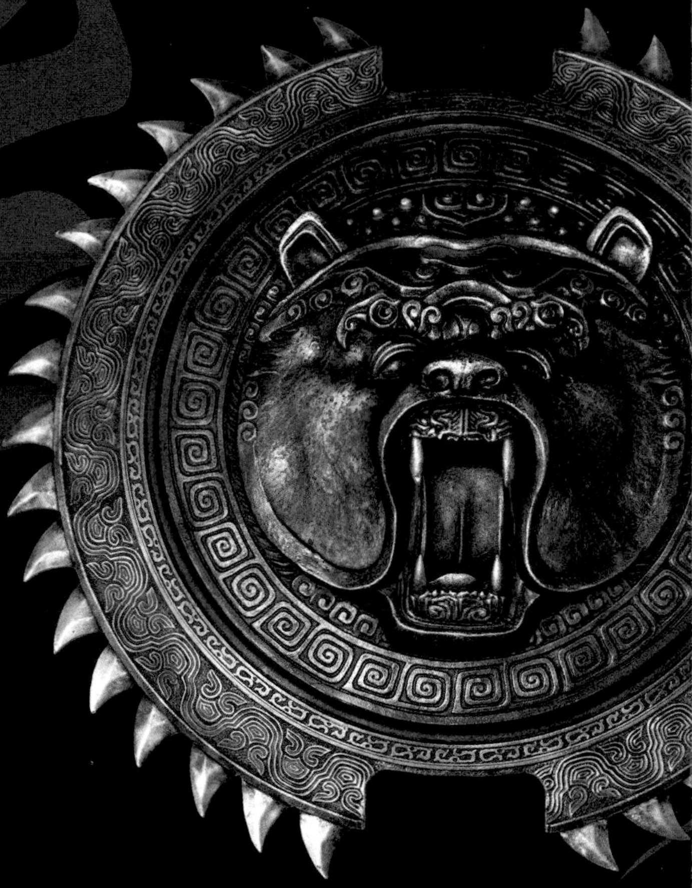

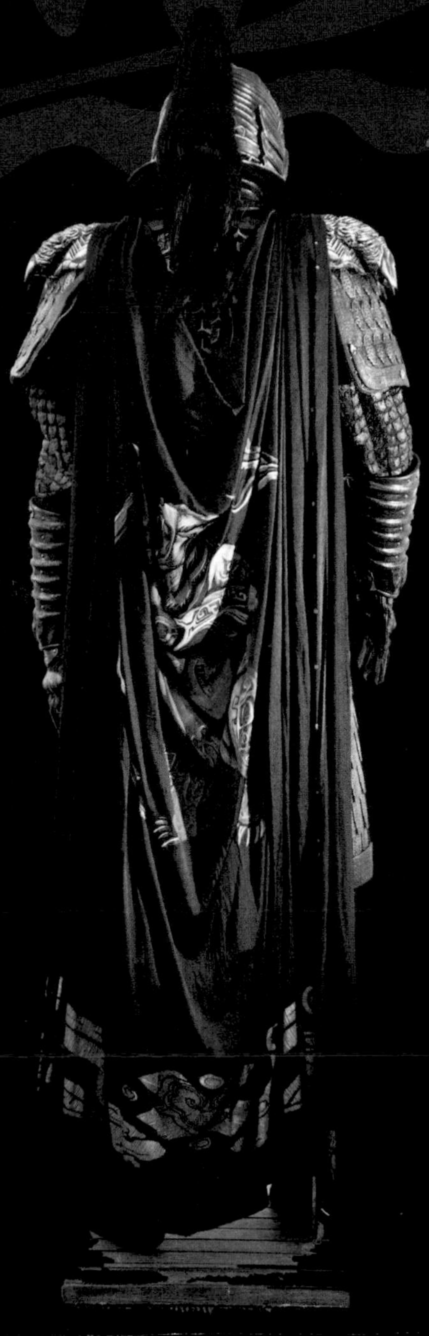

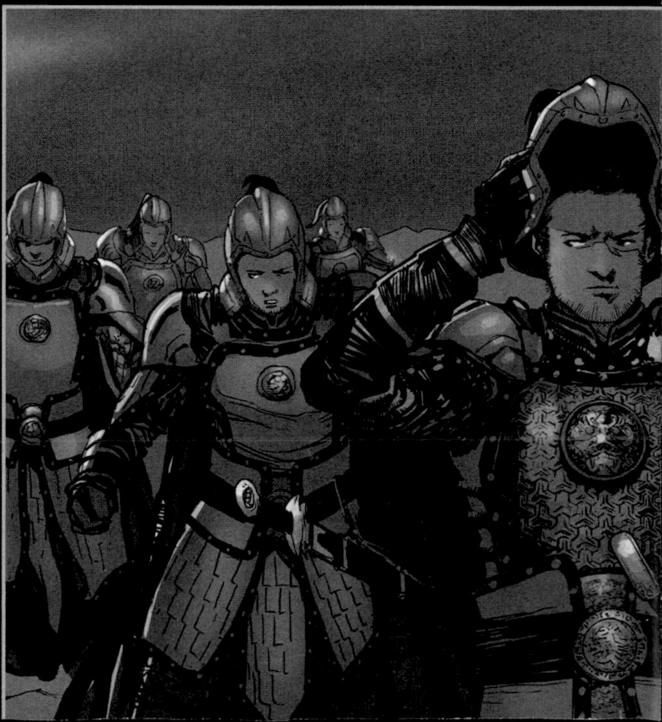

COMBAT

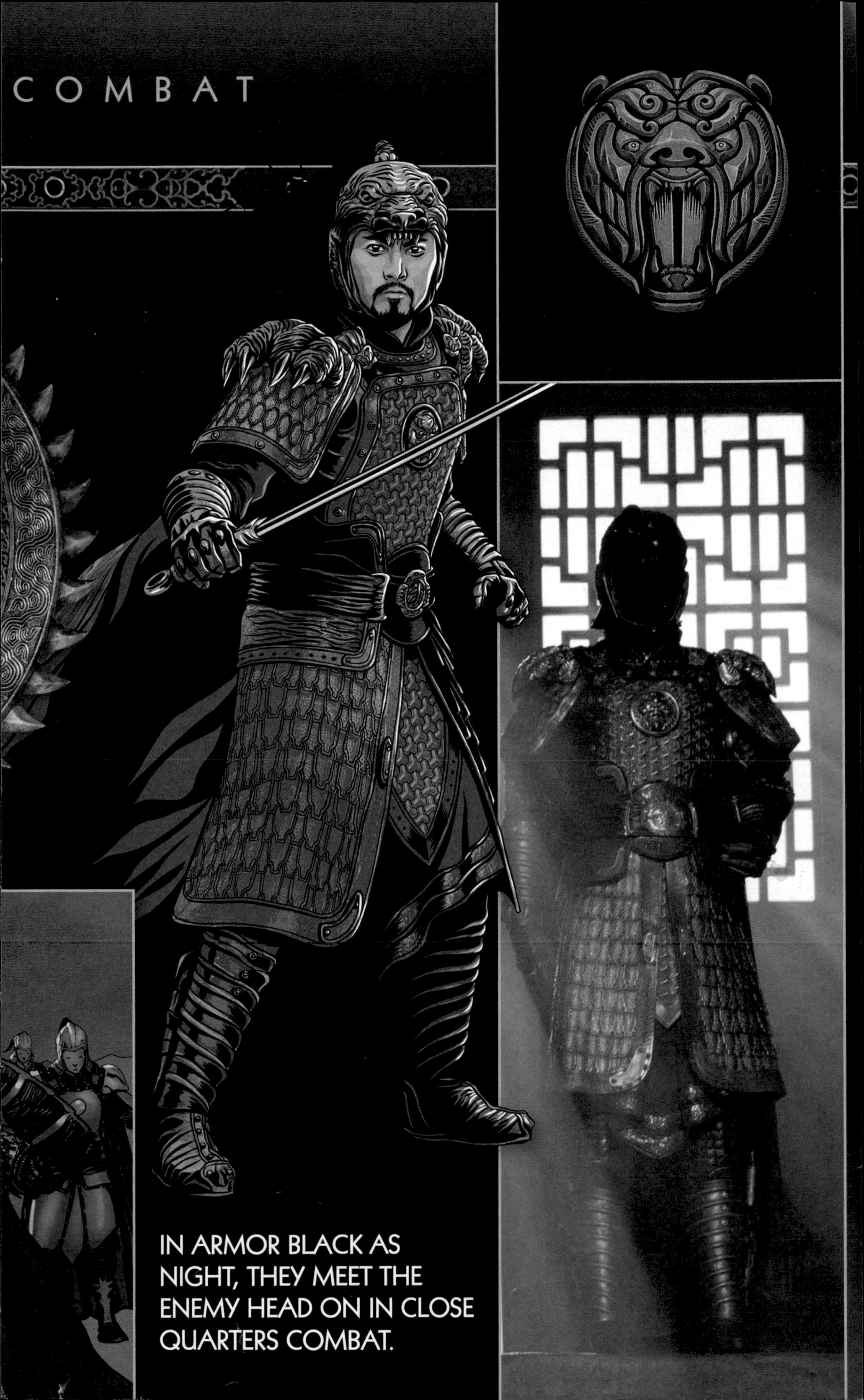

IN ARMOR BLACK AS NIGHT, THEY MEET THE ENEMY HEAD ON IN CLOSE QUARTERS COMBAT.

CRANE A E R I A L &

FEMALE WARRIORS THAT STAND HIGH ON THE GREAT WALL WITH THE GRACE AND POISE OF THE NOBLE CRANE, READY TO STRIKE LIKE A BIRD OF PREY.

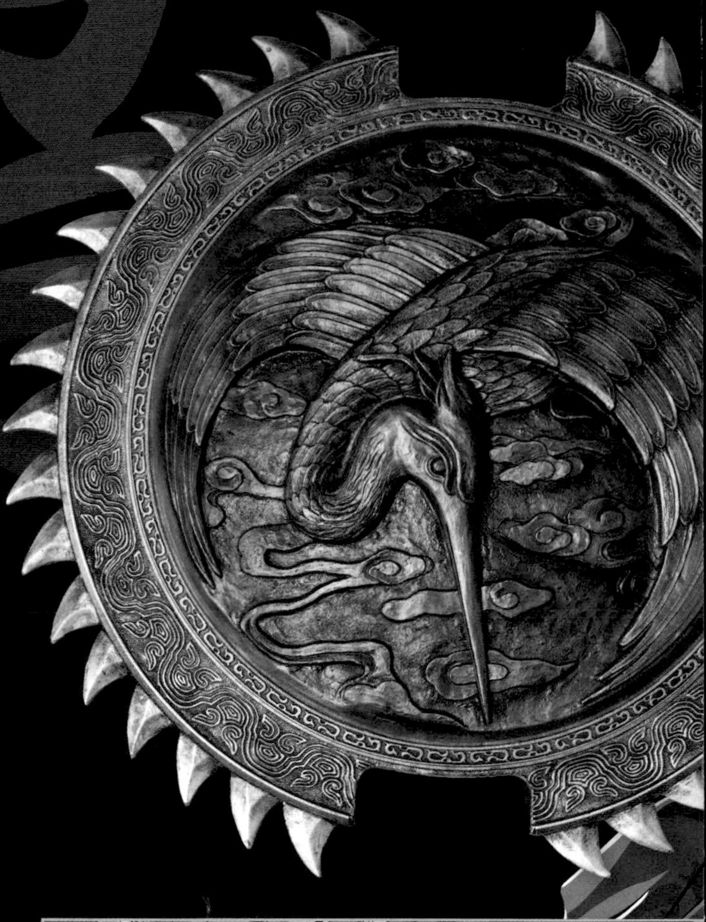

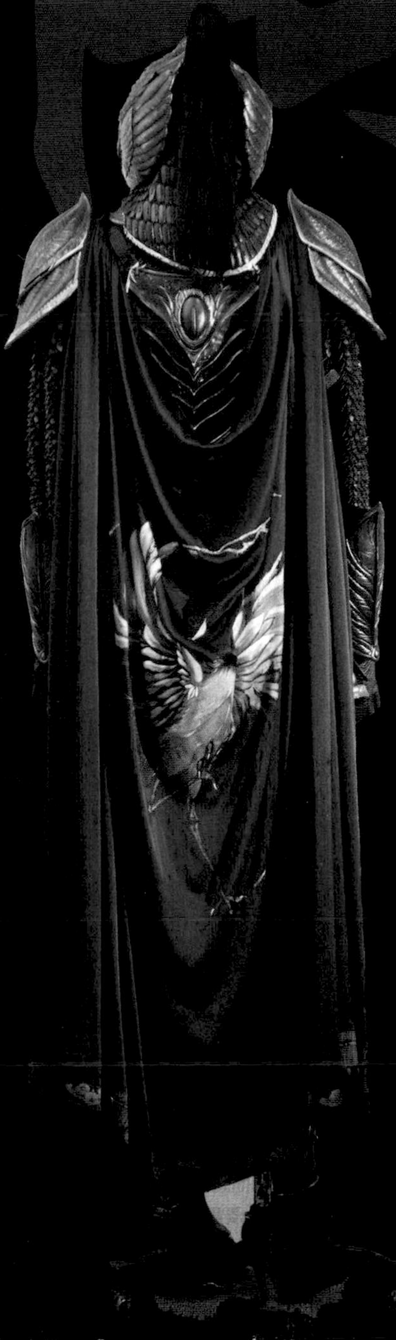

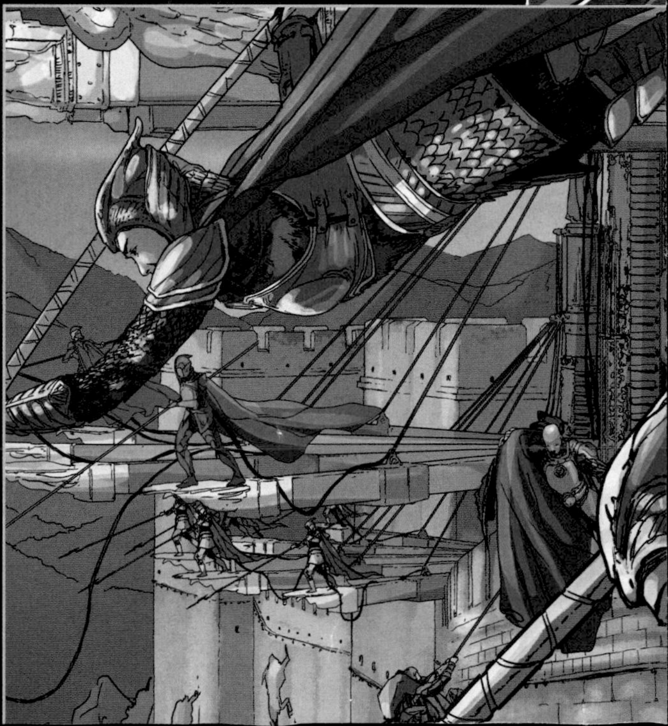

ROPES

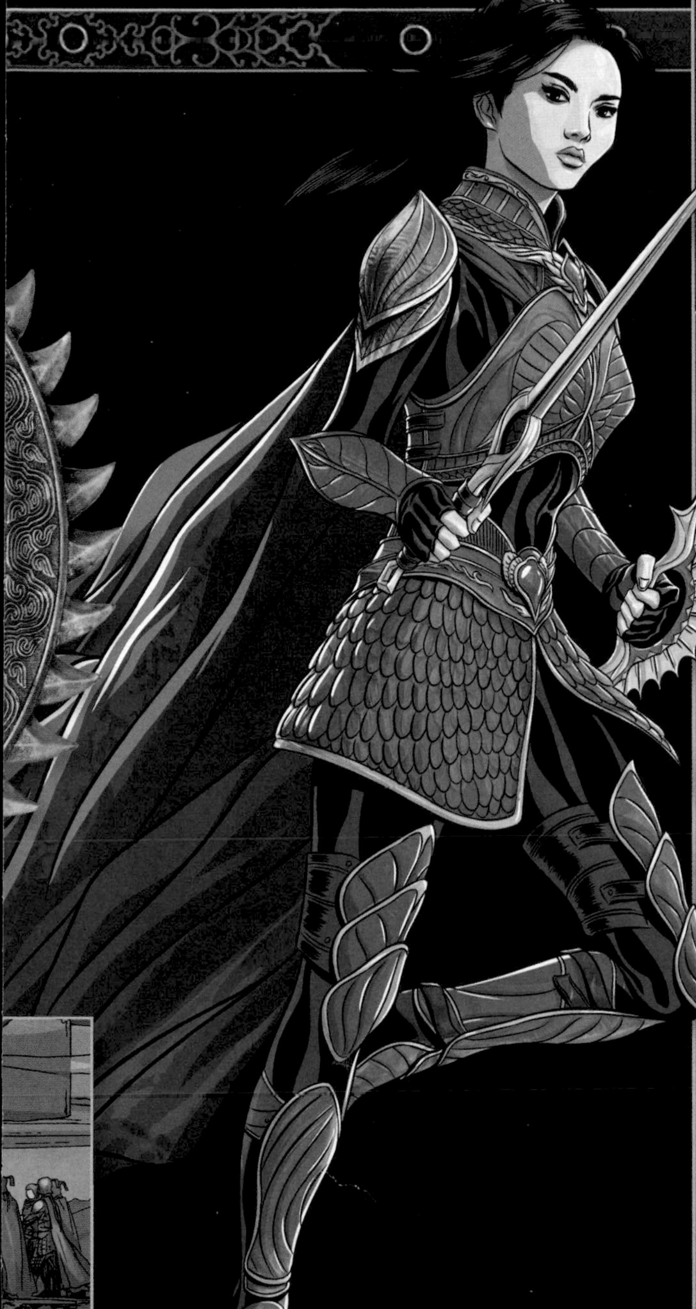

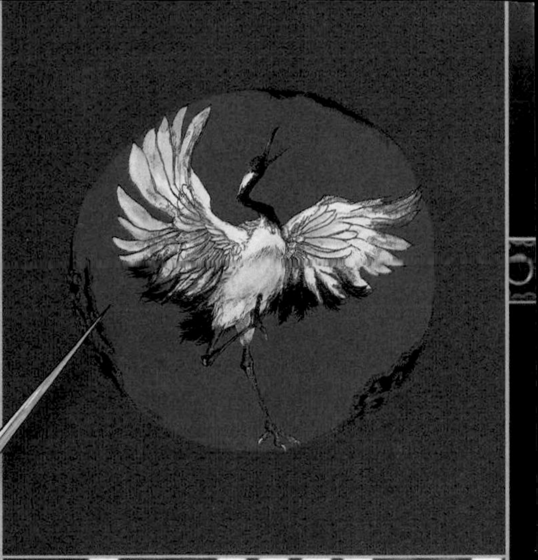

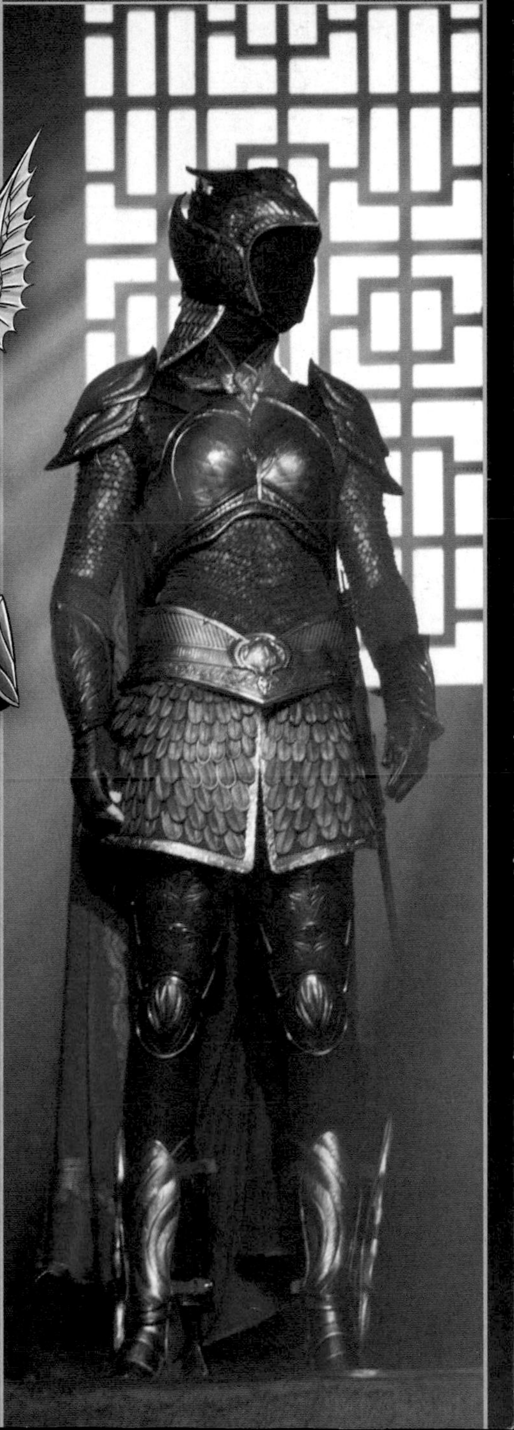

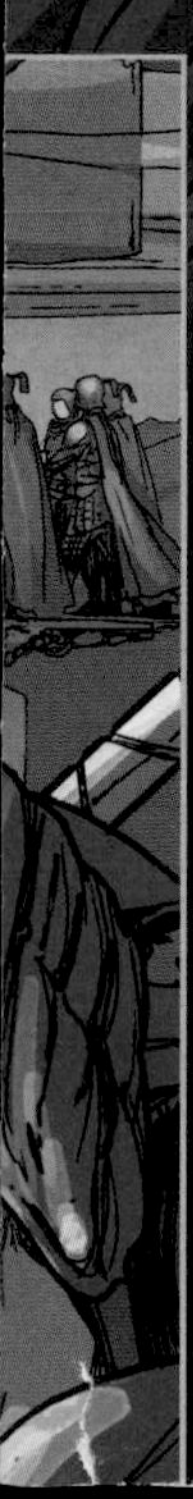

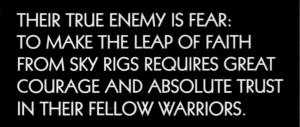

THEIR TRUE ENEMY IS FEAR: TO MAKE THE LEAP OF FAITH FROM SKY RIGS REQUIRES GREAT COURAGE AND ABSOLUTE TRUST IN THEIR FELLOW WARRIORS.

EAGLE ARCHERY

MARKSMEN WHOSE POWER LIES IN THEIR ABILITY TO PERCEIVE THEIR PREY FROM FAR AWAY LIKE THE EAGLE.

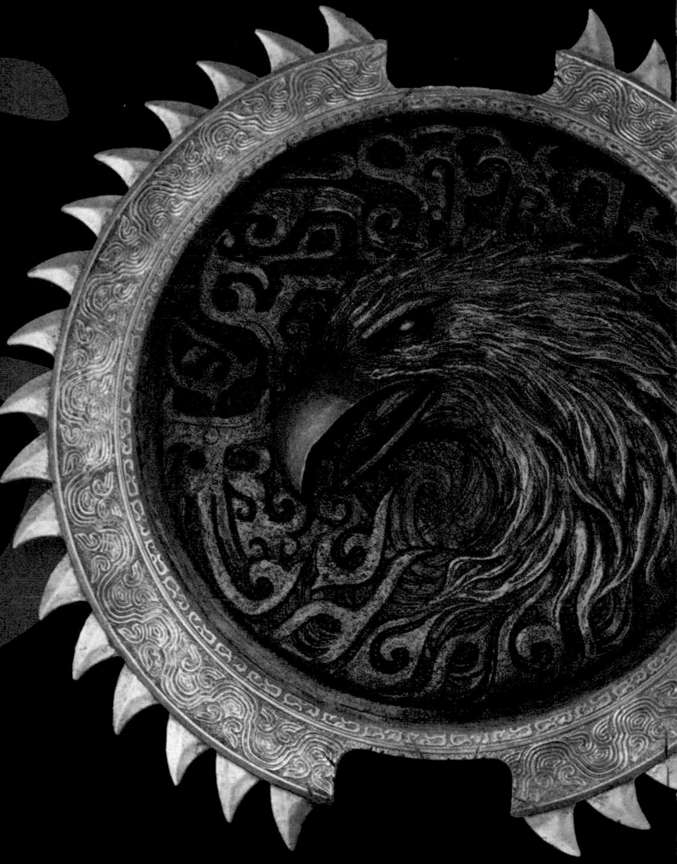

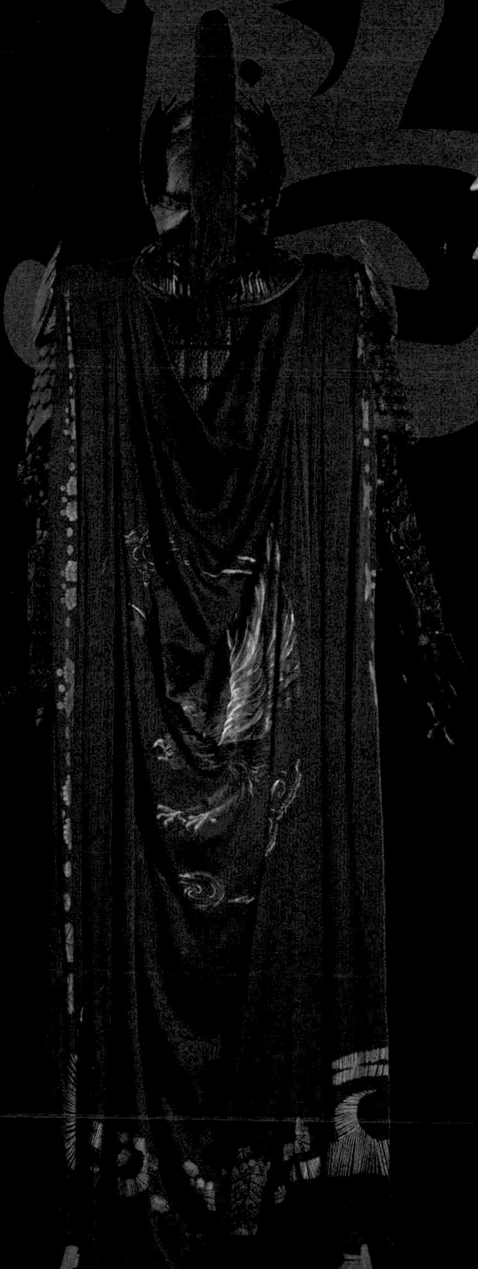

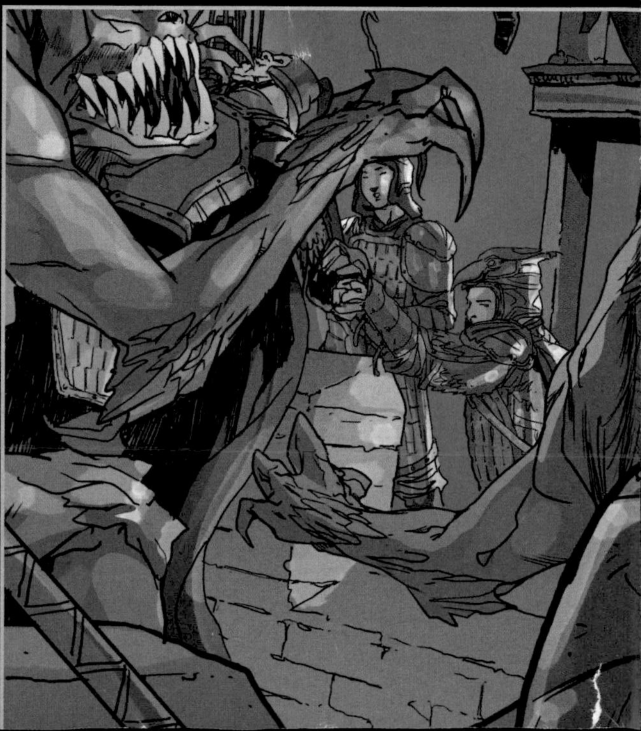

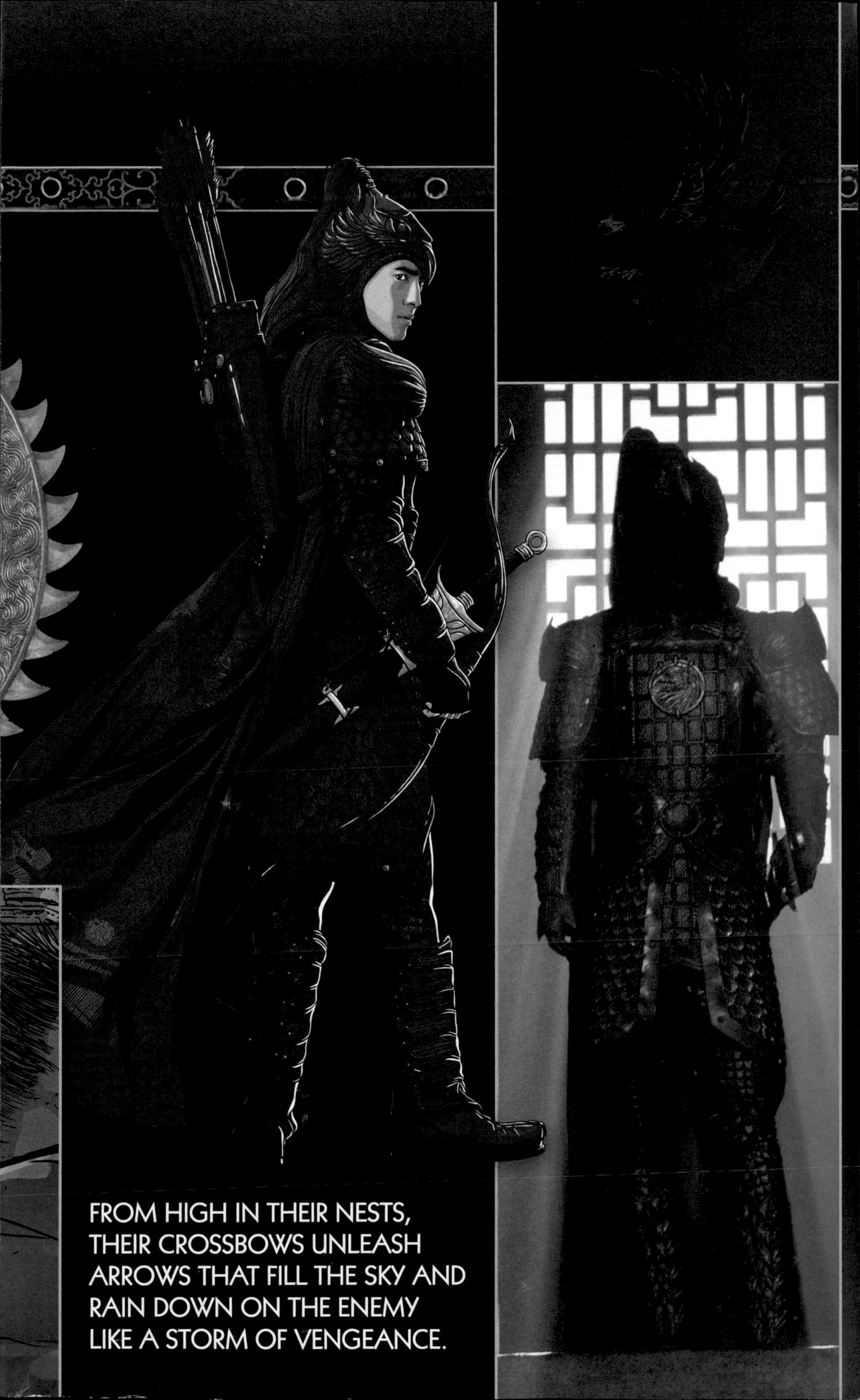

FROM HIGH IN THEIR NESTS,
THEIR CROSSBOWS UNLEASH
ARROWS THAT FILL THE SKY AND
RAIN DOWN ON THE ENEMY
LIKE A STORM OF VENGEANCE.

TIGER ENGINEERING

FIERCE WARRIORS WITH THE STRENGTH OF THE MIGHTY TIGER THAT POWER THE MECHANICAL MARVELS OF THE GREAT WALL.

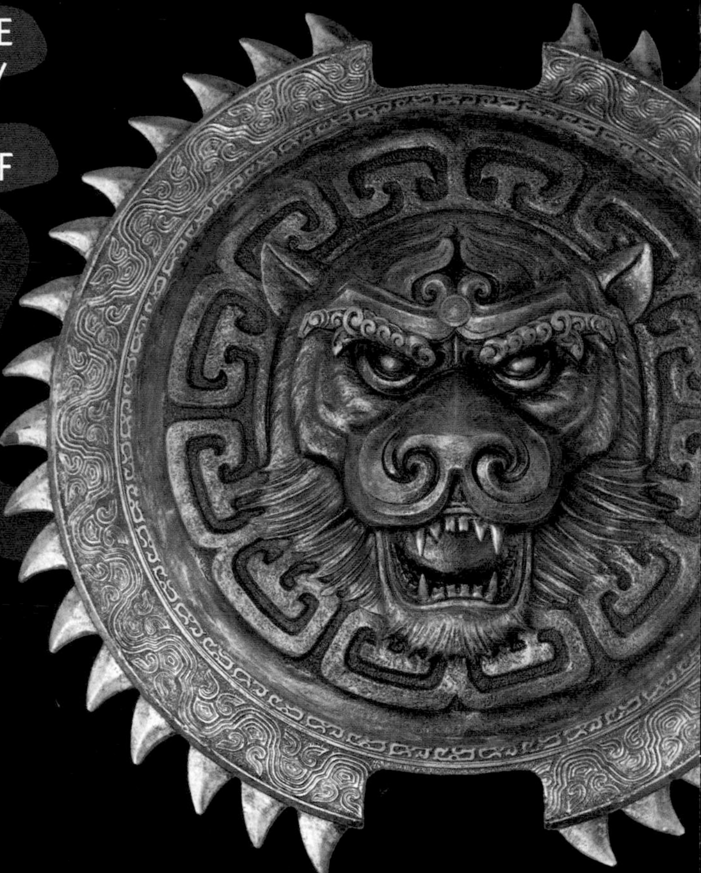

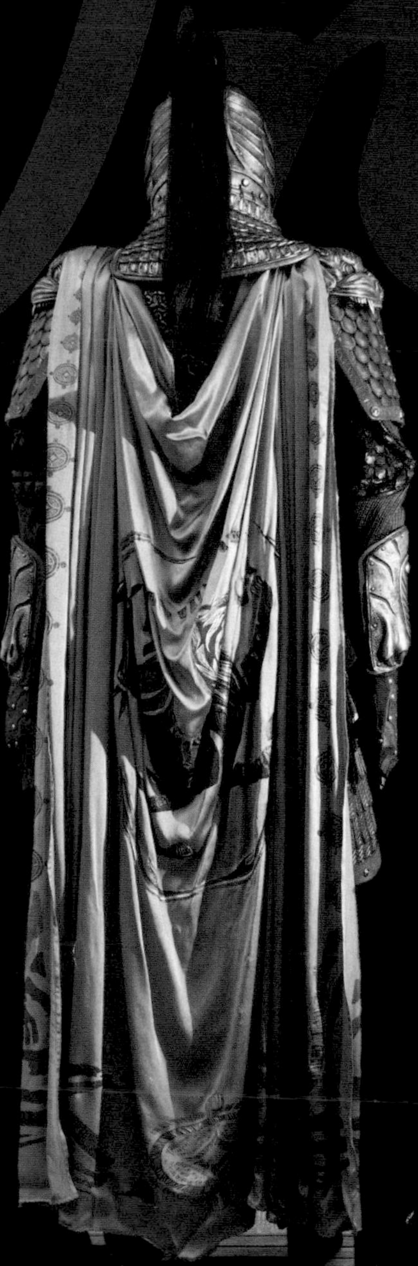

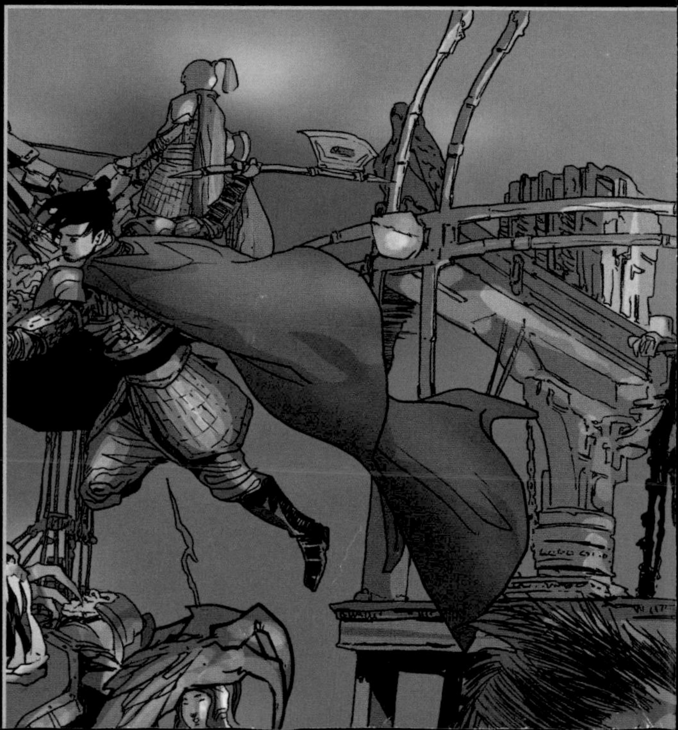

& ARTILLERY

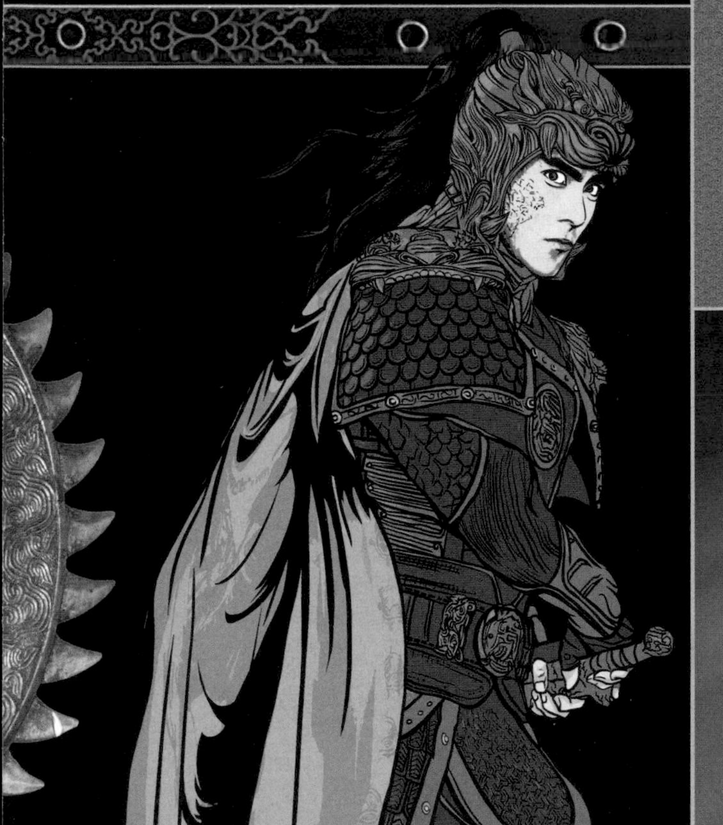

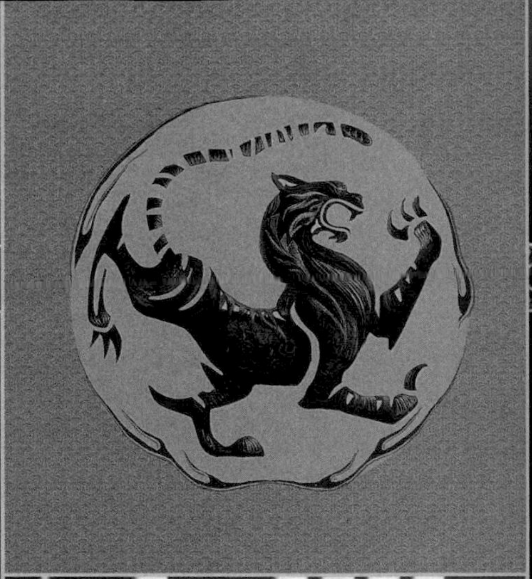

CHANNELING WATER, DRIVING THE HYDRAULICS, AND ACTIVATING THE WEAPONRY INSIDE THE WALL, THEY ARE THE BEATING HEART THAT BRINGS THIS INCREDIBLE STRUCTURE TO LIFE.

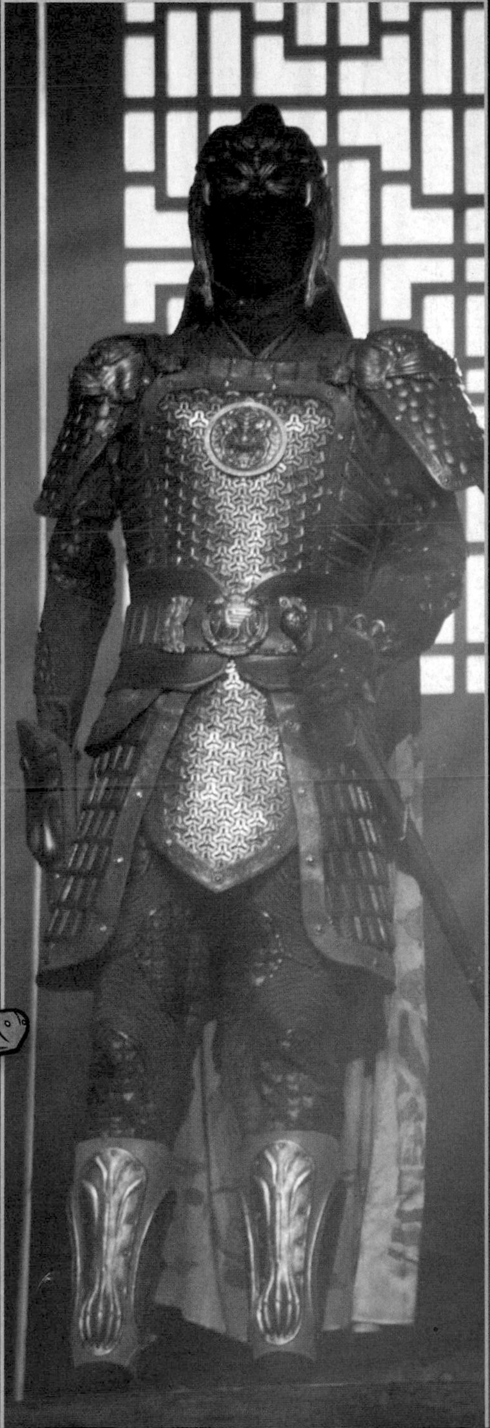

DEER INFANTRY

INFANTRY WHO SWIFTLY
GALLOP ON HORSEBACK
INTO BATTLE THAT USE SPEED
AS A DEADLY WEAPON.

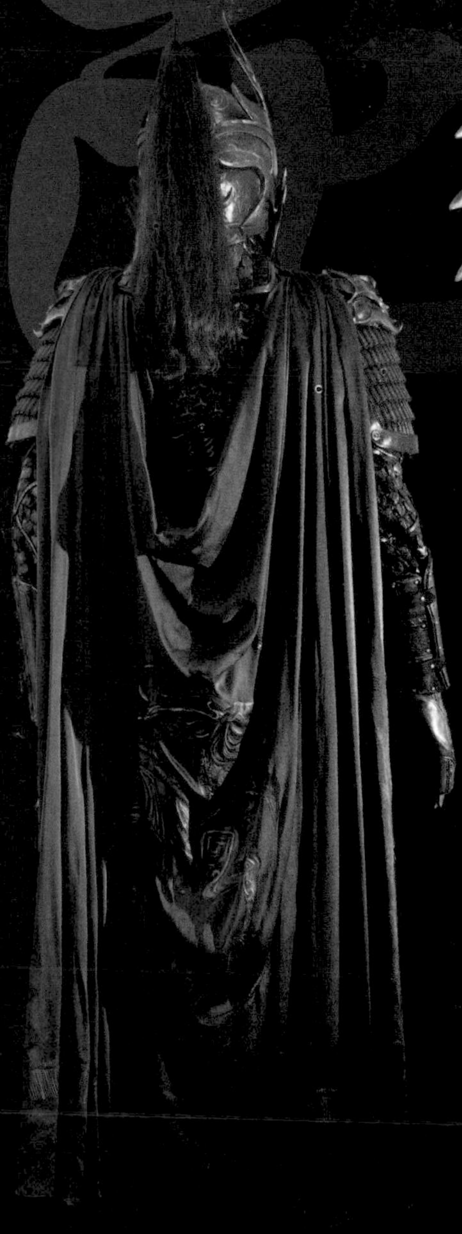

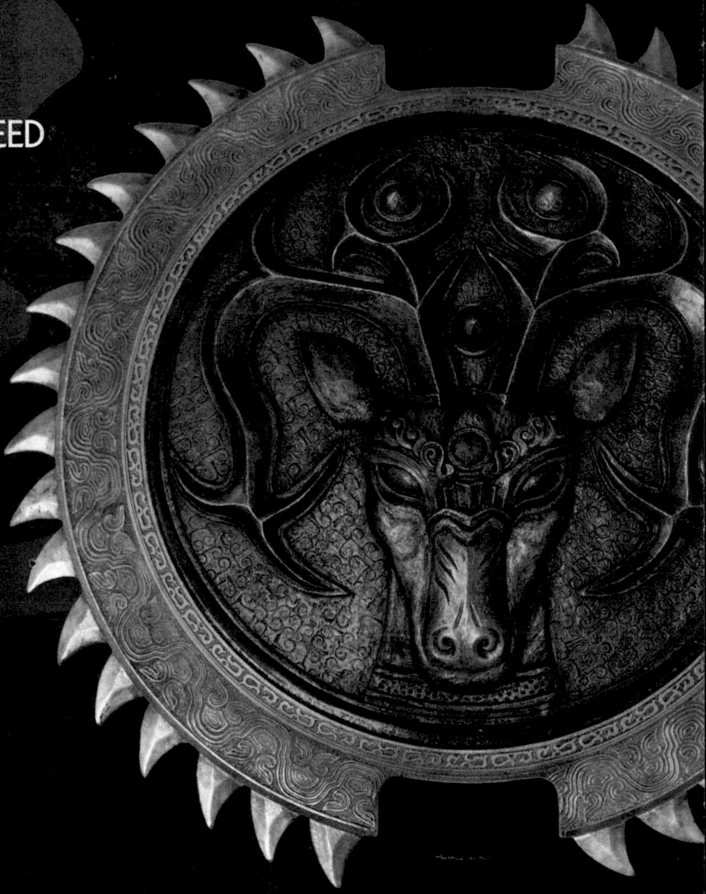

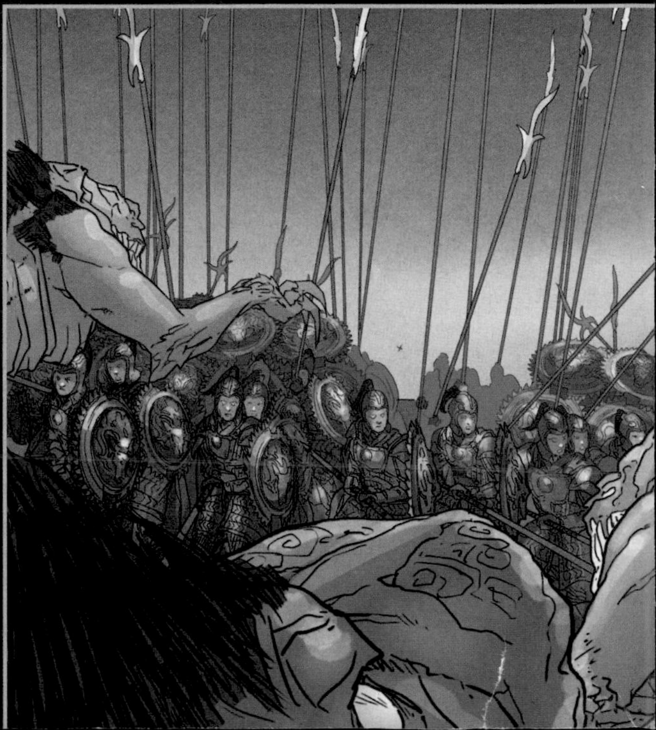

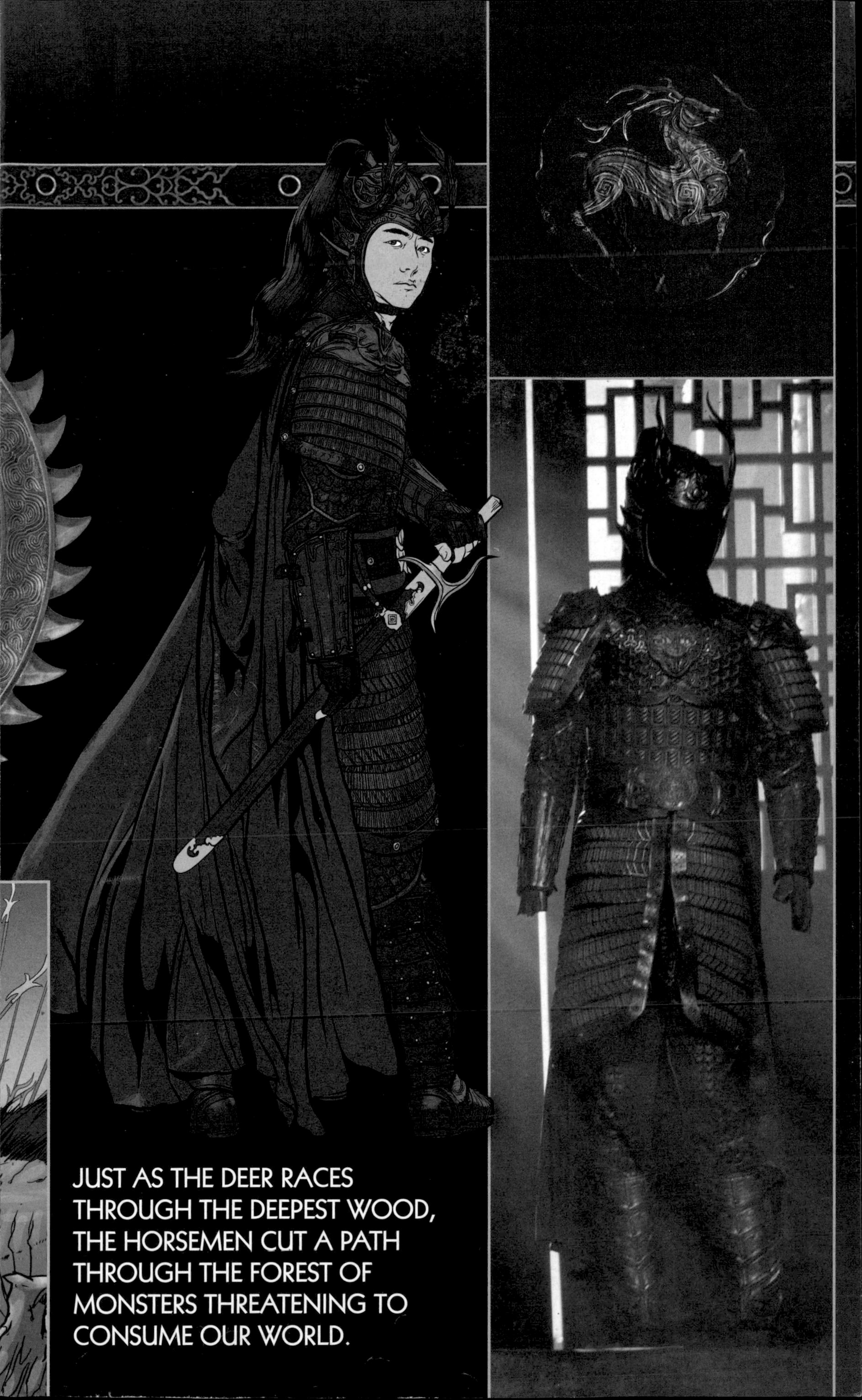
JUST AS THE DEER RACES THROUGH THE DEEPEST WOOD, THE HORSEMEN CUT A PATH THROUGH THE FOREST OF MONSTERS THREATENING TO CONSUME OUR WORLD.

THE TAO TEI

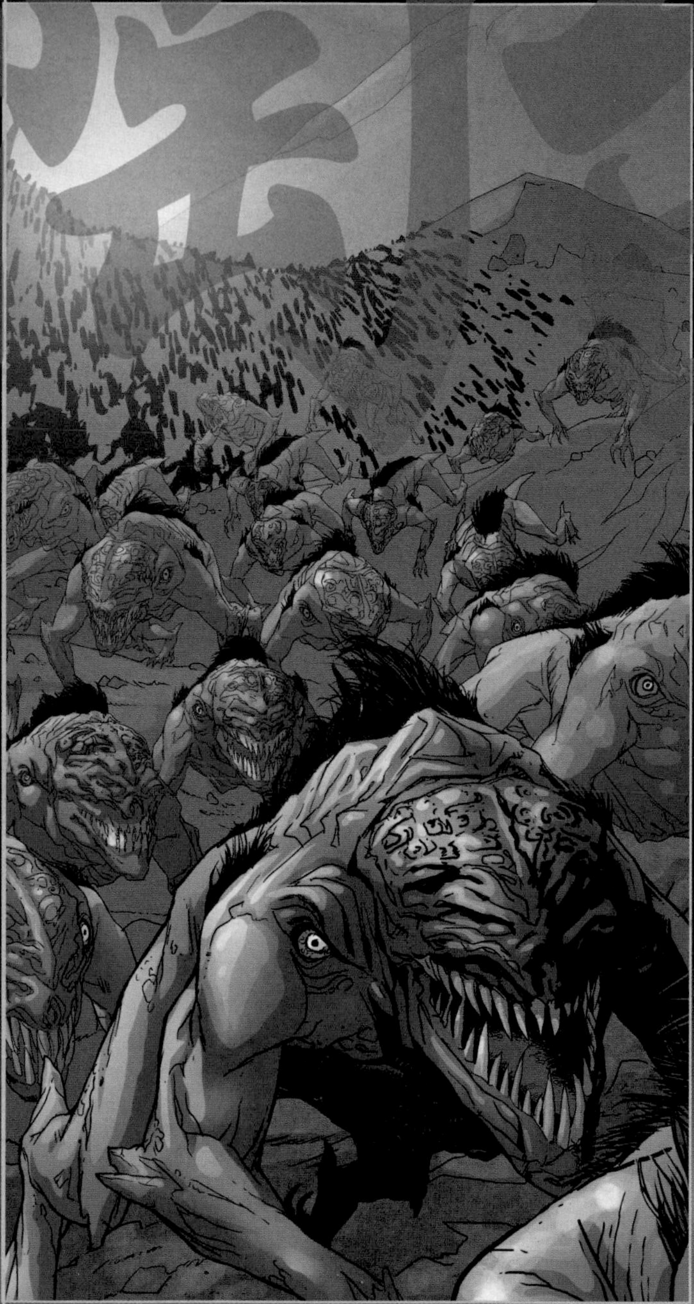

THE TAO TEI ARE MYTHICAL CREATURES BORN OF ANCIENT CHINESE FOLKLORE, AND A SYMBOL OF HUMAN GREED AND EXCESS.

A VAST, SWARMING TIDAL WAVE OF 100,000 MONSTERS SET ON DEVOURING ALL IN THEIR PATH, THE TAO TEI RISE FROM THE JADE MOUNTAIN EVERY 60 YEARS TO FEED, AND THE ONE THING STANDING BETWEEN THEM AND HUMANITY IS THE GREAT WALL.